D1422382

A Cartographic Turn

Cover design: Mirza Tursic (with Boris Beaude and Elsa Chavinier).

A Cartographic Turn

Edited by Jacques Lévy

EPFL Press

A Swiss academic publisher distributed by Routledge

www.routledge.com/builtenvironment

Taylor & Francis Group Ltd
2 Park Square, Milton Park
Abingdon, Oxford, OX14 4RN, UK

Routledge is an imprint of Taylor & Francis Group,
An informa business.

Simultaneously published in the USA and Canada by Routledge,
711 Third Avenue, New York, NY 10017

www.routledge.com

Library of Congress Cataloging-in-Publication Data
A catalog record for this book is available from the Library of Congress.

Published under the editorial direction of Professor Vincent Kaufmann (EPFL).

The author and publisher express their thanks to the Swiss Federal Institute of Technology in Lausanne (EPFL) for the generous support towards the publication of this book.

EPFL Press

The EPFL Press is the English-language imprint of the Foundation of the Presses polytechniques et universitaires romandes (PPUR). The PPUR mainly publishes works of teaching and research of the Ecole polytechnique fédérale de Lausanne (EPFL), of universities and other institutions of higher education.

Presses polytechniques et universitaires romandes
EPFL – Rolex Learning Center
Post office box 119
CH-1015 Lausanne, Switzerland
E-mail: ppur@epfl.ch
Phone: 021/693 21 30
Fax: 021/693 40 27

www.epflpress.org

© 2015, First edition, EPFL Press, Lausanne (Switzerland)
ISBN 978-2-940222-70-4 (EPFL Press)
ISBN 978-0-415-72913-0 (Routledge)

Printed in Italy

Foreword

Humans have long created maps, with the history of cartography stretching back several millennia to cave drawings and clay tablets depicting local geography. Over time, the techniques and technologies used to generate map data (e.g., surveying methods and equipment, aerial photography, photogrammatery) and to circulate them (e.g., tablets, pen and paper, printing press, computers) have gone through a number of changes, altering their forms and functions, and leading to a wider diversity of map types (e.g., topographic, thematic, statistical, cartograms, interactive). What has likewise been transformed are the ideas underpinning their construction and function, how we make sense of them, and how we use them to make sense of the world. Indeed, cartographic philosophy has mutated and diversified quite substantially over time and space with respect to the ontology, epistemology, and methodology of maps and mapping.

This is particularly the case in the post-World War II era as cartographic conceptual thought multiplied into a number of alternative viewpoints. For example, within the Anglo-American tradition, the work of Arthur Robinson and colleagues in the 1950s shifted the ontology of a map from a Cartesian representation to a mode of communication; associated work developing a communications model of cartography aimed at improving how maps were perceived and processed. This was in contrast to the French tradition pioneered by Jacques Bertin which viewed maps from a semiotic perspective as sign systems. By the late 1980s, the ontological framing of the communications model was being challenged by Brian Harley who, drawing on the ideas of Michel Foucault and Jacques Derrida, conceived of maps as social constructions that were products of power and its exercise. More recently, there has been a post-representational turn in Anglo-American cartographic theory that casts the nature of maps as ontogenetic and provisional, and frames maps as inscriptions, propositions, or actants or as a set of practices rather than simply representations.

This volatility in thinking has been accompanied by a rapid change in mapping technologies and the proliferation of maps in everyday life. The establishment and growth of computers has radically altered how maps are made, used, and shared – and by whom. Geographic information systems were initiated in the 1960s, initially as a set of university lab and national mapping agency projects. By the early 1980s, there was a well-established and expanding commercial sector and market that was accompanied by the growth of a variety of geovisualisation and remote sensing software. The rollout of the World Wide Web saw maps move online and become increasingly interactive and dynamic. By the mid-2000s, the instigation of Web 2.0 and products such as Google Maps enabled users to customize and add their own features to maps, and OpenStreetMap enabled people to contribute data directly to the production of a large-scale global mapping initiative. With the widespread adoption of smartphones and tablets, location-based services and locative media have become common applications, enabling people to be constantly geo-referenced and geo-referencing. As a consequence, the role of national mapping agencies has shifted, many more people have become active mappers, and the consumption and sharing of map products has soared.

At the same time, cartography and mapping metaphors have become increasingly important across the humanities and social sciences as means of complementing, framing, and structuring analysis and interpretation. To map – to set out places, ideas, events, findings, etc., in relation to one another – is a powerful means of sense making. This leads Jacques Levy to argue in the introduction to this book that there has been a 'cartographic turn' in the academy (and one could argue in industry as well, given the growing prevalence of location and maps as a means to organize activity and convey information through digital media). He goes further, however, to contend that this cartographic turn is a 'turn of turns' that interlinks five others: spatial, pragmatic, linguistic, ethical, and digital. Mapping, it seems, is a universal conduit for thinking about and through a wide, diverse terrain of topics and issues.

This book is about both understanding cartography and the cartographic turn. The chapters, diversely authored, are divided into four sections that consider maps as a resource, a language, a set of ethics. Interestingly, the authors are all schooled in French traditions and this is also reflected in the references, with very few citations of Anglo-American works (which, in turn, have minimal engagement with French writings). As such, the book makes an interesting counterpoint to Anglo-American cartographic theory, opening up different viewpoints and inviting both a productive dialogue and mutual learning. *A Cartographic Turn* thus performs two vital functions. First, it provides a set of chapters about the power of maps and mapping. Second, the book opens up the French tradition of cartographic thought and thinking with respect to the cartographic turn within the social sciences and humanities to a wider audience and thereby fosters an exchange of ideas that will further debate.

Rob Kitchin

Table of contents

Introduction

Mapping Is Thinkable, Thinking Is Mappable

Jacques Lévy

This book proposes fourteen texts from thirteen different authors coming from various disciplines: geography, demography, cartography, art studies, architecture, and philosophy. Some of the chapters have been written for a conference, Mapping Ethics, organised in 2011 at the École Polytechnique Fédérale de Lausanne (EPFL) by the Eidolon international network. Some other texts have been published before, between 1995 and 2000, and some have been written especially for this book. This diversity might give the impression that we have here a mere collection of independent contributions gathered only by their topic: maps and cartography. This impression would be wrong. By and large, the four simple propositions developed throughout this book are actually a single one expressed through four different viewpoints.

1. Maps convey rational, aesthetic, ethical, and personal messages – at times separately, more often together – and this mix offers fertile fields of study for the exploration of social complexities.

2. Maps are both representations of pre-existing spaces and, by their very existence, creations of new spaces. This dual nature inspires an effort to go beyond the traditional 'reflection theory' and its cartographic drawbacks and to promote a reunification of social productions, be they material, immaterial, or psychological.

3. The historical or anthropological analysis of maps as semantic objects should be connected to the production of new maps, namely those that take advantage of the powerful tools provided by digital technologies.
4. The issues of contemporary mapping should be read in light of recent innovations in the sociology of space.

Through these four statements emerges an idea : a 'cartographic turn'. The inflation of 'turns' for the last decades could certainly undermine the identification of intellectual bifurcations in social sciences ; nevertheless, the risk of that critique is worth taking. The cartographic turn can be seen as a 'turn of turns', as it connects five major switches that occur in the late 20th century :

- a 'spatial' or 'geographic turn', which shows the pivotal position of space and spatiality in the major issues of social theory ;
- a 'pragmatic turn', which rejects a structuralist (or post-structuralist) approach and places the actors, including the individuals, at the core of the self-moving social machinery ;
- a 'linguistic turn' that puts languages in a more central and open position vis-à-vis the rest of human agency in society ; IV an 'ethical turn', which corresponds to the end of 'revealed' moral injunctions and analyses the emergence of values as an historical process transcending the self ; and finally, V in another domain, the 'digital turn', which affects most aspects (techniques, languages, makers, audiences) of the cartographic 'value chain'.

Each of the chapters of this book addresses these issues from its own angle.

In the first section, 'Map As Resource', the process of mapping is related to other dimensions of thought : with the more general concept of the world in Ancient Greek societies, with pictorial arts, and with an approach to knowledge whereby a collection of heterogeneous cartographic images help the researcher find unexpected paths to research. Here, artists and scientists are closer to each other than imagined.

The following section 'Map As Language' focuses on the peculiarities of cartographic language. Maps are images that construct a discourse that is neither a classic sequential discourse nor a figurative depiction. Cartographic enunciations are rich in complexities, for example the inevitable contamination between graphic semiology and societal issues that are not necessarily conspiratorial ; or their paradoxical capacity to create new spatial realities, comparable to other spatial realities, both despite and because mapping procedures often use the dangerous resources of self-reference.

In section 3, the emergence of ethics raises two major issues for map-makers and map-users: the nature of a society's relevant components and the complexity of the relation between identity and otherness. Maps have long been the aggressive expression of an 'us' facing 'them'. But who is this 'us' in today's post-colonial world? And to what extent is 'us' or 'them' is a mere sum of 'me's'? In brief, who places whom on the map?

The last section continues this interrogation by moving to the tribulations of the author in the age of a digital society of individuals. The difficulty for a map author to be recognised as such is not new, but the massive diffusion of images on the Internet does not favour – in cartography as elsewhere – the acknowledgment of intellectual property. One of the paradoxes of the current situation, however, is that the ordinary individual has never been that considered. 'Big data' values quantity but makes the singularity of our itineraries visible, too. Moreover, any smartphone-equipped person can become a producer of new images of spatial arrangements – a cartographer.

Before the cartographic turn, technicians, historians, users, exegetes were distinct, and turned away from each other.

The time of the truly engineer-designed map is over. Maps have gained many new actors and these actors think. This book aims to modestly contribute to an enduring association between mapping and reflexivity.

Part 1
Map as Resource

Chapter 1

When Maps Reflect

Christian Jacob

Three stages in the history of Greek cartography invite us to reflect on the nature and power of these drawings that made the 'inhabited world' both visible and thinkable. Maps reflect, above all, our specific ways of seeing and our intellectual practices. Through graphic mediation, the latter aim to subject the world to a geometrical order or trace the progression of the quest for knowledge and wisdom.

The history of cartography cannot avoid a fundamental question: Why is our representation of space graphic? Although the answer varies according to the culture and society, it cannot be reduced to mere practical ends, i.e. travel, location or territorial management. The cartographic stroke is a gesture that creates a new space instead of representing it. It produces a new intellectual object whose meanings, cognitive effects and potential uses are not merely the sum of local information, measurements and empirical locations mobilised in its genesis. The visual appropriation and intellectual approaches that give maps their meaning cannot be reduced to mere signs, but rather rely on cultural categories, educational schemes, contextualised semantics, fields of knowledge, beliefs regarding worldly materiality and ends and, more fundamentally, the aptitude of the human spirit to master and model the world. The map is thus an interface, both a symbolic object that generates a sense of recognition and belonging among those who master its codes; as well as a screen upon which a society's history, vision of the world, memory, axiology and very organisation are projected.

The Map: a complex object

We cannot fully grasp the power of maps by analysing them from a geo-topographical standpoint alone. A map is not a reflection of knowledge outside of itself, for which it determines the successive steps of its construction. It constructs knowledge, produces it and gives it form, meaning that the geography of maps is not the same as the geography of travel tales or descriptions. The map introduces a new object to the field of human vision that likewise becomes an object of thought and discourse. The map is a visual matrix of complex intellectual operations – remembrance, syllogism, spatial construction, planning, foresight, location, information research – correlating different semiological elements between itself and its discursive, descriptive and fictional context. By breaking the mimetic protocol that links the map to a representation of actual space, maps can be used in conjunction with other visual devices to construct knowledge and meaning, inducing specific cognitive effects by relying on evidence from a graph. Maps share certain fundamental qualities with diagrams, tables, technical graphs and anatomical drawings: they make the invisible visible, combining various empirical, limited, and successive perceptions in an overall image, a 'mind's-eye view'. They are the culmination of a set of observations, discoveries, calculations, and hypotheses whose technical bases and logical processes can be obscured by the final result. Maps have both the power to persuade and affirm along with a rhetorical efficiency in the larger process of constructing collective knowledge and scientific communication.

Revisiting the history of cartography results in an increased awareness of the complexity of the maps-object. We will therefore analyse the levels of language and expressions specific to maps as well as the figurative codes that lead readers to use particular strategies for reading and (re-)constructing images. By exploring how writing, geometry, figurative drawing, and random topographical plots interact, we can better understand the purpose and intent behind maps in addition to the semiotic skills necessary for reading them.

Maps, like certain images, are an important component of a society's visual culture. Their construction and graphical content are strongly determined by context. Yet, the 'poetics' of maps also reflect the intellectual effects and conceptual, symbolic and social context that motivates their production and use. The map-object itself – a mere by-product – is not sufficient for reconstructing this intellectually pragmatic exercise, or for understanding the thinking or thought processes that underlie it.

In this chapter we will discuss three ways of thinking about maps based on three stages in the history of Greek cartography. In all three, the physical image will serve as a basis for understanding specific thought processes and for defining its relationship to reality, its ontological status and understanding it within the larger context of codified intellectual practices. From the first Ionian physicists to the philosophers of the Greco-Roman era, the map has seen profound changes not only in terms of geographical content or visual organisation (which is nearly unknown to us), but also in terms of how they are used, with what intent, and their intellectual efficiency.

Thinking in figures: Anaximander of Miletus

Greek tradition attributes the first map of inhabited lands to Anaximander of Miletus, a disciple of Thales, one of the pre-Socratic philosophers who developed a new type of rationality in the cities of Asia Minor. Anaximander lived during the first half of the 6th century BC. Only fragments of his work remain, mere vestiges of a treatise *On Nature*, cut out, rewritten and interpreted through layers of antique doxographic tradition. Starting from the time of Aristotle's school, in fact, philosophers and physicists have re-examined the tradition as an instrument of their own reflection.[1]

The doxographic tradition irremediably deconstructed Anaximander's treatise into a mere set of assertions, or theses, reduced to their most factual statements. Yet it is striking to consider that Anaximander's philosophical doxography (of Peripatetic origin) makes no reference to his cartographic work. It was, however, mentioned by geographers who undertook the archaeology of their discipline, starting with Eratosthenes of Cyrene (3rd century B.C.). This dissociation of traditions is instructive and suggests that perhaps cartography was only marginal in the spectrum

---

[1] See Charles H. Kahn, *Anaximander and the Origins of Greek Cosmology*, New York: Columbia University Press, 1960; Marcel Conche, *Anaximandre. Fragments et témoignages*, Paris: PUF, 1991.

of philosophical interests of those who reread the Presocratics, either in their original versions or via the first doxographies.

For the contemporary historian, the goal is to understand the map's role in Anaximander's work: Was it simply a technical digression in an intellectual process governed by pure speculation, or was it a key step in the overall understanding of Nature and the Cosmos?

From the Muses to a citizen's discourse

Anaximander was one of the first Greek writers of prose, along with Phere-cydes of Syros. The transition from poetry to prose marks an essential dif-ference in how knowledge was expressed, with one form of truth being exchanged for another – from words inspired by the Muses to writing by *ordinary individuals* who taught about the world, its genesis and the vis-ible and invisible phenomena found therein. Anaximander's work brought about a new social and political context wherein individuals could express their opinions on city affairs and the genesis of the world alike, opening it to discussion by making it public but without investing it with supernatural authority and thus closing all debate.

Such subjects did indeed involve debate and persuasion among think-ers as a way of stating their vision of the world and as a way of distinguish-ing themselves. Thales, Anaximander, and Anaximenes succeeded each other as master and pupil, answering a same set of fundamental issues: the origin, organisation, and nature of the cosmos and the origin of meteorites. Ionian physical thinking, which was not yet an established area of knowl-edge, developed in a different manner. The recourse of writing gave new status and substance to its doctrines.

Anaximander's work retraced the origin and organisation of the world, from the first principle of all things to the apparition of animal and human life. The author described the world by recalling the principle constituents in its genesis. Thus, the Earth was formed at the centre of a flaming sphere, which became the sky and was to be found at an equal distance from all points on this sphere. However, Anaximander's Earth was not spherical but rather a cylindrical volume, similar to a section of column whose height is equal to a third of its length,[2] whose dimensions are expressed in a

---

[2] See Plutarch, *Stromates* 2 (D 579); Hippolytus, *Refutationes*, I, 6, 1 (D. 559W 10); Aetius, III, 10, 2.

proportional relationship. Such descriptions are recurrent in Anaximander's fragments. For example, 'Anaximander said that the sun had an equal size to that of the Earth. However, the circle from which its exhalation was produced and in which it moves is 27 times bigger than the Earth'.[3]

This is not so much a graphic description as a linguistic one, nor so much a question of measurements as of proportion and commensurability. Yet the comparison with the stone column offers an additional, critical element as regards the cylinder's geometric form; it brings the invisible into the sphere of the visible and experiential. It is also a technical reference, as it refers to a manmade object created by a stone worker – an assemblage. That is common in Anaximander's fragments: The flaming sphere around the Earth resembles bark around a tree trunk. The openings in the air allowing for a view of the stars are like the holes in a flute, with the sun projecting fire through small openings similar to the mouth of a bellows, etc.

Analogical thought

Here we find a form of analogical thinking whose importance in Greek science and philosophy Geoffrey Lloyd proved indisputably.[4] Analogies are tools for domesticating the invisible or the infinitely distant, great or small. They bring the inaccessible into the realm of everyday experience and transform incomprehensible phenomena and entities into physical, objective realities. Technical metaphors, moreover, introduce the dimensions of assembly and construction.

Metaphor gives new visual content and mnemo-technical anchoring to a complex, speculative view of the world by moving from one register of reality to another. By making the Earth and cosmos intelligible, visualisable, and measurable, metaphor transfers these fragments of statements to us through the ages. These statements are not the result of observation but rather of deduction. Anaximander used two different types of metaphors: descriptive metaphors (the Earth is like a stone column) and functional metaphors (explaining the processes, mechanisms, and phenomena of exhalation and the diffusion of solar fire). Metaphors open the way for imagery and visualisation.

---

[3] Aetius, II, 21. 1.
[4] Geoffrey, E. R. Lloyd, *Polarity and Analogy. Two Types of Argumentation in Early Greek Thought.* Cambridge: Cambridge University Press, 1966, especially pp. 210–383.

Comparing the Earth to a column or cylinder, and showing the relationship between height and width, makes the Earth a measurable object.
The cylindrical shape of the column has its own intellectual purpose – in
this case, founding a space where a volume and its geometrical surfaces are
the basis for subsequent phases in the cosmogonic narrative.

This is the intellectual context in which Anaximander's map, which
belongs to the same category of intellectual processes as analogies and
metaphors, must be placed. No longer are we in the realm of mental or
discursive images but of an actual graphic projection on a tablet. The map
was part of the overall modelling process of the cosmos; Anaximander's
disciples were able to understand its architecture and assembly, from the
concentric circles surrounding the Earth's cylinder to the centre of the
celestial sphere, to the map of the Earth itself, which corresponded to one
of the two flat ends of the column's section.

Geometric thought

Nevertheless, a map involves moving from a volume to a plane, and thus
transferring technical objects and processes in the abstraction of a drawing
made geometric. Anaximander is representative of this early Greek geometry, where the use of graphic figures was extremely important. His teacher,
Thales, is typically credited with the creation of a set of applied and theoretical works. The latter is depicted as having both the qualities of an engineer
interested in the flow of rivers, the Nile's floods, and olive harvesting and
those of a geometrician interested in the basic properties of figures (the triangle, circle, and line), independent of any materialisation or empirical reference. For instance, it was his abstract reflection on geometric shapes that enabled Thales to recognise the 'similarity' of regular figures, such as equilateral
triangles.[5] Observation and the drawing of figures played an essential role
by isolating part of an object, superimposing two forms, placing one within
another, or dividing a symmetric figure into two equal halves. It was through
these graphic exercises that the general properties of figures were defined.

Anaximander's map is nearly completely unknown to us. From Herodotus's critique of mid-5th century maps,[6] it can be deduced that the latter
were very geometric (e.g. a circle drawn with a compass that an equatorial

---

[5]   Maurice Caveing, *La constitution du type mathématique de l'idéalité dans la pensée grecque*,
      doctoral dissertation, Université de Lille-III, 1982, t. 2, p. 541–542.
[6]   Herodotus, *Histories*, IV, 36.

line could divide into two halves). Miletus, a Greek city at the frontier of the Persian Empire, was an important base for colonial expeditions and a commercial hub between the Aegean and Black Seas. Moreover, legend speaks of an Anaximander of Miletus as leading one of these expeditions. Even if much geographical information about Miletus exists, we cannot assume that Anaximander's map successfully synthesised all of this topographical information and was destined for use by travellers and navigators.

What is known of Anaximander's work suggests that his map was part of a greater movement of logic that sought to model the world, domesticating the invisible and unthinkable through geometric figures and empirical objects that allowed for better understanding of that which was seemingly inaccessible. Moreover, Thales's interest in applied geometry and measurement (e.g., estimating the distance of a boat on the high seas), leads one to believe that Anaximander's map may have also fulfilled such practical ends. However, it is likely that the first tried and tested map in the Greek world was part of a larger speculative project and that the geometric drawings (namely the circle and line, as well as perhaps a sketch of the three-continent cut-out) played the same role as metaphors in cosmological discourse. Thus, the map is an excellent example of the thinking of Pre-Socratic physicists. Tradition attributes the expression, 'Apparent things provide a vision of that which is hidden', to Anaximander.[7] This lapidary expression emphasises the power of inference, allowing human intellect to reach the inaccessible through the mediation of the visible. One may ask if modelling and, in particular, maps may be two such forms of mediations, making the invisible visible, something that can be experienced, and allowing one to 'see' that which lies beyond the reach of the senses.

The map as a Euclidean calculation machine

There is very little information regarding the evolution of Greek cartography between the 6th and 4th centuries BC. In fact, we must refer to Strabo, at the beginning of the Christian era, in order to have a comprehensive view of Alexandrian cartography, especially that of Eratosthenes (3rd century BC), who is only known through indirect tradition.

---

[7] Sextus Empiricus, *Adversus Mathematicos*, VII, 140. We cannot elaborate on this quote here. G.E.R. Lloyd, *op. cit.* n. 4, p. 338-341 puts it a framework of analogical thought, and rightly associates it with Herodotus's thinking on the source of the Nile, conjectured, by analogy, with the source of the Danube : II, 33. This reasoning is supported by the Ionian map's symmetric organisation.

A discursive object

The Alexandrian map is, above all, a discursive object. Modern restitutions of Eratostenes's map reintroduced evidence of a physical, materialised figure into our reading of Greek geographers. This occurs when Strabo refers to an unseen device, which he describes and deconstructs in a set of propositions, affirmations, and measurements, providing fodder for criticism and rectification. Strabo was familiar with Alexandrian cartography. However, there is no proof that he ever drew a map himself, or that he had even had one on hand during the writing of his *Geography*. By linking the discursive forms of periegeses and journeying through Alexandrian cartography, which was clearly stated in his first two books, Strabo invites reflection on a new status and new uses for maps which, after over more than two centuries, finally became a transferable device.

If modern historians of Alexandrian science often systematically reconstruct its frameworks, foundations, and content by reorganising the logics reused by ancient traditions in their discursive projects, then it also seems important to make this tradition the focus of historical enquiry and to find clues therein regarding particular forms of knowledge acquisition and transmission. What is it about this absent, invisible, immaterial map, whose evolution and transmission could be observed in the works of the Peripatetic Dicearchus and the Platonic Eudoxus, Eratosthenes, Hipparchus, Poseidonius, Polybius, and Strabo himself, from the 4th Century BC all the way up to the Christian era?

Anaximander's map was groundbreaking. From the outset, it represented everything, and had the power both of a metaphor and of an intellectual model. It was a 'black box', leaving little room for critical deconstruction or even its own perfectibility. Also, the development of geography, with Hecataeus of Miletus and Herodotus, seemed to be governed by a different paradigm, where perfecting the geometric model was abandoned in favour of a comprehensive and cumulative model of knowledge that was better able to integrate new information brought back by travellers.

Strabo describes one point in the development of geography where maps lost their ontological power, or at least required constant justification. Hence, maps went from cartographer to cartographer, allowing them to verify routes, correct positions, and add new ones. Maps were both a basis for reasoning, calculations, and syllogisms and the result of these different intellectual operations – both the end and the means. They were geography's workshop, the successive steps of its work being *places*, and an archive where predecessors' work could be re-evaluated.

A step forward in knowledge

The Alexandrian map was a complete cosmological master plan rendering the world visible and intelligible. Its legitimacy relied less on checking the validity of the calculations and mathematical developments that allowed for its creation than on its coherency relative to an image of the cosmos as a whole, which could also be expressed through metaphor and description. Geographers in the Alexandrian tradition used figuration less as a means of constructing an overall, definitive image than as a way of translating the corrections and additions resulting from new topographical data into a graphical form. The map therefore simultaneously presented the state of geographical knowledge while allowing for its advancement, the end of a process of data transformation, and a starting point for its critical examination. The adoption of a technical language – that of geometric demonstration – helped describe the steps in drawn rendering and the reconstitution of data and calculations underpinning it. The map was therefore broken down into a multitude of local situations and problems. If the first two books of Strabo's *Geography* are any measure of this, the reader himself can use the geometric drawing to verify the coherency of a set of measurements or denounce their absurdity.

What was the purpose of the Alexandrian map, insofar Strabo represents it? It was an instrument for processing and transforming information. It later became a synoptic place where discoveries, experiments, explorations and various measurements could be recorded and passed down, through the flood of books and information that converged in Alexandria's library. It was a tool for creating order where disorder, dispersion, and distraction reigned. Maps filtered information, retaining only that which was geometrically translatable and could be plotted on a Euclidean plane. They were also abstract places of storage, calculation, and measurement, crossed by parallel and perpendicular lines that did not veritably correspond to the lands they represented but that fostered discussion amongst cartographers. These lines indicated latitudes and longitudes of inhabited lands, defined alignments allowing for the graphing of points from north to south and from east to west. Cartographers retained only the statements from travel journals, exploratory reports of Ptolemaic admirals or elephant hunters that were likely to be poured through filters of successive decantation, thus eliminating subjective points-of-views and travel anecdotes – the myopia of travellers journeying between a point A and a point B. What was left was the mathematical refinement of measurement in stages that can be broken down into partial measurements, permitting axes to be drawn, gaps to be evaluated, points to be aligned, and, most importantly, new measurements to be produced by syllogism and thus new figures drawn. Eratosthenes's orthogonal-projection map is therefore a seemingly strange device that summarises information in a conventional and codified way, and on the limited surface of a 'board', reveals that which books could not. The Euclidean map allowed proven intervals to be displaced from one region to another on the Earth and calculations to be delocalised in the surprising form of mental voyages: The parallel running through Brittany is the same as that at Borysthenes; Meroë's parallel is also located at the southern capes of India, while Byzantium, as depicted in gnomon's shadow, is situated at the same latitude as Marseille and, hence, 3,700 parallel stages from Borysthenes.

It is a space of equations, where measurements are mobile and cumulative. The device gives formal and intellectual coherency to data manipulation. However, the accuracy of the lines and distances, in Hipparchus's opinion, only thinly disguises their fragile foundations. Only astronomical measurements – not Eratosthenes's geometric patchwork – allow for the position of places to be established with any certitude.

When maps invite a step back

Nothing indicates that Hellenistic cartography emerged from a geometrical framework entirely aimed at creating order, parallelism, and 'symmetry' out of the disorder of data. Eratosthenes's map is also emblematic of a characteristically Alexandrian process, as it reflects the Platonic formation of a scholar enamoured by deviations and accurate measurements, the harmony of the world, historical chronology, geodesy, and geography. In other words, it is a discipline that aims to resorb the multiplication of signs.

Certainly in the Greek world, we could not find any source with the least mention of maps used for trips, of *portulan*-based navigation, or of maps used for political and military purposes.

An instrument of conquest

Maps are tools for the long-distance, mathematical conquest of the world, starting from the Alexandrian centre. They allow for places to be positioned in a space of global commensurability. The most striking trait is the interaction between the graphics and the logical and discursive operations to which they give rise. Strabo's texts hint that graphics were a diagrammatic device, an ensemble of lines allowing longitudes, latitudes, and deviations to be defined, among which polygons are inscribed. Maps lend themselves to a surprisingly abstract, intellectual vision of the world. They are a view of the spirit, not only in terms of their instrumental value in the geographical process (verification, proof, persuasion, controversy, etc.), but also in terms of the simplicity of viewpoints they invite, i.e. understanding inhabited lands as geometric plans structured by lines, in which figures are embedded. We must rise above the realm of the senses and empirical viewpoints to seize the inherent order of things in these graphic constructions. These constructions provide both an overall vision as well as details; their efficiency comes from consistently and simultaneously showing the many mathematical relationships that have been successively inscribed.

Does this mean that these maps have remained enclosed in the geometers' cabinets, in the Museum of Alexandria, or in Athenian philosophy schools like Aristotle's Academy? Undoubtedly. However, this does not preclude the circulation of other maps that are potentially more schematic and archaic in terms of their representations of inhabited lands.[8] However, it is clear that it was not these maps that organised the Greek vision of the world, coming as they did from the Hellenistic world. For those with access to the teachings of grammarians and rhetors, Classical works provided important geo-ethnographic references. Dionysius Periegetes's *Description of the Inhabited Earth* (2nd Century AD) attests to the preponderance of literature in geographical teaching, even if the text itself, in all likelihood, relied on maps. Of the latter, it suggests the broad outlines to the imagination of its readers simply by virtue of descriptive language.

---

[8]   See, for example, Plutarch, *Life of Theseus*, 1.

A cosmic point-of-view

The intellectual efficiency of maps, however, cannot be reduced to syllogistic operations and the complex treatment of topographical data, as attested to by Strabo. The technical work of constructing maps, of verification, and of calculation seems to have been a highly specialised activity that involved an infinitesimal number of scholars, according to conservative estimates. On the other hand, we hypothesise that Hellenistic cartography had a major impact in philosophy schools. An instrument of scientific instruction in the same way as different types of celestial spheres were, they may also have offered a physical and visual basis for spiritual exercises, whose fundamental role in different Greco-Roman philosophy movements Pierre Hadot underlined.[9] Stoicism, medium Platonism, and cynicism were examples of the spread of *kataskopos* (sic.), an 'over-view' of the terrestrial world, resulting in a relativisation of human values and accomplishments, as well as the adoption of the intellectual point-of-view of a soul discovering the beauty and order of the world beyond the shimmering appearances and limited knowledge of men. In this exercise, where the subject is removed from the world of the senses, from superficial things towards terrestrial regions where the Earth is seen in its totality, the map as a celestial sphere is a support for meditation. Their sensory and physical anchoring points allow for a positioning of the mind's eye beyond the corporeal envelope, to bring the gaze and the soul closer to divinity.

To consider a map is to adopt a cosmic perspective, free from the mist of the empirical world, and achieve comprehensive understanding. They ask us to take a step back, to detach ourselves from the illusions of the human world, vain knowledge, and all that distracts from essential activities, knowledge of self and the search for wisdom. Maps are also lessons in morality: to free ourselves from earthly vanities, glory, and riches. These traditional themes of the Cynic diatribe are notably relayed by Lucian, who several times played on the theme of the aerial view of Earth, with the epistemological and ethical effects of a scale change.

Following such a spiritual itinerary liberates the soul from its corporeal envelope. Maps encourage us to follow scenarios of ascension and

---

[9]   Pierre Hadot, *Exercices spirituels et philosophie antique*, Paris: Etudes Augustiniennes, 1981; - *La citadelle intérieure. Introduction aux* Pensées *de Marc-Aurèle*, Paris: Fayard, 1992 (notably Chapter 3, '*Les pensées comme exercices spirituels*') – *Qu'est-ce que la philosophie antique ?* Paris: Gallimard, 1995.

ecstatic visions, which authors like Maximus of Tyre, Philo of Alexandria, Seneca, and Marcus Aurelius each describe in their own way.

Geometry was the instrument in this ascetic view, as Maximus of Tyre, a contemporary of Emperor Commodus, explains. Thanks to geometry, maps were able to extend his field of vision to the entire surface of the Earth, as a magnificent spectacle of the celestial sphere in orbit with all its stars: 'Do you see this vast, this immense sea, covering the greater part of the Earth, and uniting its different regions, which you had never heard spoken of before now, and which you can never hope to see?' Geometry is a chariot that soars like an eagle: 'Oh you, who are a stranger to these sublime regions, I charge myself with leading you there. I will build for you a light skiff. I shall trust you to geometry…'.[10]

A philosophical form of contemplation

Manuals of astronomical vulgarisation, like that of Geminos, or of geography, like that of Dionysius Periegetes (which purports to be a voyage of the mind above the Earth); maps and celestial spheres, full or armillary, define an intellectual field wherein scientific study is a propaedeutic to forms of philosophical contemplation. Eratosthenes himself describes in the poem *Hermes* a cosmic vision of a celestial sphere and of the Earth, where the eye can move from the Milky Way to terrestrial zones. Such was this immediate, intellectual vision that a long mathematical work later materialised through cartographic mediation. 'Scipio's Dream' in Book VI of Cicero's *Republic* invites the reader to contemplate the nine nested spheres that make up the Pre-Copernican universe. As the centre, the terrestrial sphere is described in detail, with climate zones and four inhabited worlds symmetrical one to the other. This cosmic view of the Earth underlines its structure and geometrical order: the soul sees the world's order while the empirical view focuses on the armillary sphere or a cartographic diagram. This is one source of the tradition of medieval, schematic world maps with 'zones'.

The iconography of celestial spheres, particularly Torre Annunziata's 'Philosopher's Mosaic' (1st century AD), perhaps describes a Hellenistic worldview, bringing us to the heart of the intellectual and spiritual

---

[10] Maximus of Tyr. *Dissertations*, XXXVII, 8.

practices taught in philosophy schools.[11] The highly visible sphere in the foreground, amidst a circle of studious philosophers, is not only the basis for an astronomy lesson in the technical sense of the term, but also undoubtedly lends itself to a larger discussion and to meditation. It is a strange device whereby philosophers surround the object, looking at it from the outside (in other words, from nowhere), project a mental view to inside of it, contemplating its mechanics and immensity, plunging their thoughts into the centre of this infinitesimally small point which is the human world.

The spread of celestial mechanics in Hellenistic culture, though dependent on mathematical knowledge, can also be explained by the use of this type of miniaturised model in meditative and contemplative exercises, where the mind's eye takes over from those of the body and moves from the visible to the invisible, and from the sensory to the intelligible. Perhaps one of the goals of scientific instruction in philosophy schools was to achieve wisdom through the experience of the soul traveling through the world's sphere.

Hence, maps from the Hellenistic and Imperial Era had a much greater impact on cartography, strictly speaking, than history suggests. Reputed cartographers were either associated with philosophy schools or established in Alexandria. These individuals appear to have been highly specialised astronomers and geometricians more interested in the theoretical dimensions and mathematical concerns inherent to the creation of maps than to their political and practical implications. Philosophy school students' training included initiation to geometry and spherical astronomy. It is within this framework that geographical maps were able to leave their mark, for all that remains of them are records of the eye's and mind's view on our world, a practice that allowed for philosophical meditation on the world's order and the hierarchy of its values. Maps also allowed for a certain level of abstraction, heightened thinking by successive degrees: they defined a physical location, an external position, and a distance relative to the human world.

---

[11]   For a more detailed discussion of this mosaic and a different interpretation from that expressed here, see K. Gaiser, *Das Philosophenmosaik in Neapel. Eine Darstellung der platonischen Akademie*, Heidelberg: Carl Winter, Universtitätsverlag, 1980.

The user's viewpoint

From Anaximander to the philosophy schools of the Greco-Roman world, maps have evolved not only in terms of their geographic content, cosmological assumptions, and geometric foundations, but also in terms of viewpoint and the type of intellectual processes to which they lend themselves. Greek maps were interfaces between the visible and invisible, and they played an instrumental role in forms of speculative thought that allowed the human mind to understand that which was inaccessible to the senses. Modelling the Earth was part of a larger cosmological project; it was the basis for archiving geographical knowledge, was subject to the codes and laws of Euclidean geometry, and was the catalyst for an intellectual and spiritual journey that led to a theoretical outlook on the world. The Greek map is a record of both successive intellectual projects and specific cultural practices.

Anaximander's map was unquestionably simple. However, it was also comprehensive, and simultaneously circumscribes everything within clear contours, thereby defining the scope of knowledge accessible to human reason. It was also subject to the rules of a form of geometry that appeared to be the architectonic principle of the cosmos. Between Athens and Alexandria, the nature of maps changed. Their geometrical structure offered a new visual and intellectual object by translating the empirical data of texts into a universal language. Maps succeeded in showing the geographical places described in texts in relation to one another, in terms of both distance and symmetry. They indicated spaces inhabited by people, revealing the major alignments that only geometry can demonstrate and breaking down their expanses into juxtaposed, measurable shapes. Here, viewpoint cannot be dissociated from calculation. Geometry allows us to see space and Earth, free from all contingencies, as relationships and mathematical distances. Maps therefore elicit viewpoints and require technical processes similar to those used to understand geometrical figures: measurement, comparison, division, and assembly. These spaces of syllogism are devised to produce order. Cartographic metaphor, which can be seen in the Hellenistic and Greco-Roman world, demonstrates the importance of the imaginary vision born of the drawings of geometricians, which led to a disincarnate, intellectual point-of-view. They were the origin of apocalyptic scenarios wherein the truth of the world was discovered without meditation or spiritual journeys, leading to the relativizing of the scale of terrestrial values. As all proportions were equal, maps shares certain psychagogic properties with Tibetan mandalas.

What maps reflect, above all, are the viewpoints and worldviews of their users (and forms of rationality in particular), as well as the use of graphical mediation to tame the invisible.

First published in French: "Quand les cartes réfléchissent" © *EspacesTemps Les Cahiers*, 62-63, 1996, Penser/Figurer. L'espace comme langage dans les sciences sociales, pp. 36-49.

Chapter 2

Maps in Perspective
What can philosophy learn from experimental maps in contemporary art?

Patrice Maniglier

One might expect from a philosopher writing about maps that he or she propose a philosophy of maps. However, my point in this paper is precisely to argue that maps cannot be treated as mere *objects* for philosophical investigation, given that they are themselves *models* of speculative activity. Along with mirrors and paintings, whose resemblance with things has been used to conceptualize the relationship between an idea and its object, maps have always been used to express particular *images of thought*. From Port-Royal's concept of sign to contemporary neural maps, through Deleuze and Guattari's notion of the *map* to counter the paradigm of representation, maps have been extensively used as instruments to reflect upon the relationship between thought and the world. Indeed, this relationship between the mind and the world is both *intentional* (the mind is that *for which* there is a world) and spatial (the world is that *in which* the mind has intentions).

My contention is not only that philosophers should take seriously those figurative devices by which thought tries to conceptualize its own activity, but also that much of art has consisted – and still consists – in exploring such devices. As I will argue here, the history of perspective shows that the most abstract and speculative conceptions of the philosophical issue of the relationship between the mind and the world are deeply correlated with the invention of figurative techniques, in general, and of spatial representations, in particular. Maps and perspective images have followed largely parallel paths. Both imply cross-fertilizing intersections between science and art, both were invented or reinvented during the Renaissance, both closely associate the problem of intentionality with that of space, both are techniques of projection from one space to another. Perspective and cartographic images have constantly functioned as rival images of thought. My aim in this paper is to use this analogy to sketch a methodological frame in which current explorations of cartography by contemporary artists can be used as an intellectual instrument to tackle the philosophical issue of the relationship between the mind and the world.

Mapping / Thinking

That maps are not only food for thought but also tools for thought can be illustrated through several examples from a virtually inexhaustible list.

One of the most cited examples is the excerpt from *Port-Royal Logic* (1861 [1662]) where Arnaud and Nicole use the notion of map first to illustrate the notion of signs in general (I, 4), and then to illustrate the notion of *natural signs* as opposed to *conventional signs* (II, 14). Louis Marin (1971) remarked that maps are the last in a series of natural signs comprised of I) *mirrors*, II) *portraits* and III) *maps*. Interestingly enough, natural signs are characterized not so much by the fact that their relationship to their object is 'motivated' (as Saussurian semioticians would have it), as by the fact that they clearly manifest themselves as signs. Indeed, one can say figuratively of a natural sign that it *is* what it means, without leading to any confusion. For instance, 'we might say without introduction and without ceremony, of a portrait of Caesar – *This is Caesar*, and of map of Italy – *This is Italy*' (Arnauld & Nicole, 1861 [1662]: 157). On the contrary, someone who has decided to call all cats 'dogs' cannot say, 'A cat is a dog', without having explained her new convention, i.e. 'The *new* name of the cat is *dog*' (as if, when pointing at a map of Italy, we had to say 'This is *the map of* Italy'). The interesting observation here is that, because the sign *resembles* its object, the fact that it is *different from it* does not need to be made explicit. Resemblance is not a factor of confusion but rather a manifestation of duality. Maps thus appear as the mimetic sign most akin to conventional signs. The map of Italy looks like Italy less than the portrait of Caesar looks like Caesar, which itself resembles its object less than an image in a mirror resembles the object reflected. The map is an image on the verge of becoming a word.

Oddly enough, it is for the exact opposite reason, i.e. because they consider maps as non-mimetic signs, that Gilles Deleuze and Félix Guattari use the notion of map in *A Thousand Plateaux* (1987: 12). They contrast cartography and decalcomania to clarify the concept of *rhizome,* which is arguably the most central concept in their philosophy: 'The rhizome is altogether different, a map and not a tracing. Make a map, not a tracing. The orchid does not reproduce the tracing of the wasp; it forms a map with the wasp, in a rhizome. What distinguishes the map from the tracing is that it is entirely oriented toward an experimentation in contact with the real'. One reason for this appeal to the notion of map seems to be that maps are things to be used: a map does not refer to a territory as an image refers to an object, but rather as a tool to explore this territory. Thus, maps do not need to *look like* what they map; they simply need to preserve a certain number of significant relationships between elements that can actually be pragmatically connected by the user. In other words, although Port-Royal logicians tended to emphasize the mimetic aspect of maps while Deleuze and Guattari emphasize its pragmatic aspects, notably both use maps to offer a metaphor for thought in general. One might say they convey their philosophy of the mind through the way they talk about maps.[1]

But maps are not only used by philosophy as a model for thought. Contemporary neurosciences tend to describe the relationship between the brain and the world as a cartographic one. Neural patterns would consist of *maps* of their objects, and not of arbitrary transcriptions comparable to linguistic symbols, as has long been argued.[2] Furthermore, the notion of *code* seems to be more generally challenged by that of *map.* This is particularly notable in genetics, where the concept of code has been, and remains, so important.[3] The discovery of Hox genes demonstrated that parts of the chromosome were linearly correlated with the body plan of the organism along the anterior-posterior axis. It is not absurd to say that there have been

---

[1] Another particularly interesting example of a philosopher using the concept of map as a concept of concept is William James. See During, 2011.

[2] For a 'symbolic' conception of thought, see Fodor, 1975. For a 'cartographic' conception of the brain, see for instance Edelman, 1992 or Damasio, 1999.

[3] A good illustration of the domination of the symbolic conception of the gene can be found in France in Monod (1970) and Jacob (1970).

at least three competitive metaphors for considering thought and the brain – mirror, language, and map – the latter being perhaps the most convincing at present.[4]

Maybe even more importantly for the future, in this age of information proliferation, synthesizing massive data corpuses quickly has become a necessity. Hence, the linear representation of data through lists still dominant today might one day be replaced by a more cartographic one. Warren Sack's *conversational maps* offer a view of what is being *said* in one community that does not imply any linear hierarchy between the data (as do Google searches, for instance), but rather enables the user to have immediate access to the different options within this universe of discourse.[5]

It is thus clear that maps are used in all disciplines that deal with the very nature of thought as models for the activity of thinking. Should we then say that thought is, in essence, cartographic, as Italian critical geographer Franco Farinelli seems to suggest in his important book, *De la raison cartographique* (2009)? Should we argue that all signs are cartographic by nature? I think not, and for a very simple reason: there is more than one concept of what a map is. Consequently, any attempt to define thought 'as a form of mapping' (instead of mapping as a subset of cognitive activities) remains empty so long as a definition of mapping has not been provided.

My contention, however, is that maps are important for understanding what thinking is *precisely because* of (or thanks to) this very diversity. *First*, there are other such kinds 'reflective objects', perspective images being one of them, as we will see. *Second*, there is such a wide variety of forms of mapping that each conception of thought can express itself in contrast to the others by promoting one mapping practice versus another. Instead of arguing for some enigmatic cartographic *essence* of thought, I suggest taking the practice of map-making as an *experimental site* for speculative conceptions of thought. My hypothesis is that differences in the way maps are made (and even in the way their significance is appreciated) can be correlated with differences in conceptions of thought.

This approach to maps means approaching maps as 'dispositifs', in Foucault's sense, i.e. a field of variants, each consisting of a different combination of heterogeneous objects (e.g. words, images, movements,

---

[4]   Alain Prochiantz (2000) has insisted on this generalization of the concept of map.
[5]   See http://web.media.mit.edu/~lieber/IUI/Sack/Sack.html and http://hybrid.ucsc.edu/ConversationMap/EmpyreArchive/Manual/index.html

geometrical figures, instruments, etc.), versus a 'structure', where the variants are homogeneous (e.g. linguistic objects or myths or kinship attitudes, etc.).[6]

Perspective as a case-model: how figurative arts contribute to speculative philosophy

This approach to maps can be clarified through a comparison with perspective. It is well known that perspective has been recognized as being closely associated with philosophical conceptions of both the world and the relationship between the mind and the world. Erwin Panofsky's celebrated article, *Perspective as a Symbolic Form* (1991 [1927]), emphasized this relationship. While perspective was often considered a technical solution to a problem as old as humanity itself – that of producing convincing images of the world – and while it was discussed by the artistic avant-garde of the early 20th century on this ground, Panofsky argued that it was rather the expression of a 'worldview' that was specific to a particular time and inseparable from it. This worldview had cosmological aspects (it promoted an infinite, acentred space, as in Giordano Bruno, Nicolas de Cusa or Blaise Pascal, as opposed to the centred, finite space inherited from Aristotelian physics),[7] as well as ethical and political ones. For instance, it reconciled subjective freedom with objective reality. Indeed, the fact that my view of the world is distorted by my specific position in it does not prevent it from being perfectly valid for others, since the rules of perspective enable me to transform it into that of others; I can determine what the world would

---

[6] Foucault defines a 'dispositif' as: 'Un ensemble résolument hétérogène, comportant des discours, des institutions, des aménagements architecturaux, des décisions réglementaires, des lois, des mesures administratives, des énoncés scientifiques, des propositions philosophiques, morales, philanthropiques, bref: du dit, aussi bien que du non-dit. Le dispositif lui-même, c'est le réseau qu'on peut établir entre ces éléments.' ('Le jeu de Michel Foucault', 1994: 299). Since then, much literature has been produced on the concept of 'dispositif' and its applications in various domains of art (cinema, theatre, new media, maps, etc.).

[7] This shift from one conception of space to the other is described by Alexandre Koyré (1957). The intuition of an infinite, acentred, homogeneous space is perhaps best captured in Pascal's phrase: Nature is 'an infinite sphere, the centre of which is everywhere, the circumference nowhere' (1958 [1670], §70).

look like from where you stand.[8] To characterise the relationship between this *figurative technique* and those of *speculative notions*, Panofsky (1991 [1927]: 41) borrowed from Ernst Cassirer the concept of 'symbolic form', in which 'spiritual meaning is attached to a concrete, material sign and intrinsically given to this sign'.

However, there are at least two sets of reasons why this notion of symbolic form seems unfit to accurately capture the relationship between the speculative ('spiritual') and the figurative ('material'), so characteristic of the history of perspective. The first is, quite simply, anachronism. Perspective cannot be thought to have an already well-conceived 'spiritual meaning' encoded in a 'material sign', given that the formulation of this spiritual meaning came a century or two *later* than the invention of perspective. A quick look at the dates of birth and death of Brunelleschi (1377–1446) and those philosophers who arguably spelled out the cosmological and ethical notions Panofsky considers as defining the worldview perspective supposedly conveyed (Giordano Bruno: 1548–1600; Descartes: 1596–1650; Kant: 1724–1804) should suffice to prove that the story does not stand.

Rather, the reverse relationship was true. It was figurative technique that helped construct speculative notions. A good example is Descartes' conception of thought. In the Fourth Discourse of his *Dioptrics*, to argue that ideas do not need to *resemble* their objects in order to refer to them, Descartes draws from perspective images, in which circles are 'better represented' by ovals and squares by lozenges (Descartes, 1985: 165). In the *Order of Things*, Michel Foucault (1970) argued that once *resemblance* ceased to be considered, the only way by which something could refer to something else was one of the most important events in the history of modern thought.[9] It so happens that this event was *conditioned* by the invention of perspective. Philosophers were able to give meaning to what they thought because they had concrete ways of *making thought apparent to itself.* Generally speaking, perspective enabled not only Descartes, but Leibniz, Berkeley, and many others to substitute the notion of *resemblance* for that of *projection* as the defining concept of the relationship between ideas and their objects.

---

[8]   The arbitrariness of the *point of view* was particularly emphasized at the dawn of perspective. Alberti (1950 [1436], p. 78) famously wrote: '*Dove a me paia, fermo uno punto*', I fix a point wherever I like.

[9]   For a commentary, see Maniglier, 2013.

The other reason why the concept of symbolic form cannot account for the relationship between figurative techniques and metaphysical speculations is that it considers perspective a unified technique. The fact is that there is nothing like *perspective in general*. There are different ways of constructing a perspective image. It is this variation that makes perspective such an interesting terrain for philosophy; it opens up a kind of *experimental site* to explore the relationship between the way things *appear to us* and the construction of the space where the subject for whom there are appearances is related to the objects that appear or, to speak more philosophically, between the *intentional relationship* (being for) and the relationship of *coexistence* (between with). This is one of the lessons that can be drawn from Panofsky's article, particularly from his comparison between 'Antique perspective' and 'Modern perspective', as Hubert Damisch argued in his *Origin of Perspective* (1994). This line of research has since been superbly developed by French philosopher Lucien Vinciguerra in his *Archéologie de la Perspective* (2007). He shows that Alberti, Piero della Franscesca, Leonardo da Vinci and Dürer had neither the same theory of perspective nor the same practice of it. For the first three, paintings were thought to be made of the same material as the world they depicted (coloured surfaces combined on the surface of the canvas, sections of visual pyramids, intersecting devices, etc.). Dürer, on the other hand, appeals to elements that are heterogeneous to the image (coordinates on the frame, as in the famous perspective machines), thus anticipating Descartes' *dualist* conception of the mind. In fact, the first historical appearance of the notion of Cartesian coordinates can be found in Dürer's perspective machines, which used a grid that defined each point on the image by two points on the frame of the canvas. But even among the three Italian masters, the techniques varied, with their divergent conceptions of the nature of the world and of the relationship between the mind and the world. For Alberti, the world was made of individual surfaces combined within the painting to depict a situation (*historia*) as the well-measured proportion between those things. For Da Vinci, things were not surfaces but transformations in process. Painting captured the transformational nature of the world in an atmospheric, essentially unfinished image. More generally, Vinciguerra shows how the material details of the devices used to create perspective images (the hand, the eye, the frame, the surface, the line, etc.) are important for an intellectual history of perspective.

In other words, while it is inaccurate to relate one figurative technique called 'perspective' to one supposedly 'modern' worldview, it is not absurd to explore the relationship between art and metaphysics, as long as we compare *sets of variations* and not unique entities. Perspective relates to philosophical issues not because it symbolizes a positive conception of the world, but rather because it enables philosophers to experiment with the relationship between appearance and coexistence, i.e. to vary a parameter and see its impact on the metaphysical understanding of the image.

Strikingly enough, this experimental situation continues today. One can consider the attempts to overcome what was perceived by the early 20th-century avant-garde as the limitations of perspective as an extreme variation within the perspective paradigm, as Hubert Damisch rightly argued. Traditionally, the main objection to perspective by futurist, cubist, and suprematist avant-gardes was its inability to capture the subject's movement and thus reflect what it means to represent the world in modern conditions, i.e. when the subject is moving or constantly changing. It is widely recognised that perspective images require a single, motionless eye. However, it is rarely noted that this requirement came with another: the institution of what Panofsky called a 'systematic space' – that is, a relative but infinite, homogeneous, global space. A perspective image is a projection of the entirety of a virtually infinite space into a single point. It so happens that modern geometry, especially following Bernhard Riemann's *On the Hypotheses which Lie at the Foundation of Geometry* (1854), has shown that local invariance within what is called a 'neighbourhood' does not ensure that the connection between those neighbourhoods will preserve *global* invariance. It is impossible to infer from the local form of a space its global structure.[10] For instance, an entity living on a Möbius strip will preserve its orientation locally but not globally, since a whole loop on the strip inverses right and left. Or, more simply, a space can be *locally* flat and *globally* spherical, as the Earth is for us. In other words, the inference from local to global requires *movement*. To know the global structure of the space in which one is, one must move on it.

This argument can be expressed in terms of perspective. Russian mathematician Andrei Rodin writes (2007):

'In the Cartesian setting any viewpoint was in the view of any other. In the Riemanean setting, a given viewpoint has in its view only a (small)

---

[10]   The best philosophical introduction to this mathematical revolution I know of is by David Rabouin (2010).

part of other viewpoints. Other viewpoints are behind its *horizon*. The usual notion of horizon (the limit of visibility existing due to the spherical form of the earth) is perfectly relevant here; the globe with human observers on its surface is a sound model of manifold but not only a metaphor. Each observer can see some other observers but nobody can see all the observers at once. This brings the distinction between local and global properties of a given manifold: 'local' refers to a neighbourhood of a given observer covered by his or her viewpoint, and 'global' refers to the whole thing (the globe with observers on it). [...] Imagine that one of them travels, taking viewpoints of all other observers met on her way. Using her memory this traveller can arrange for communication of all other observers, even when most of these observers are found outside of horizons of each other. (However in the case when each observer is out of the view of any other, this wouldn't work because the traveller wouldn't know where to go.) The global communication so established can perform (and does perform unless the given setting reduces to Cartesian one) features which cannot be possibly detected from any particular viewpoint. In particular the property of Earth of being ball-like can be tested only by a traveller but cannot be detected by an immovable observer. Such properties are called *topological'*.

In other words, the fact that the connection between the mind and the world cannot be considered as a face-to-face, isolated relationship and must be conceived as a form of *communication* is itself expressed as a variation with the perspective paradigm, where local perspectives bound within finite horizons replace global perspectives with a vanishing point at the infinite.

My point here is that we should approach maps in the same spirit. For one, it might be worth trying to correlate the many ways of making maps with dialogically opposed conceptions of the relationship between the mind and the world. Moreover, mapping itself, as a figurative technique for depicting space, might usefully be contrasted with perspective precisely because of how it answers to the problem of the relationship between a non-local conception of space and a philosophical concept of intentionality.

Comparing maps and perspective

The comparison between mapmaking and perspective as regards their respective philosophical significance has been put forth by American art historian Svetlana Alpers in her 1984 masterpiece, *The Art of Describing: Dutch Art in the Seventeenth Century*. There she argues that there are two paradigms of representation in classical painting: the Italian one – perspective – and the Dutch one – cartography.

Mapmaking and perspective have much in common. Both emerged during the Renaissance at a time when the arts attempted to rival the sciences. Both manifest a historical shift from a *symbolic* to a *representational* conception of space (the space of the image is not used to express a thought but to represent another space).[11] Both, however, distanced themselves from a mimetic conception of the relationship between the image and what it represents, and both substitute the notion of *resemblance* with that of *projection* of one space into another one. Edgerton (1975) even argues that it was through his interest in Ptolemy's *Geography* and the projective techniques described therein that Alberti was led to formulate the rules of perspective.[12] For both, this implied that the representational nature of the image (be it a map or a perspective image) relies not on the individual relationship between an object and a specific portion of the image, but on the relationship between two spaces (or structures). Indeed, just as Panofsky shows that the most important philosophical shift in the invention of perspective was to have proven that *how things look* is determined by their *position* with respect to the viewer, maps likewise establish a close link between what one might experience (or see, touch, encounter, etc.) and where one is. Ultimately, both required a global conception of space. In other words, space is not constructed by a juxtaposition of localities but is immediately given as a systematic grid within which localities are defined with systems of coordinates.

However, Alpers argues that Dutch painters conceived of their work as a form of mapmaking in contradistinction with their Italian counterparts. Vermeer's famous *Allegory of Painting* (1665–1667) is particularly striking in sense, although maps are present throughout the artist's work.

---

[11] As far as maps are concerned, this shift can be observed in the quite brutal transition from symbolic maps to Leonardo's *Map of Imola* (c. 1502), for instance, which illustrates perfectly the geometrization of the image characteristic of the time.

[12] See also *Cartes et Figures de la Terre* (1980: 244).

Her main point is that the cartographic model used by Dutch painters is based on a conception of painting not as *narration* but as *depiction*. Indeed, the invention of perspective was motivated not by the will to create illusionist artefacts or replicas of perception, but as a way of retelling a story (*historia*), i.e. conveying the sense of an event belonging either to the mythological tradition or to the holy Christian repertoire. It was meant to awaken in the viewer a sense of *witnessing*, thus implying a strong emphasis on the *subjectivity* of the image, its narrative and its spectacular content. In contrast, the Dutch would have vindicated a more objective, neutral, informational conception of their work. Maps do not tell a story; they inform about a (part of the) world.

In addition to this basic contrast comes a series of others. Perspective images have depth precisely because they open on a *scene*, while maps are mere surfaces, more like a page in a book. Perspective images belong to the realm of seeing and separate image and text, while maps must be *read* and thus combine visual and textual elements. Perspective images are illusionist (analog) while maps are informational (digital). Perspective provides a partial, though idealized, *analogon* of experience, while maps have no experiential ground. Perspective images still look like the things we perceive, while maps look nothing like anything we experience. Perspective images are subjective, while maps are objective. In the same line, a perspective image is clearly and immediately locatable within the world it represents – i.e. it is always possible to infer from a perspective image from where it has been taken – whereas maps illustrate the paradox of a view from nowhere. Perspective images can be categorised with scenography and drama, while maps are more similar to lists and registers. Moreover, perspective implies a *many-to-one projection*: the whole is projected onto one of its own points, whereas in maps, everything is not captured in one point but through a *many-to-many projection*. This implies both a change in scale and a change in nature, i.e. going from an immersed experience to a quasi-linguistic account. Ultimately, perspective implies the absolute immobility of the viewer, who is reduced to her visual existence. Maps, on the other hand, imply something more akin to the infinite speed of the eye, although they still refer to a potential *moving* body.

All of these contrasts are summarized in the following chart:

Perspective	Maps
Depth	Surface
Seeing	Reading
Perception	Language
Illusionist	Informational
Exclusion between visual and textual	Conjunction of visual and textual
Subjective	Objective
Localised	Non-localised
Dramatisation	Description
Immersion	Distance
Scenography	Analysis
Story	Register
Many-to-one projection	Many-to-many projection
Motionless eye	Eye at infinite speed

Table 1 Perspective and Maps: Differences.

However, in spite of the many contrasts, maps may not be better suited to determine the ability of figurative techniques to provide a model of representation for a world in which both the subject and the object are in movement. Although maps are obviously made for subjects in movement, to help them navigate in their environment, they do not incorporate move-ment *within* representation. The subject for whom an image can appear in perspective is ascribed by the image itself a unique position within the very space represented. On the other hand, the subject using a map has no particu-lar localisation. But there is not more movement in absolute immobility than there is in infinite speed. Of course, one of the most common uses of a map is precisely to locate oneself on this map ('You are here'). The map itself, however, does not preclude the possibility of looking at a space, and even interacting with it, from a place that it is not located on the map (e.g. NATO chief commander looking at a map of Belgrade from NATO headquarters outside Serbia). A map is actually defined by the dis-location of the user: it creates a non-local representation of a particular space so that I can *be* some-where and have a *representation* that is independent of this location. While perspective implies the fiction of a subject's motionlessness, maps imply the fiction of a subject capable of flying over a territory at infinite speed. In both cases, the 'Riemannian' issue of the connection between neighbourhoods for which rules of compatibility are not a priori self-evident is avoided.

As a matter of fact, the same historical shift can be observed both in the invention of modern perspective and in modern mapping. Franco Farinelli has argued that the modern paradigm for maps appears with the concept of *continent*. Indeed, the first atlases that appeared at the end of the fifteenth century were *isolaria*. An isolarium is a kind of atlas in which each island, i.e. a unit of land bound by the sea, is represented on the same scale as any other one; Eurasia would then occupy one page, while the island of Jersey would occupy another, and so on. This convention is strikingly similar to Panofsky's description of 'premodern' painting, in which each object had its own 'organic space'. However, just as the notion of 'organic space' gave way to that of 'systematic space', where it is not the appearance of the object that dictates the type of space it is in, but rather its position within an a priori abstract space that determines the way it looks, the invention of the notion of *continent* implied that cartographic units were no longer determined by the contingencies of landscape. On the contrary, a piece of land occupies an independent, abstract, cartographic space (a continent). Of course, some might object that the notion of *continent* is far from capturing the idea of abstract space, since it is a concrete whole. What is striking is that there exists an equivalent transitional invention in the history of perspective, which Panofsky called 'partial planes'. While the entire painting does not obey to the laws of perspective, a part of the painting – e.g. the ceiling or the carpet – presents a partial realization of the *concept* of perspective, as though the *structure* of the space were juxtaposed to the agglomeration of the volumes. This is particularly obvious, for instance, in the ceiling in Duccio's *The Last Supper* in Sienna (1301–1308), or in the carpet in Lorenzetti's *Madonna with Angels and Saints* (c. 1340, Pinacoteca, Sienna).

All of this points to one conclusion: the modern notion of cartographic space is just as global and indifferent to movement as was the concept of space embedded in perspective.

However, this is not the end of the story. Not only have mapping technologies been dramatically modified in recent times, but art has continued to engage with maps, so much so that a subgenre of contemporary art called *map art* has emerged. It is therefore worth asking how this new historical condition impacted maps' capacity to contribute to a new, 'non-global' representation of the world.

Digital media and cinematic maps

Contemporary maps have seen and are still undergoing a historic transformation, similar to the one that took place for perspective with the invention of cinema at the dawn of the last century. The cinema introduced movement within perspective representation. The cinematic image is produced according to the laws of perspective, since it is a photograph. At the same time, it also builds the movement of the viewer's (theoretical) eye into the image. In film, movement is not a possibility of the image (as if the image could stay still or change); it is its very essence. A motionless shot of an empty room where everything is still will nonetheless be the expression of an event (becoming) and not the description of a situation (being). Even though, in practice, it might be indistinguishable from a photographic slide, it inherently implies that something *might* happen. This *potentiality* is linked to the fact that the limits of the image are not that of a frame, as Bazin remarked: they are essentially mobile limits, since something might always come into the field.

Gilles Deleuze coined the term 'movement-image' to emphasize that although we know that cinematic images are produced by the swift replacement of one image by another on a rotating reel, we do not experience an image *first,* and then that either something moves within it (e.g. a stagecoach moving from the left to the right of the screen) or is replaced; we experience the movement immediately. It is neither the movement *of* the image (as we do not see an image independent from a change) nor the movement of something *within* the image (as it is the whole that moves): it is movement in itself – not the movement *of* an object but movement *as* an objet. We do not see stills or the reel, but the unity of change. 'Cinema does not give us an image to which movement is added, it immediately gives us a movement-image. It does give us a section, but a section which is mobile, not an immobile section + abstract movement' (Deleuze, 1986: 2–3).

I want to argue that digital technology has introduced something similar in maps. Paper maps are to virtual maps what photography is to cinema. A map on a GPS receiver or on Google Maps is not individualised as a map in the same way a paper map of Paris and its suburbs produced by the National Geographic Institute is. While the latter can be seen as a portion of a greater map, while it is shared by many users and remains identical to itself as we move, a GPS map is essentially *moving* – an essentially mobile section. This is also true of Google Maps and Google Earth maps. Although it might seem counter-intuitive to argue that Google Maps are moving in the same way that GPS maps are, we must not be misled by the fact that movement in the former is not automatic, whereas in the latter, it is correlated to the user's movement. Indeed, a map on Google Maps or Google Earth is designed for the user to navigate *within the map itself.* Each map is a part of a larger map, and is essentially, continuously linked to all the other maps that would appear were we to zoom in or out or explore part of the map beyond the 'field'. It is crucial to note that, in both cases, the map seen on the screen is not merely an instantaneous version of a paper map, which could be almost immediately replaced by another instantaneous map. The important point here is not interactivity but mobility *within representation.* Just as Deleuze argued that cinematic film does not simply go from one image to another, in the same way, we must acknowledge that we do not go from one map to another: immediately, we find ourselves between one map and another. In other words, there are only *movement-maps.* Not movement *of* a map, but the movement *as* a map. Either because our movement in the territory transforms the map we see on our GPS device (or on the window of the game we are playing), or because we navigate within the map (on Google Maps), the map we see is merely a point of view *on* a virtual set of trajectories that we can perform *within the map* – a 'mobile section', not of an actual global map but of a virtual map in the making. I do not mean to say that we can easily change our maps; I mean that our maps are mere sections of changing maps – *cinemaps.* The ontology of the map has changed, and the mapping unit is now comparable to a shot in cinema.

This, I contend, changes the problem of globalisation. An individual paper map could be thought of as having been carved from a single, actual (possibly infinite) map. The global had priority over the local, as if there was a global map that was carved up into an arbitrary number of local maps (think of the image of France on an IGN map that locates the map you handle within the greater map of the country you might obtain by adding all of them together). With cinematic maps, this is no longer the case. As odd as it may seem, the global map no longer exists in the digital age, although the technical conditions of possibility of such maps comes with the globalisation of the mapping process (through satellites). A cinematic map represents not a territory but rather a virtual change. The whole is not an actual theoretical map, but rather a set of all the possible combinations of movement-maps – which is simply something that cannot be actualised as such. The whole and the parts belong to different ontological levels; the whole is not comprised of parts. Even more significant is the following observation: suppose one starts with a map of Paris on Google Maps and then zooms in on the fifth arrondissement. The latter image is not contained *within* the former one, firstly because they are both generated the same way, and secondly because together they constitute a movement-map exactly like the one displayed on a taxi's GPS receiver during a ride. It is no more logical to say that the map of the fifth arrondissement is 'in' the map of Paris I started with, than it is to say that the close-up shot of Clint Eastwood's eyes in *The Good, the Bad and the Ugly* is 'a part of' the image of the panoramic shot that immediately precedes it. The whole is not made up of smaller maps stuck one to the other, but rather of map-trajectories intersecting one another in different ways, more akin to the unity of a film than to the unity of a paper map.[13] A particular map does not so much represent part of a territory as express a moment in a trajectory within the map. In other words, it has become a *temporal* unit as much as a spatial one.

Contemporary art experiments with cinematic maps

This new technological context has inspired artists to use new technologies to explore figurative artistic ways of representing the world. The use of maps by artists of course predates the invention of GPS technologies, and the presence of maps in contemporary art is massive.[14] My intention is not to review all or part of this production, but to single out one work that I believe is particularly representative of how the problem of representation can be reformulated when one accepts that there is no global map, but only different ways of editing cinemaps. Japanese artist Masaki Fujihata, who combines perspective and GPS in a very original way, will be my focus here.[15]

In his 1992 work, *Impressing Velocity*, he installed for the first time a camera on a GPS device to record his ascent of Mount Fuji both cartographically and visually. The work is displayed in 3-D through a stereoscopic interactive apparatus. The viewer does not see a map in a traditional sense, but rather a series of trajectories represented as thin white strings on which he or she can navigate. It is a map, but a map produced by the

---

[13] Bruno Latour emphasized this flatness of digital technology and argued for what he called a *monadology*. See November, Camacho-Hübner & Latour, 2010.

[14] There is an impressive bibliography on the topic: 'Cartographies', 2011. GNS, Global Navigation System, 2003; Buci-Glucksman, 1996; Harmon, 2009; Lemonnier & Brayer, 2004; Tiberghien, 2007.

[15] On Fujihata's work, see During, 2012: 50–56.

artist's movements, instead of movements being located on a map. The
user can also click on certain points along the trajectory to launch a one-
minute video showing the visual immersion of the artist at that particular
point in his ascension. Masaki Fujihata commented on this work, saying
that it enabled him to compare two kinds of memory: 'objective' memory,
resulting from the recording of an experience situation onto an external
recording (here the GPS screen), and the 'subjective' memory of the person who experiences the situation in a first-person perspective (here the
video recording). However, the goal of the work is clearly also to compare
two kinds of duration: the duration of movement of a point on a map, and
the duration of an image. In other words, it combines maps and perspective; the movement on a map appears to be a pasting of movement-images.
The continuous movement of the map can be contrasted with the discontinuity of the movement-image.

This opened up to a series of works entitled *Fieldworks*,[16] which are
meant to represent collective memory by using GPS and a video camera.
Impressing Velocity features two main innovations. First, it is no longer
a one-person experience. It involves an immediate relationship with the
group. For instance, in *Fieldwork@Alsace*, commissioned by ZKM, the
artist uses a bicycle to wander about and across the border between France
and Germany many times over. He stops each time he meets someone and
records this encounter, however brief. Whereas in *Impressing Velocity*
the connection between the image and the map was somewhat arbitrary,
convention now stipulates that two spaces meet where two human beings
communicated. Communication and space converge. Space is constructed
as a social reality: it is made of nodes between trajectories and not points
within some abstract, continuous space. Since the video recordings act as
landmarks in the rather intricate web of lines, we can say that the space in
which we navigate is made of the communication between human beings.

The second innovation concerns the orientation of the screens. The
viewer now not only sees the space in 3D, but also the orientation of the
screens in this very space. In *Impressive Velocity*, the videos and map were
not part of the same image. In the latter work, they create a kind of odd
space together, where the black emptiness striped with white GPS lines
seems to be populated by *invisible moving images* like those displayed
on the screens. Each screen appears like a window opening on a qualitative space, in which another window opens from a different point of view.

However, it is impossible to recreate the overall experience of this qualitative space using videos. Although the depth of the perspective image built in the cinematic object and the orientation of the screens gives the viewer the impression that each video is a point of view on the positions of the other videos, it is also clearly impossible to connect those two visual spaces together in a straightforward manner. The relationship between the two is entirely dependent on the movement of the artist. The 'compatibilisation' of these images is warranted by the continuity of the artist's movements from one encounter to the other. In *Fieldwork@Alsace*, the artist's play with an invisible border takes its whole significance from this background. The problem is indeed to connect people with one another, to create the sense of a common world, a shared environment, and, at the same time, awareness of the variations and possible ruptures within this environment through the body's movement from one encounter to the other. Fujihata replaces the objective notion of space as something that is *given* – before and outside our experience of it – with an *intersubjective* notion of space that suggests that the space *on which* (or in which) we live (move) is comprised only of the experience we make of others' experiences. It is the merger of cartographic and perspective space in a single type of image that is the key innovation of *Fieldworks*.

Fujihata has simultaneously invented a completely new kind of montage, a new kind of perspective and a new kind of map. He has, in fact, succeeded in merging the three most important spatial figurative techniques: perspective, cinema, and mapping. His work is a remarkable illustration of how the tradition of artistic experimentation with maps in dialog with perspective continues today. Artists' experimentation with new media to investigate new kinds of representation of space is just beginning. More is undoubtedly to come. My point here was not to give a synthetic representation (a map!) of these experiments, but rather to suggest a methodological frame with which to approach those experiments and, more particularly, to emphasise their philosophical importance. Since history shows that the patching together new figurative spaces is often correlated with the construction of new metaphysical systems, it might be worth paying closer attention to what artists are doing with maps.

References

Cartes et Figures de la Terre, 1980. Paris: Centre Georges Pompidou.

'Cartographies', 2011. *Les Carnets du Paysage*, n° 20, automne/hiver 2010–2011.

GNS, Global Navigation System, 2003. [Catalogue,] Paris: Palais de Tokyo.

Alberti, L.B., 1950 [1436]. *Della Pittura*, ed. Luigi Mallé, Florence: Sansoni.

Alpers, S., 1983. *The Art of Describing: Dutch Art in the Seventeenth Century*, Chicago: University of Chicago Press.

Arnauld, A. and Nicole, P., 1861 [1662]. *Port-Royal Logic*, trans. Thomas Spencer Baynes, Edinburgh: James Gordon.

Buci-Glucksman, C., 1996. *L'Œil cartographique de l'art*, Paris, Galilée.

Damasio, A., 1999. T*he Feeling of What Happens: Body and Emotion in the Making of Consciousness*, London: Harcourt.

Damisch, H., 1994. *The Origin of Perspective*, trans. John Goodman, London: MIT Press.

Deleuze, G., 1986. *Cinema 1. The Movement Image,* trans. H. Tomlinson & B. Habberjam. Minneapolis: University of Minnesota Press.

Deleuze, G. & Guattari, F., 1987. *A Thousand Plateaux*, trans. B. Massumi, Minneapolis: University of Minnesota Press.

Descartes, R., 1985. *The Philosophical Writings of Descartes*, ed. Cottigham et al., Cambridge: Cambridge University Press.

During, E., 2011. 'Cartes et graphes: les usages du concept chez James et Bergson', in Stéphane Madelrieux (ed.), *Bergson et James: cent ans après*, Paris: PUF.

During, E., 2012. 'An Architecture of Movement: Masaki Fujihata', *Art Press*, December 2012.

Edelman, G., 1992. *Bright Air, Brilliant Fire: On the Matter of the Mind*, New York: Basic Books.

Edgerton, S.Y., 1975. *The Renaissance Discovery of Linear Perspective*, New York: Harper & Row.

Farinelli, F., 2009. *De la Raison cartographique*, trans. K. Bievenu, Paris: DL.

Fodor, J., 1975. *The Language of Thought*, Cambridge: Harvard University Press.

Foucault, M., 1994. 'Le jeu de Michel Foucault', in *Dits et écrits*, t. III, Paris: Gallimard.

Foucault, M., 1970. *The Order of Things*, London: Tavistock.

Harmon, K., 2009. *The Map as Art: Contemporary Artists Explore Cartography*. Princeton: Princeton Architectural Press.

Jacob, F., 1970. *Logique du vivant*, Paris: Gallimard.

Koyré, A., 1957. *From the Closed World to the Infinite Universe*, Baltimore: Johns Hopkins Press.

Lemonnier, A. & Brayer, M.A., 2004. *Le dessus des cartes. Art contemporain et cartographie*, Brussels: Institut Supérieur pour l'étude du langage plastique (Iselp).

Maniglier, P., 2013. 'The Order of Things', in Falzon, O'Leary & Sawicki, eds., *A Companion to Foucault*, Oxford: Wiley-Blackwell.

Marin, L., 1971. 'A propos du signe naturel: cartes et tableaux', in *Etudes sémiologiques: Écritures, Peintures*, Paris: Klincksieck.

Monod, J., 1970. *Le Hasard et la Nécessité*, Paris: Seuil.

November, V., Camacho-Hübner, E., & Latour, B., 2010. 'Entering a Risky Territory: Space in the Age of Digital Navigation', *Environment and Planning: Society and Space*, vol. 28, 2010, pp. 581–599.

Panofsky, E., 1991 [1927]. *Perspective as Symbolic Form*, translated by Christopher S. Wood, New York: Zone Books.

Pascal, 1958 [1670]. *Pensées*, New York: Dutton.

Prochiantz, A., 2000. *Machine-Esprit*, Paris: Odile Jacob.

Rabouin, D., 2010. *Vivre ici. Pour une éthique locale,* Paris: PUF.

Rodin, A., 2007. 'Rationality and Relativism', in J. Olafsson and J. Raikka (eds.) *Rationality in Local and Global Contexts,* University of Turku.

Tiberghien, G.A., 2007. *Finis Terrae. Imaginaires et imaginations cartographiques*, Paris: Bayard.

Vinciguerra, L., 2007. *Archéologie de la Perspective*, Paris: PUF.

Chapter 3

The Cartographic Dimension of Contemporary Art

Marie-Ange Brayer

Geographic maps can be found in every artistic movement since the *Avant-garde* of the early 20th century. What maps have been used, and in what ways have artists' techniques been seized? This transversal journey questions the entry of this instrument of 'measurement' into an opus that has become the geographic map.

Marking and measuring

Until the 19th century, the geographic map was understood as a parable of painting, similarly limited to transposing the world onto a planar surface. In the Middle Ages, the geographic map was considered an imago, like a painting or sculpture. Maps and works of art allowed for the displacement of one's point-of-view and multiple points-of-view, even offering 'several 'points-of-view' simultaneously but favouring none, from whence comes an iconic mobility [...]; the 'real' object is deconstructed in multiple ways'.[1]

---

[1]   Zumthor, Paul, 1993. *La mesure du monde. Représentation de l'espace au Moyen Âge*, Paris: Seuil, p. 353.

This dispersive vision was to become more widely practised during the Renaissance. Rationalised space from a central perspective reclaimed a monocular vision, assigning a fixed point-of-view on the world. Thus, at that time, paintings and maps resembled a grid of mathematical coordinates. Yet, no distinction was to be made between the act of painting and that of drawing a map during the Renaissance, as Leonardo da Vinci, who was employed as cartographer in the service of Cesare Borgia, surely witnessed. In the 17th century, maps and pictorial space were still visible strata that overlapped and covered one another, even if their respective surfaces were starting to separate from one another, pushing the map's pictorial quality towards its margins in the form of ornamentation. In *The Allegory of Painting*, Vermeer creates a *mise en abyme* with a map as the pictorial surface in an enclosed space. The map's knowledge is treated as a luminous field. By equating it to an act of seeing, the map is illuminated and signed as a painting.[2] Yet, its surface is clouded, and the map does not offer the same visual fluidity as the luminous pictorial space. A profound change occurred in the 17th century, with the movement from a finite world to an infinite universe (Koyré), with the projective geometry of Desargue, who used 'cartographic' projection models, as well as Kant's intellectual systematisation by way of diagrams and tables. Having become the 'paradigm of classic episteme',[3] the picture-map and its thought matrix became a substitute for painting-maps. 'So that the world could become representable in its entirety, maps in their frames had to cease being thought of as "paintings", in order to be read and considered as pictures'.[4] In the 18th century, Alexander von Humbolt (*Ansichten der Natur*, 1808) marked an important change in the conception of landscapes from aesthetic to scientific, and from artistic literature to geography.[5] Yet, it was not until the 19th century, the century of positivism and rationalisation, that an irremediable schism between painting and maps occurred, forcing the latter into the category of science under the new label of 'cartography'.

[2]   Cf. Arasse, Daniel, 1989. 'Le lieu Vermeer' in *La Part de l'Œil*, Topologie de l'énonciation', n° 5, Bruxelles, pp. 7–26.
[3]   Jacob, Christian, 1992. *L'empire des cartes*, Paris: Albin Michel.
[4]   Damisch, Hubert, 1980. 'La grille comme volonté et représentation' in *Cartes et figures de la Terre*, CCI, Paris: Centre Georges Pompidou, p. 40.
[5]   Farinelli, Franco, 1981. 'Storia del concetto geografico di paesaggio' in *Paesaggio. Immagine e realtà*, Galleria d'Arte Moderna, Bologne: Electa, pp. 151–158.

Although it lies beyond the scope of this paper to retrace the historical journey of the modes of representation found in works of arts and geographic maps, the fact remains that maps reappear in the art of the Avant-garde at the beginning of the 20th century and most artistic movements thenceforth, leading to a peak of production in the 1980s. How can the map's surprising fate across all of contemporary art be explained? What maps are concerned? In what ways have artists dealt with them? The birth of modern cartography in the Renaissance was simultaneous with the discovery of the New World, as well as with the development of central perspective in the fine arts. In the same way that perspective was akin to a spatial measurement system that separated the observer from the object observed, humanist geography – in setting rational limits to the world – delimited space as a measurable table in all of its parts. However, this unitary space, which existed for several centuries, burst at the beginning of the 20th century. Euclidean space was cut up, and a differential topography as developed by Poincaré and Einstein created a relative plurality of spaces. From that point on, there would no longer be a single space to serve as an absolute reference, but infinity of qualitatively and quantitatively different spaces. Since space no longer had any precedent, perspective, which had up until then been a privileged system of measurement, was disaggregated. Maps, however, drew these differential spaces together. The analogy of geographic maps – which are both plans and frameworks – with paintings allowed artists to free themselves from figuration, while reinstating a new representational order beyond all mimicry, despite the map's referentiality. Maps display a pictorial surface whose inherent segmentarity offers a substitute for the 'indivisible' space of works of fine art. Maps call for fragmentation and preventing any unitary reconstruction of space. Thus the Avant-garde of the 1920s seized maps as fragments, as heterogeneous pieces in a pictorial space that had become an arrangement, an assemblage. As such, maps play the role of space-time convertor, or a surface for exchanges between images and their factual referents. The map's 'linear, fragmented, story-like, or descriptive character is opposed to images' instantaneity'.[6] This syncopated description found in maps displaced paradigms of pictorial space and made maps into tools to extend the pictorial horizon to the geographic horizon. By leaving the workshop behind to work outdoors in nature or in the city, the Land Art and conceptual art movements saw in the map a way of extending a work's spatiality into real

___

[6] Jacob, op. cit., p. 44.

space, with the body in motion as the new measure of space. Faced with the 'post-modern loss of site'[7], a new-found 'extroversion' of creation became the hallmark of and instrument for making maps.

Yet the map is also a language combining words and images. Simply looking no longer sufficed; seeing meant *reading*, and in this hybrid act, vision became objectified. What is more, maps turn the subjects into observers and assign them a double topological function: an external one, and another that is projected towards the space's interior. 'In looking at geographic maps, sight is inseparable from the referent's construction'.[8] That is why works with maps demand more from the spectator. Maps (carta, forma, charts, maps) – etymologically, a support which is written upon – were used by artists as an objective pictorial substrate. The map is a nomadic referential space, a mix of distance and proximity, a doubling of sight concerning both detail and a more synoptic view. Confronted with a crisis of references and territories, maps in contemporary art bring together multiple elements: pictorial fragments, grids, supports, frames, peripheries, routes, and an accumulation of visible layers which produce a syncopated, folded, overturned, hatched, and reified representation that could never provide a stable reference but rather calls forth a plurality of referential spaces. In this way, the map is an instrument for reconstructing the space-time that is broken apart in works of art.

The map is an anti-genealogy of space where 'spatio-temporal multiplicity' converges (Deleuze/Guattari). The map is not one, but appears to be a super-positioning of maps, one on top of the other, which never stop moving. 'Voyages through different spaces, voyages through an exfoliated variety of maps. You have to lose yourself from one space to another, from one circle to another, from one map to another'.[9] As Gilles Deleuze wrote in *Rhizome*, the map is no longer a painting, nor a layering, but has become a rhizome, a plateau. If maps are no longer layers, how can they still measure space? This notion of measurement would have to be entirely re-evaluated by contemporary artists. From Duchamp's *Triple étalon* to Robert Morris' *Three Rulers* (1963), the measurement system would have to take its own measure and implode in order to transform the map into a

---

[7]   Louis Cummins, 'Une dialectique Site/Non-Site. Une utopie cartographique' in *Parachute*, Montréal, n°68, pp. 42–46.
[8]   Jacob, op. cit., p. 349.
[9]   Serres Michel, 1974. *Jouvences sur Jules Verne*, Paris: Minuit, p. 150.

'dimensional marking' of territory.[10] The map as a geometric foundation for the world, a grid of coordinates and measurements, has become a tool for addressing the foundations of representation. Even when a map seems to offer itself as a form of measurement, it no longer refers to a single point-of-view in a closed system of representation, but instead resembles a mark or imprint in the factual matter of reality. This mark would be a discontinuous measurement unit, a fragment of designated territory, an indicator of an intermittent spatial system for marking which does not allow for the reconstruction of a territory's unity. In the map's epistemology in contemporary art, reference slides towards conjecture, and measurement towards marking as a displacement of inscription. The map's continuous stroke is sectioned into an arrangement of dotted lines, creating strategies of de-territorialisation and overturning visible layers where maps as a view of a territory offer themselves as instruments for reflexive measurement, and where representational space and real space come together. The map has thus become a potential plan for multiple inscriptions.

A lost fragment

The geographic map emerged at the beginning of the 20th century, in metaphysical paintings such as Giorgio de Chirico's *The Melancholy of Departure* (1916). In the foreground, a triangular-shaped map with no inscription is spread out; dotted lines trace a maritime trajectory of islands along ports of call. The map lacks any place or name, except for the itinerary leading from one unknown point to another. In the same year, *Still Life: Turin in Spring* and *La politique* borrowed the same representational device. Each time, Chirico concentrated on the representation of physiography through hatching and shadow zones that suggest cliffs or frayed mountain chains. The map only represents one part of the territory, arbitrarily interrupted by edges of the pictorial space. At the same time, it is framed like a painting – a painting deprived of orthogonality corresponding to a tangle of frames in the background. The land this 'chorographic map represents could only be to one imaginary place; the map here is merely a trajectory, a displacement borrowing the most fluid element – the ocean – while the land, bristling with obstacles, remain unknown. During his metaphysical period, and in

---

[10] Deleuze, Gilles & Guattari, Félix, 1980. *Mille Plateaux. Capitalisme et schizophrénie*, Paris: Minuit, p. 388.

The Metaphysical Muse (1917), Carlo Carrà seems to be inspired by the representations of maps found in Chirico's works. The same rendering of terrain can be found therein, as can an absence of any location. A picture within a picture – the only instance of representability – the map serves as an outlet for an impasse to representation. In another of Chirico's drawings, in the middle of a frame with no canvas, hanging on an easel, a map is the only 'painting', the only form of representation, though it is full of shortcomings and is traversed by a-territoriality. The map becomes an atopical description. In Chirico's metaphysical interiors, the map incarnates the impossibility of a pictorial place, become a drifting fragment.

While the first maps appear in metaphysical interiors, they are found again later among the Dadaists, especially Francis Picabia. In his 1918 work *Les îles Marquises*, the geographic reference is limited to the cursive writing of the phrase '*Les îles Marquises*', which accompanies a drawing of a sexual mechanism The Dadaists advocated mockery of territory, as evidenced by Picabia's collage *Cure-dents* (1925), in which seven toothpicks are placed on a trivial point of the German map and in a starburst trace out virtual directions in space. From 1920 onward, Raul Hausmann incorporated maps into his collages, such as *Tatlin at Home* or *Dada siegt*. In the latter collage, Hausmann wrote the word 'Dada' three times: first in the slogan '*Dada siegt*', across the map cut out in the shape of a hemisphere and on the cerebral hemisphere of an open human skull. 'Dada' is likewise stamped on every territory, whether cerebral or geographic. In the beginning of the 1930s, Kurt Schwitters would sometimes insert the transport network maps or representations of the globe in his Merzbau collages, the globe representing heterogeneous topography amidst second-hand ripped papers or newspaper cuttings. In this case, the map was a sampling of one reality among others.

Like the Dadaists, the Surrealists developed a poetic way of mocking territory. In the *Surrealist Map of the World* (1929), Paris appears in Germany, while Russia, Alaska, Greenland, and a host of islands take up most of the map. The map became a subjective territory, a malleable surface upon which surrealist artists could move lines at will. However, Surrealist literature gave the map a key operative role, which is described in *Les itinéraires du Paysan de Paris* by Aragon or *Nadja* by Breton.[11] In the 1930s, Marcel Mariën also included many maps in his collages, such as those cut into the shape of fish floating in the sky (no inscription) in *Le Miroir du Monde*.

---

[11] See the text: Hollevoet, Christel, 1995. 'Quand l'objet de l'art est la démarche', Exposé, 2, pp. 112–123.

Another example is *Recherche d'un pays natal* (1939), where the reading of the map is inverted, preventing the viewer from deploying a synoptic point-of-view. In Joseph Cornell's boxes, from the late 1930s onward, cosmographic maps of planets and constellations were associated with symbolic objects. Here, the map is a microcosm within the macrocosm of the box, a search for a native place in the cosmographic infinity, a universal foundation for knowledge in all scientific domains which never ceases to withhold itself. In *Europa nach dem Regen 1* (1933) by Max Ernst, we find the pictorial map once again, with neither borders nor reference. The line of a maritime route, lacking any toponym or territorial rendering, is reminiscent of Chirico's maps. Paul Klee also made topographic paintings, such as *Classical Coast* (1931). In 1943, Marcel Duchamp did a cover project for *Vogue* magazine featuring George Washington. Duchamp placed Washington's profile in front of a horizontally oriented map of the United States. For Stephen Bann, Duchamp jointly used, 'the register of image, diagram, and metaphor (according to the subdivisions of the category of icon as defined by Pierce). The side-shot of the president (image) was turned into a map of the United States (diagram), and both were obviously linked metaphorically'.[12]

This brief overview of the use of maps in art in the first half of the 20th century highlights their role as elements of disorientation, motors for metaphysical or surrealist wandering and poetic/political mockery of territory. The map was manifested either in the form of a 'silent' pictorial stretch, furrowed with multiple crevices, without any indication of names (metaphysical painting, Ernst and Klee); or as fragments, a collage of heterogeneous elements incorporated into a transgressed pictorial space. Regardless, in these works, maps do not establish place; they are detached from any fixed reference, branching out into the imagination or multiplying existing places until their very disappearance.

The map as pictorial field

The collage approach in art appeared immediately following World War II and continued in the 1950s in certain works by Robert Rauschenberg, who integrated maps in the form of collages (*Road Map*, 1950). At the end of the 1940s, William N. Copley created a complex collage, *New World Map*

---

[12] Bann, Stephen, 1988. 'Truth in Mapping' in *Word and Image*, *Maps and Mapping*, London, vol. 4, n°2, April–June 1988, p. 508.

(1948), combining cartographic figuration and representation, description and measurement in a single image. Fragments of geographic maps fill a female silhouette, the head of which is a clock. The image is accompanied by a text entitled, 'Description of the New Round World Map'. On the right is a ruler that, in measuring the person, also measures the geographical space. In this anthropomorphic map, it is the body that measures territory in the representational space that, with Land Art, extends into real space.

From the end of the 1940s, artists used maps as pictorial substrates. As part of the Cobra movement, Pierre Alechinsky was one of the first to use geographic maps among other media, including notarial acts and nautical maps in particular, upon which he would trace pictorial calligraphy. In this case, the map acted as an historical, objective medium, bringing to Alechinsky's works the narration of a pictorial space teeming with lyrical subjectivity. In the 1980s, Julian Schnabel and David Diao, in the Cobra style, revisited this pictorial approach to maps.

In the same period in the 1950s, Ellsworth Kelly created a surprising collage, *Fields on a Map* (Meschers, Gironde), which was a pictorial suggestion of the topography of a region where the artist had lived. The landscape was divided into geometric parts. This stratification by way of stages foils any horizon or territorial unit. The space was no more than a graph without titles. In 1957, Yves Klein enveloped a globe with his IKB blue and entitled it *La Terre bleue*. In the same manner, in the planetary reliefs of 1961, such as *Planétaire (Bleu)*, the map is not an exteriority. However, through a process evoking printing, it becomes the territory – a cosmic one, in this case – that escapes all recognition, since it is the configuration of a mental space.

In 1961, Jasper Johns painted his first map of the United States, *Map* (1961), a work somewhere between the painting inspired by the gestures of abstract expressionism and the objectification of territory. In a publication in 1964, John Cage described Johns's approach for creating this work: 'He had found a map of the United States showing only State boundaries... So he transcribed this map's geometry on a canvas and then copied the map in freehand, respecting its proportions. Then, with a change of tempo, he set about painting quickly, varying brushstrokes and colours, and working everywhere at once instead of starting at one point, finishing one spot, and then going towards another. He gave the impression of always coming back again and again over the painting, each time incompletely... He then used a stencil and traced out each State's name or abbreviation. Having done that, it still was not finished in any way, because he continued painting and coming back over what he had already done... I asked him how many processes had been used in this work. He thought about it and answered, "It is only one process"'.[13]

Johns's artwork accumulated pictorial strata while preventing some primordial territory from being found. The map's partitioning was endlessly transgressed by pictorial gestures that continued to spill over their boundaries, thus negating any notion of centre. As John Cage shows, the pictorial process is paratactic and dispersed, never ceasing to deploy itself laterally, without privileging any particular spot. The space is in-between the subjectivity of brush strokes and the objectivity of the substrate. The addition of state names lends an objective marking to subjective pictorial layers that transgresses any measurement. In his 'all over' compositions, Johns used a perceptively planar grid (i.e. map, flag, target), where surface and depths were combined. As in the *Flags or the Targets*, the pictorial space is opaque, devoid of any devoid of depth. The substrate (the map) is also the plan. *Map* (1962–63), like the former one, was done in wax. The space is depicted as an opaque marquetry, where the painter's gestures once again overlap geographic divisions. The map series ended in 1967 with *Map* (based on Buckminster Fuller's Dimaxion Air-ocean World), which used Fuller's geodesic projection scheme. This world map problematised pictorial representation through an arrangement of fragments and marquetry stuck together. The layout of the elements in the work accentuated the centrifugal movement.

The irregular geometric cuts of the outlines evoke a map that would have been folded like an origami sculpture, offering no meaningful reading or any type of spatial continuity. For Jasper Johns, the map was an instrument with which to undermine pictorial space, allowing him to foil the interior of the representation, implode its references while incorporating other, equally arbitrary ones from geographic maps. His painting was reduced to a moving inscription that slid between layers with no hierarchy, thus totally flattening space-construction procedures.

Territorial rhetoric

At the end of the 1950s, Manzoni was the first artist to use the geographic map as a figure of visual rhetoric to state procedures for representation.

---

[13] Cage, John, 1964. 'Jasper Johns: Stories and Ideas' in *Jasper Johns*, New York: Jewish Museum, p. 22.

The work, entitled *8 Tavole di acccertamento* (1958), included a map of Ireland and another of Iceland. Both maps featured repeated associated letters of the alphabet as well as the application of fingerprints. The map of Ireland was reduced to merely an outline of the watercourses, lakes, and city names. The map of Iceland also featured names and watercourses, as well as some contours whose curves evoked fingerprints and could be read as topographic strata. In this work Marzoni likened the territory to a fingerprint, which can be read at the same scale as the map and whose subjectivity was inoculated in the assumed objectivity of the representation. Just as the letters of the alphabet are at the same scale, the maps of Ireland and Iceland have identical proportions. The territorial representation shifts like that in a rhetorical figure, beyond all referential inscription.

A similar representational device was used in the *Tavole zoogeografiche* (1968) by Claudio Parmiggiani, where the black-and-white spotted cow-skin is used to represent the continents (i.e. Australia, America, Africa…) superposed over five photographs. This is an ironic background, considering the allegorical representations of continents in the legends of old maps. Instead of a symbolic figure, the continents are represented in identical formal proportions, which correspond not to geographical references but to the background (the cow skin) itself.

This territorial rhetoric is found again in Marcel Broodthaers's miniature atlas, entitled *The Conquest of Space: An Atlas for the Use of Artists and Soldiers* (1975). In this work, the countries are all represented on an identical scale, fictionalising their geographic referent in a utopian manner. Luciano Fabro's first map, *Italia, carta stradale* (1968) marks the beginning of a series which continues today. It uses the map of Italy as a rhetorical figure, which Fabro reworks in every form and material. Often, Italy is represented hanging 'by its foot' in empty space, thus becoming an autonomous cartographic object subjected to every possible distortion. The map is merely an outline, the fringes of a territory. Freed from every frame of reference, it literally levitates in a space with no inscription. While Fabro's first map was a road map, most of those that followed kept only the county's contours, with no inscription whatsoever. The map is no longer the substrate of a representation; the material, which always varies, plays the role of cartographic representation and is identifiable through the repetition of a single figure: a country's border – be it Italy's or Germany's.

The territory-map

More and more maps have appeared since the beginning of the 1960s. In 1961, Daniel Spoerri made a *Traité topographique du hasard* using everyday objects strewn about a table. In 1962, George Maciunas drew a *Plan for the City of Wiesbaden*. In the same year, Constant conceived his *Labyratory,* while Wolf Vostell – the 'de-collager' – organised an event around the *Petite Ceinture* in Paris. Mimmo Rotella realised *Italia* in 1963, a 'decollage' of the map of Italy. In 1964, Stanley Brouwn did his first *This Way Brouwn,* while Addi Köpcke showed an audience a *Plan de la bataille de la Marne* during a performance at Aix-la-Chapelle on June 20, 1964. All of these works from the first half of the 1960s used the map in different ways, some based on pictorial indexation (the extradition of a map from its normal territory, like Johns); others based on an anonymous, subjective map (Brouwn); and yet others using demonstrative (Köpcke) or tearing gestures (Vostell, Rotella). In some cases, map and territory overlap, and in others, they disjoin. In each case, however, the map indicates a point of view on reality. The variable geometry of this cartographic perspective is combined in a representation that escapes the status of form. Where indeed can form be found between map and territory? In the shift from one to the other? 'It is however the map which precedes territory – a mock precession – it is this which engenders territory', wrote Baudrillard.[14] In contrast, we posit that there is no anteriority of map to territory in processes such as Land Art or conceptual art, but that territory is created with maps and maps are created with territory simultaneously. Map and territory are defined relative to each other, each acquiring meaning based on the other in functional reflexivity. It is this simultaneity between the two procedures in the constitution of space which goes backward from the inscription of a work of art into a predefined space. The territory-map is thus an equivalence of the two terms, a conjunction abolishing all notion of substrate.

In 1967, at the Dwan Gallery in New York, Carl Andre covered the gallery's floor with a map on which visitors walked. '[…] Immersed, rectangular "islands" [were] placed at regular intervals. Maps became immense and solid grids, topographic limits, emblems of continuity, interminable coordinates without equators or tropics',[15] wrote Smithson about

---

14 Baudrillard, Jean, 1981. *Simulacres et simulation*, Paris: Galilée.
15 Smithson, Robert, 1968. 'A Museum of Language in the Vicinity of Art', *Art International*, March 1968 cited in: Tiberghien, Gilles A., 1993. *Land Art*, Paris: Éditions Carré, pp. 163–196.

this map. In that installation, Andre included the map and the territory, without trying to combine them. The notion of substrate was entirely maintained. As Smithson wrote, the map remains a topographical limit. Though understood as a surface for inscription, its coordinates shifted according to visitors' position on its surface. Meanwhile, starting at the end of the 1960s, in Christo's wrappings, the notions of map and territory overlapped. Thousands of square metres of cloth stretching over natural surfaces both concealed and revealed the territory. Yet, it was about more than just covering-over; it was about the interface between map and territory. For Gilles Tiberghien, Christo's process was about neither maps nor tracings (*calques*), but rather an 'intermediate reality'.[16] Christo's wrappings are, in fact, more like castings of a territory, which became its imprint. The map here is but a converter between moulding and printing, beyond all representation of territory and formal constitution.

For Dennis Oppenheim as well, separating map from territory, which are embedded in one another, was impossible. *Annual Rings, Frozen River: St John River at Ft. Kend, Maine,* from 1968, where he traced rings at the border between Canada and the United States, is one such example. The growth rings of a tree were cut through by the arbitrariness of a political border. Here we find a map within a map, where the 'natural map' traced by Oppenheim was just as arbitrary as the political delimitation of the territory that it overlapped. This work likewise lacks a substrate; the map was congruent with the territory.

Through the dialectic between site and non-site, Robert Smithson's works also made map and territory inseparable. Only the map can take into account the entropic place developed by Smithson, since it already conveys this entropy on its own. The non-site is akin to a map pointing out a specific place on Earth's surface. For Smithson, 'the old landscape of naturalism and realism has been replaced by the new landscape of abstraction and artifice', and 'the landscape [started], then, to seem more like a three-dimensional map rather than a country garden'.[17] The map became a medium for revealing the world in its structure, comparable to crystallography, with which Smithson was obsessed. The map is a convolution, a rotation of space-time with no centrality, such as in *Gyrostasis,* where the frame turns into itself, abolishing in its spiral movement any notion

[16] Gilles A. Tiberghien, op. cit., p. 171.
[17] 'Aerial Art' in Holt Nancy (ed.), 1979. *The Writings of Robert Smithson*, New York: New York University Press, p. 92.

of border, of frontier. Non-hierarchical, stratigraphic, and caught in a lateral expansion, the map does not cease to move the territory. *The Map of Glass (Atlantis)* (1969), a map of accumulated glass debris, shows this in an entropic landscape transversed by light, a geological amassing of a fractured, crumbled temporal construction. This map makes reference to a mythical place, Atlantis. Smithson also created a map of Lemuria (*The Hypothetical Continent of Lemuria*, 1969), an imaginary country whose map was made of shells. A drawing of the work is accompanied by a map of its location, an island in Florida, to which Smithson added the presumed location of Lemuria. Three maps, with different degrees of representation, are simultaneously presented. The accumulation of shells is an 'objective' map, referring both to its factual location (an island in Florida), and its hypothetical location (Lemuria). The juncture of these three maps creates a total loss of location for the site; the map is a curveball within a map that, itself, refers to another map. No order of measurement is possible. The natural and empirical map of shells, the geographic map, and the map drawn by Smithson offer a fractured, atomised territory laminated in heterogeneous layers of the visible. The map, according to Smithson, could also be compared to mirrors, which he arranged in a natural setting (*Mirror-Travel in the Yucatan*). Maps and mirrors are used both to fragment the visible – dividing it into facets – and to absorb it in incessant movement. They officiate as instruments, not to impose an inscription of the work but to carry out a process of movement within the territory itself. In the same way as the mirrors were not placed on the ground but set into it, Smithson's maps functioned within the territory itself, making its objectivisation impossible. That is why *Spiral Jetty* can be understood as a map within a territory. In the same way, *The Map of Glass*, a coagulation of unstable mirror fragments, 'collapses' – in Smithson's own words – its representation. The image literally collapses into the territory. In this case, the map is a vector of absence, that of an original site.

Since 1968, Lothar Baumgarten has used geographic maps, the references of which are denounced as an 'invention': 'The world, without a map, has no contours, no limits, no forms, no dimensions'.[18] *Feather People* (1968) is a double map of North and South America upon which feathers bearing the names of indigenous tribes are glued, the existence of which tribes is re-imposed on the map that obliterates them. Meanwhile, *Night Flight* (1968–69), a map of Central Europe featuring Germany, Poland and

---

[18] Christian Jacob, op. cit., p. 51.

the Baltic Sea, is partially 'camouflaged' by earth, which seems to delimit the natural borders of the map. In this work, the land and its map simultaneously coexist, one in the other, the object and its representation. *Homage to M.B.* (1972–74), where the names of North American tribes are painted on feathers, is also a type of map since, for Baumgarten, the map is a segment, like a feather. Feathers are thus mobile maps without contour or border, where various topographies are deployed, autonomous spots as unities that give rise to a space beyond all syntax. Thus, in Baumgarten's work, the map went from being a physical object to being a metonymic device, leading to its gradual invisibility. Consequently, the map subsisted only as a process of visual language structuring, which the artist has deployed in space. With the map, Baumgarten freed himself from the status of both object and site, transgressing the hegemonic invention of space stretching from the eponymous gesture of the discoverer to the cartographer and substituting sensorial instruments in the construction of identity. Mobile maps were made of urucu pigment, feathers, charcoal, colours, and writing, with no inscription, in a fusion of territory and map.

In 1969, *Domaine d'un rouge-gorge/Sculpture* (Robin's Domain/ Sculpture) by Jan Dibbets achieved perfect congruence between map and territory. After finding the 'domain' of a robin in a park, Dibbets installed barriers near the woods where the bird lived and gradually moved them every day, taking the robin further and further from the woods. In this work, two maps are nested: the artificial one that the artist constantly moves, and that of the robin who adopts this new map in its 'natural' territory.[19] Map and territory coexist simultaneously, as the robin's natural territory is absorbed and displaced by Dibbets' map, a map whose measurement has been transformed into marking. Dibbets used the barrier as an 'indicator' of the robin's territory to understand space as dimension and rhythm. The moving barriers created a 'melodic landscape', as analysed by Deleuze and Guattari in *De la ritournelle*, where the refrain gives rise to a moving territorial arrangement. 'Refrain refers to any means of expression which trace

---

[19] 'After having carefully measured the domain, I placed barriers 1 and 2 near the edge of the little wood where the bird often went, but far enough away from its territory so that curiosity would incite it to fly towards its borders. Every day, I slightly displaced the borders until the moment when they were isolated from the little wood. Friday, May 16, this part of the operation was finished, and the bird often came to sit on the barriers'. Dibbets, Jan, 1969. *Domaine d'un rouge-gorge/Sculpture 1969*, Cologne, New York: Seth Siegelaub Verlag Gebr. König.

out a territory, and are developed in territorial motifs and landscapes'.[20] Dibbets played on the 'ritual' nature of the robin's territory to alter the parameters, and to 'interiorise' other marks. 'A territory is always de-territorialising, at least potentially, always moving towards other arrangements, other than if another arrangement causes a re-territorialisation'.[21] This is how Dibbets created what Deleuze called a series of 'shifts', constantly moving from one territorial layout to another. The map's plan and the territory's extent were recovered, in a way, thanks to a measurement that became a mark, a 'rhythm', 'refrain', or a distance modulator and transfer from one plan of inscription to another.

Negative maps

Negative maps can be distinguished by their absence of inscription and the impossibility of their representation, such as *Folded Map* (1967) by Robert Smithson, a map folded like an origami sculpture to prevent territorial unity from 'unfolding'. Similar to the geological folds of Smithson's other maps, *Folded Map* is an elliptical representation, bringing the map back to its primary segmentarity. 'The material unity, the smallest element of the labyrinth, is the fold'.[22] The map thus returns to its state as a particle of space-time; it includes the process of representation. Other maps roll into themselves, creating a circular territory that always comes back to the same point, like in *Site Marker no. 3* (1967) by Dennis Oppenheim, or *Geografia dell'attenzione* (1971) by Mario Nanni, a topographic map rolled around a cylinder. In 1973, Baumgarten wrapped a stick in a map of Europe, thus hindering a synoptic vision of the map. The stick was added to the silhouette of a bird painted on a wall, scattered with stars, thus forming an astronomical map. Its placement in the territory thus occurs without any reference. The map is no longer a surface for projection or an autonomous 'framework' for reference, but rather is transformed into an instrument for surveying the Earth itself. We can also cite *Globus* (1968), by Claudio Parmiggiani, a deflated balloon wherein the representation of the Earth, compressed into a bottle, escapes any logic of visual measurement.

---

[20] Deleuze Gilles & Guattari, Félix, op. cit., p. 397.
[21] Ibid., p. 402.
[22] Deleuze, Gilles, 1988. *Le pli. Leibniz et le Baroque*, Paris: Minuit, p. 9.

Other negative maps are marked by absence. As Smithson himself declared, 'What is interesting about the non-site is that, differently from the site, it sends you towards the borders… In a way, the non-site is the centre of the system and the site itself is the limit or the edge'.[23] It is in this way that the map of the *Mono Lake Nonsite* (1968) deliberately refers to the empty map of Lewis Carrol's *The Hunting of the Snark*. In this map by Smithson, territorial representation – little more than a narrow fringe allowing for no recognition of the space – is pushed to the limits. Perhaps it is the interval between this border and its beyond that is significant for the map, a map understood as a reversal of the visible, always on the border.

In *Map* (1967), Terry Atkinson and Michael Baldwin also express mapping through its negativity. The map here is comprised of the borders of two U.S. states, Iowa and Kentucky, while a list enumerates the other states not represented on the map. The map exists in the gap between its empty space and the one 'full' of toponyms, in a lack of reconciliation that gives it all its meaning. Starting in 1964, Stanley Brouwn's maps also incorporated this 'absence'. *This Way Brouwn* plots the paths of passers-by, whom Brouwn asked where they had come from and were going. Here, the territory's objective unity is understood by its subjective description. When there was no drawing but only an oral description, the page remained blank, and Brouwn stamped onto the bottom of it 'This Way Brouwn'. In these 'mute' maps, the space was revealed without writing, if only that of the artist's nominal imprint. In 1966, Stanley Brouwn created a work where the unity of territorial representation was virtually cut off in the literal sense. Suspended from a sheet of paper are a pair of scissors that seem on the verge of cutting along dotted lines that form a broken trajectory through space, as if they could divide up the real and, simultaneously, its representation. This dissociated territory, in which the artist tries in vain to reassemble the pieces, re-emerged in a more recent work, *Winter Jacket* (1986), by Bill Woodrow. In this work, a sewing machine fails to reassemble the pieces of a geographic map already interspersed with empty spaces. Another piece, *Territori occupati* (1969) by Alighiero e Boetti, was embroidered with silhouettes of occupied countries that emerged like islands floating in a space without inscription, commenting on the oppression of territorial occupation. The embroidered map, however, is an addition that demonstrates the emptiness and ineffectiveness – absorption into a space that denounces

---

[23] 'Discussions with Oppenheim, Heizer, Smithson' in *The Writings of Robert Smithson*, op. cit., p. 177.

its artificial construction. In *Garden (A World Model)* (1973) by Oyvind Fahlström, we find an equally fragmented world. Inspired by comic strips, Fahlström's maps, somewhere between Pop and Fluxus, reveal a satirical political universe. Here, a world map, like a plant emerging from a flowerpot, is cut up into multiple territorial blooms, impeding any continuous reading of space.

Other works from the same era, such as *Hole in the Sea* (1969), use a non-territory seemingly beyond any cartography, and based on a loss of inscription. Barry Flanagan plunged a cylinder into the sand and waited for the tide to cover it. He then removed the cylinder, which caused an ephemeral 'hole in the sea'. There was certainly no map involved in the proper sense. Yet, there was a clear marking of a territory – an inverted, absorbed map, so to speak, in a negative construction of territory. By burying the cylinder, Flanagan defined the limits and created a framework. Even when this banished any inscription, a zone was both geographically delimited and a landmark – defined by its negative nature and its absence – affixed in a territory's expanse. The inscription was made by a void, accepting a loss of the site, which could not happen without first having traced out a perimeter.

During an exhibit organised by Seth Siegelaub in 1969, uniting a dozen artists working around world, Lawrence Weiner threw a rubber ball into part American/part Canadian Niagara Falls. The exhibit was itself a mapping process, which the catalogue's cover also advertised. Even though Weiner realised a work beyond any inscription, except that of the moving water, the geographic map was the implicit, dichotomous substrate (Canada/The United States). Operating on the very matter of the reality, where a ball fractures geographic orientation, it literally 'pierced' every map and territorial representation. The space was built around a 'clinamen', generated by the act of throwing the ball into the water.

Location Piece n. 7 (1969), by Douglas Huebler, is also a type of negative map. Snow was taken from Bradford, Massachusetts, and sent – melted – to Oxford, Ohio, where the container was left uncovered so the liquid might evaporate. A map is also the substrate of this work, which is comprised of two photos showing the beginning and the end of the work and whose cartographic trajectory – invisible but structural – determines its final state. Whether it is in *Negative Board* (1968), by Dennis Oppenheim, or *Double Negative* (1969), by Michael Heizer, where a road hewn into the rock hinders central viewing, the eye withdraws to the periphery. The only thing left of the map is a border, a zone defined by its negative space, and the viewer's non-centric perspective.

Trip-maps

Trip-maps[24] include many types of maps. The following are but a few examples:

1. A mnemonic map recreates a trip that has just been made, as with Stanley Brouwn, where the act of drawing a map relates to the memory of a displacement. In *Cartes de la mémoire* (ca. 1973–76), Roger Welch asks a guest invited to a performance to make his own map of his movements around the city, recomposed with the help of objects (little wooden cubes, woolen string, etc.).

2. The map as a basis for an action recreating movement. In the context of Situationist derivatives, the *Guide psychogéographique de Paris* (1957), by Guy Debord, is a territory cut into unmeasured units, combining subjective movement in urban space where the itinerary forms the map. In *Buried Poems* (1969–71), by Nancy Holt, each addressee receives a batch of information, including a map, allowing each to dig up a poem that evokes his or her personality, which has been buried in a location chosen by the artist. *Buried Poems* is thus completed by the addressee's itinerary in search of the poem.

    In 1969, Dibbets performed *Paris. 20 points sur la grand-route autour de Paris*. Along a driven itinerary around Paris, a tape recorded a voice that named twenty landmarks. The work was at the interface between the map and the movement it led to, sectioned into time units. The same year, Dibbets asked a certain number of people to return a flyer to the address of 'Art & Project' in Amsterdam. He then made a list of the flyers received accompanied by their location on a map (from Amsterdam, Belgium, the Netherlands, Luxembourg, and elsewhere), starting from Amsterdam.

3. The objective substrate map on which the artist draws a representation of movement:

    a) The reversible map: The artist's movement follows the lines of a map, establishing reversibility between the map and real space. As soon as the end of the 1960s, On Kawara drew one-day trips on maps, layering trajectories inoculating a subjective time in the map's objective extent.

    b) The diagram map: The movement begins in a geometric form traced on a map. In the *Land Art* context, Richard Long traces geometric

---

[24] See Christel Hollevoet, op. cit.

shapes on a map (squares, circles, straight lines, etc.), which determine his own route through nature. Congruency is produced between the figure drawn on the map and that made in space. The map's geographic horizon is literally stretched onto the real space. The map acts as the motor of a *step* through space.

Douglas Huebler's works bring together strata of heterogeneous movement on a map's plan. In *Site Sculpture Project Variable Piece #1 New York City* (1968), Huebler draws three concentric squares on a map whose angles depend on the placement of stickers on two lifts for square 1, on an immobile support for square 2, and on mobile vehicles for square 3. In this way, the plane, the elevation, and the trajectory are all united. There is no other horizon than that of movement, the 'vehicles making a horizontal plan depending on their random movements'.[25] The map is an inscription surface where geometric shapes themselves are the mobile part of a work about space. We see nothing other than the parameters of this intervention, which is done simultaneously on several planes: the map, the coordinate tracings, and the actual markers. The map is proposed as a marker, not a measure; it is reabsorbed in its structure as index, a space-shifter. Thus, it is both a non-object and a function.

c) The supplemental map: The artist's movement adds his own itinerary to a map. For example, Hamish Fulton recorded the convolutions of his many trips through nature on a map, without following predetermined geometric shapes like Richard Long. Another example is Jan Dibbets's *Carte du voyage du 1er juin au 30 septembre 1969*, where he records the lines of his own movement. In *Map of Sound Paths* (1977), Max Neuhaus added a network of sound trajectories to a map of the United States.

'The map is not an object, but a function',[26] and it is as a function that the map has become the influx of movement in space. The map functions as a mediator between 'represented space' and 'real space' (Christian Jacob). The metonymic functioning of the map allows one to go from one level of inscription to another through constant shifts in point-of-view, perspective, de- and re-territorialisation, and the reversal of subjective and objective. This sphere of influence prevents any secularisation of thought, which never ceases

---

[25] cf. 'Douglas Huebler 'Variable, etc.', FRAC Limousin, 1993.
[26] Jacob, op. cit., p. 29.

to transition from the map and its actualization in the real world. The index-like structure of the map acts as a motor for movement, a loss of inscription that reconfigures modes of representation.

The dismantled grid

In *Soft Manhattan # 1 (Postal Zones)* (1966), Claes Oldenburg made a grid opaque by using aggregates of blocks overlapping one another, representing the postal zones of Manhattan. These modular constructions, which make an ironic allusion to contemporary minimalist processes, fragmented any cartographic unification of space. *Boîte contenant une carte Montmartre avec une fermeture à glissière* by George Brecht (1967) is a map of Montmartre with a zipper crossing it. In this case, the map is metonymically treated as a transitive function capable of opening onto real space. In *Photograph of Part of Manhattan with the Area Between the John Weber Gallery, the Former Dwan Gallery, and Sol LeWitt's Residence Cut Out* (1977), Sol LeWitt cut a triangular shape into an aerial view of Manhattan. Each side of the triangle traced the trajectory between three places – the John Weber Gallery, the former Dwan Gallery, and Sol LeWitt's own place of residence. The aerial view's cartographic space includes the map as marked out by Sol LeWitt in this way, contradicting the perspective space and any notion of *grid* and substituting an opaque surface of non-inscription. In the installation project *Voice of America* (1975) by Vito Acconci, a series of slides showing aerial views of the United States was projected onto a floor transformed into a map, while a reticular assemblage of ropes stretched across a room twenty centimetres from the floor delimited an arbitrary grid and interfered with the cartographic projection. Around 1970, Wolf Vostell made the projection plan of a map opaque by using geographic maps partially covered by a layer of concrete, reifying the territorial representation. If 'the grid is the emblem of modernity',[27] as Rosalind Krauss wrote, it is indeed dismantled in Post-War works integrating maps. The grid is a 'structure', a non-projective view through a space that offers itself as 'a transfer where nothing changes place'. Otherwise, the map is 'modular', at once a projective space and an aggregate of differential spaces, which operate like a 'clutch' upon real space.

27   Rosalind Krauss, 1979. *Grids. Format and Image in 20th Century Art,* New York: The Pace Gallery; Akron: The Akron Art Institute.

More recently, since the end of the 1980s, Guillermo Kuitca painted road maps on mattresses. The maps became opaque objects in space, a kind of palimpsest representation reflected like a stratum amongst other layers of paint through which it was transparently read. With Hermann Pitz, map fragments cover cardboard boxes scattered in space, under a lamp's halo. The map is significant from an optical point-of-view on the world.

Confronted by a territorial logic of fragments, the grid as a unitary reconstitution of space can no longer remain. While the map still indicates positions, these positions must be read in relation to a mobile subject, spread over many places. The map preserves 'fragmented appropriations of the reality' (Jacob) in contrast to the grid's totalizing, which re-forges a secular unity of the subject.

Stretching the pictorial horizon to the geographic horizon, the map's system of measurement is constructed at the same time as it is implemented in real space. The recourse to the geographic map used as prosthesis can be explained by a crisis in spatial reference. Maps have provided an intermediary status between representation and object, a collective inscription value, overruling subjective forms. While the concept of 'imaginary geography' is valid in literature, rare are the maps in post-1945 art that are purely 'imaginary' – these 'fantastic geographies' being the trampoline of a pure interiority. Even when they rely upon subjectivity, maps measure a referential space – that in which we live – and displace its parameters. Instigating a transfer from a 'form' to a process of 'formation' of a discontinuous and heterogeneous space, the map offers a privileged instrument for the loss of inscription in contemporary art.

This article was written for publication as part of a research project at the French Academy in Rome, Villa Medicis.

First published in French: 'Mesure d'une fiction picturale. La carte de géographie', *Exposé*, 2, 1995, Pertes d'inscription, pp. 6-23. ©Éditions HYX.

Chapter 4

What the Atlas Does to the Map

Elsa Chavinier, Carole Lanoix,
Jacques Lévy and Véronique Mauron

The 6th century. In the Byzantine church of Saint George of Madaba, a small town located in present-day Jordan, mosaic workers were getting to work. Tessera by tessera, a map was being made, and on it, an out-of-scale Jerusalem magisterially displayed. Home to a population and a religious symbol, the city is one of those places that, being more important than others, takes up more space. In 6th-century Madaba, several mosaic artists created spatial representation consistent with their perception.

December 2009. Several days had passed, but the results of the 'anti-minaret vote' still troubled minds in Switzerland (see also Chapter 7, pp. 167-170). The questions always hovered around the same issue: what image was Switzerland projecting of itself? Critiques were flying. And then, along came a map – a map that might set everything right again.

An approach: unsolvable problems, improbable solutions

Fourteen centuries and the advent of modern technology separate these two maps. Although graphic expression, as well as the principles of deformation

Fig. 1 Map of Madaba, Byzantine Empire, 6th century.

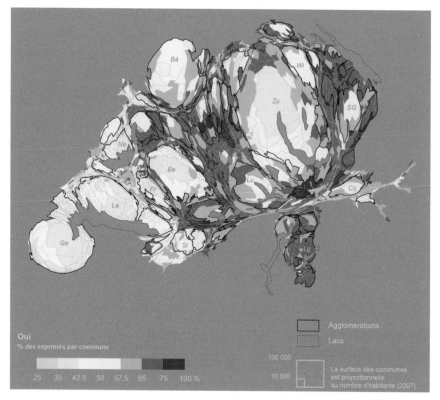

Fig. 2 Map of the anti-minaret vote, Switzerland, 2009.

and systematisation, has changed, these maps are similar in many respects. Contrary to all expectations, both provide a representation of space based on the same principle. We know that all spaces are not equal, that all spaces in the world are not of equal importance, and that the homology of many maps omits something essential about people that should be present in our description. Both of these maps offer a representation that attempts to overcome this limit. The mosaic of Madaba is a cartogram much like the electoral map of Switzerland. Is it an anachronism? Absolutely. It is even more of an anachronism when the existing gap between these two maps is measured. Over 14 centuries, the domestication of the invisible through mathematical reasoning advanced, bringing non-Euclidean maps or not explicitly cartographic spatial representations, into the tumult of error. Obscure cosmographies with no scale or orientation were rejected, and the oils of Flemish painters working alternately on portraits and maps were discarded.

Yet, we can measure how these cartographies from 'before the fall' – another time and place in the history of cartography – might be useful when read like the maps of today. All we had to do was take a close look at the Madaba Map (which we did), that treasure well known to cartographic historians and art historians, and yet largely ignored by cartographers. The technology is easy to implement; we are all familiar with cartograms. What we propose is discovering that which has not yet been invented.

This is in no way a gratuitous exercise, an abstract game, or an aesthetic distraction. Unanimous in the critiques of maps today are their shortcomings. Some even speak of modern cartography's aporia of representing the world and contemporary spaces, and imagine closing the cartographic 'stage'. The map would have had its day and fulfilled its function, but this day and function would now be expired (Torricelli, 2003).

In fact, 'normal' or 'standard' cartography has difficulty extracting itself from a domain of excellence where there is no longer a monopoly. The map was born of the demands of mathematical reasoning, a survey of a world discovered using a single metric of measurement. This map, thereby born of 'modern times', has now become obsolete. In this way, the map – conceived as a way of representing land – is incapable of representing mobile space (see chapter 11, 'Mapping the World Mobile Space'). Designed to establish borders, it is awkward with limitless spaces. Hence, as a kind of anchor, it does not know what to do with the experience of 'polytopic' spaces. Maps are made for population counts, not for understanding societies.

If the turning point in the social sciences did indeed take place in the area of geography, and while a *geographic* turn in the social sciences is becoming increasingly manifest, cartography has not yet experienced this double revolution. Cartography's move into the digital age has changed many things, but has not modified the field's organising principles. While techniques for producing cartographic objects have completely changed, the objects produced have changed very little. The certification processes in the space of the map, which can be labelled under the triple sign of homogeneity, exclusivity, and simultaneity, have not evolved (Chavinier, 2008). Worse still, the cartographic device offers formal and intellectual consistency to cartographic images and tends to transform arrangements and layouts into geographic beings (Retaillé, 1996), which does little to encourage paradigm shifts.

How can we move beyond this simple recognition? In the light of current developments in geolocation applications, some soberly envision a future of 'maps without a map' (Nova, 2009). However, we think that because the map comes from the construction of an invisible space, the materialisation of an abstract material order (Jacob, 1992), we must go far beyond the principle of a simple room in which to record geolocated data.

Our inquiry is thus developed in two stages: what maps does the 21st century need? How can original approaches help us create these maps? For the first point, we shall identify several challenges.

Maps blurred with the world?

1. The challenge of urbanisation. Cities and urbanity are everywhere. Today, how can we represent that which was reduced to mere 'points' in classic cartography, when the urban world has become the 'natural habitat' of human beings?
2. The challenge of globalisation. Projection was the fundamental tool for the cartography of the Earth. What does this mean for the social, lived reality of an ever-increasing world population?
3. The challenge of the individual. Traditionally, maps provide information regarding masses and averages. What happens when each individual becomes an actor, in particular an undisputable spatial actor?

4. The challenge of mobility. Modern cartography uses models to keep track of flows. To what extent do maps contribute to representing current dynamics? How can Euclidean geometry be made to coincide with other types of spatial representations linked to movement and rhythm?

5. The challenge of duration. Representing temporal dynamics has become easier, thanks to animated images. Yet is this a real solution? Temporal change is not movement in space, and much would be lost were the two confused. How can maps express these temporalities?

6. The challenge of a layered world. Representing a multi-layered world is what geographic information systems do. In this area, has the map become overly complicated to the point of becoming a hermetic language understood only by cartographers?

7. The challenge of technology. Technology adds an additional layer of complexity to the six aforementioned challenges. In order for cartography to progress, which of the array of current technologies should it use? These technologies, which evolve rapidly, often provide unexpected solutions, as digital technology facilitates flows and transfers.

In order to move in this direction – the second point of our inquiry – we have developed a three-stage approach.

I. First, to flesh out the idea of *cognitive elsewheres*, we have built a corpus (see Appendix 2) that includes maps from different iconic universes: 'ancient maps', 'non-Western maps' and contemporary artwork that share a close relationship with the cartographic project and language.

II. In order to relate this corpus to contemporary scientific issues, we will discuss the notions of anachronism, comparison, and the particulars of working with images. This development has been incarnated into a specific methodological device, the *atlas*, which, in our opinion, seemed capable of making this 'hybrid forum' of maps work.

III. Finally, returning to the initial questions, we evaluated the contribution of this approach, while accepting that the initial formulations have been modified and enriched through the experiment. We will implement this complex edifice by metaphorically using two animals that, though they share similarities, are quite different: the cuttlefish, which represents the 'backbone' of our cognitive expectations, and the jellyfish, with its many tentacles unified under one flexible umbrella-like body, which represents the open nature of the 'message' of our corpus.

As we shall see later in this chapter, we chose two main modes – the itin-erary and the grid – which, each in their own way, united our empirical materials. This was the case for the first stage of the approach, described above. We then combined many of our initial questions, notably points 3, 4, and 5, and, indirectly points 1, 2, and 6. To conclude, we will review the contributions of the 'jellyfish' to the 'cuttlefish' or, in other words, measure the productivity of our method relative to our initial questions.

Cognitive elsewheres: appropriating otherness

Once again, we have brought the scientific map and the contemporary artistic map together for the purposes of innovation and cognitive contri-bution. In the art world, maps and artwork have had powerful ties since the Renaissance. In 1336, Petrarch undertook the ascension of Mount Ventoux and contemplated a vast stretch of territory, thus giving birth to the 'land-scape'. Not long after, in Tuscany, painters laid the foundations of classical perspective to order space. At that time, the latter grappled with questions relative to planes, projection, and spatialisation with as much acuity as cartographers. In the 16th and 17th centuries, painters were called upon by the sponsors of cartographic series to work together with cartographers and mathematicians. Ignazio Danti created the famous gallery of Italian maps at the Vatican in Rome. The visual culture of this period materialised in the form of curio cabinets, where maps existed alongside globes, works of art and natural objects. In the Dutch Republic during the 17th century, the map was a pictorial element unto itself. Several of Vermeer's works feature maps, such as the map of the United Netherlands, which appears in *The Art of Painting*. A single copy of this map that so aptly illustrates the link between cartographic representations and painting has been found. This relationship is even stronger in painting from Northern Europe, which gives special importance to the treatment of surfaces. A shared perspective was established between painters and cartographers (Alpers, 1983). In the 19th and 20th centuries, with the development of scientific disciplines and art's plea for autonomy, the domains belonging to cartography and painting grew distant and developed their own techniques and modes of expression.

However, in the 19th century, the technical drawing skills of cartographers producing maps approached certain artistic currents (Neo-Classicism, for example). From the 1960s onward, maps and artistic images engaged in a new dialogue. Pop Art, New Realism, the Situationist International, and Land Art used and created maps, bringing the power and language of cartography to the forefront. Cartographic elements continued to be used by artists in the 1990s and 2000s. Now, the joining of cognitive and aesthetic ties between cartography and art is once again possible, based on the modus operandi of our era.

In the field of contemporary art, exhibitions and publications have highlighted the relationship between the fine arts and cartography, for instance *Mapping* (New York, 1994), *Map* (London, 1996), *Orbis Terrarum, Ways of World Making* (Antwerp, 2000), GNS (Paris, 2003), *Le dessus des cartes* (Brussels, 2004) and *The Map as Art: Contemporary Artists Explore Cartography* (New York, 2010) to name several of the more notable ones. More recently, London has been home to two exhibits: *Magnificent Maps: Power, Propaganda, and Art* (London, 2010), and *Whose Map is It?* (London, 2010). Our investigation to discover maps from contemporary art systematically took us to the latest editions of the Venice Biennale (1999–2011) and the Dokumenta in Kassel (2002–2012). In addition, we have also found artists' maps from other thematic and monographic exhibits presented in modern and contemporary art museums, centres, and galleries in Europe in the past five years.

In this way, we have built a corpus of contemporary artistic maps, some of which have been analysed and introduced into the general corpus of research maps.

The analysis of these maps followed a protocol that used a common interpretive framework for all the maps chosen. Our line of questioning was two-fold. First, we attempted to describe the object in its history and context and to understand it on its own terms. How was the map made (visual means and materials)? What does it show? In what context was it produced? Who made it? Then, we addressed research questions relative to the object described, for instance: What innovation does this map convey? To what family does it belong? What does it say about space and how people use it?

Appendix 1 is an example of such a descriptive document. It consists of several cartographic works by Hélène Gerster, a young Swiss artist who has been creating installations, drawings, and objects that directly relate to the world of geographic mapss for several years.

Plates of the atlas: setting up maps

The establishment and analysis of a heterogeneous, diachronic corpus that includes ancient maps, foreign maps, and non-cartographic maps in stricto sensu (i.e. from contemporary art) required the development of a method that could link maps to one another. Our thinking was based on two authors – Marcel Détienne[1] and Georges Didi-Huberman[2] – developing two approaches – comparing and setting up – as well as a tool: the atlas. The maps were studied as maps but also as images with semiological and aesthetic qualities. Images, both trans-historical and trans-generational, are space. Creating the plates of an atlas has become one of the intermediate goals of our research. The plates themselves are made up of several maps that 'do not know each other'.

Firstly, we re-examined the atlas, a work of geography par excellence and codified by the discipline. The traditional geographic atlas, essentially a catalogue of all the maps on a given theme or of a given territory, has given way to de-centring rather than classification, tranversality rather than cataloging, expansion rather than depletion. What follows is a proposal of known plates as transversal decompartmentalised, transgressive compositions that renounce all typology. Our goal was to create a montage of these comparable and incomparable maps.

The plates for the atlas were created through comparison and assembly. Following Marcel Détienne's lesson, we constructed points of comparison and through experimentation with our 'card game' (of maps), aimed less at juxtaposing maps but rather at multiplying them. Disassembling and reassembling cartographic reasoning and upsetting chronology resulted in unexpected reactions and relationships, novel questions, and original formulations. We sought the smallest common denominator as our basis for comparison, going beyond differences through conceptualisation with no illusion of creating a depthless universalism, and not considering the map as the very basis of the cartographic act.

We modelled the mounting of our map plates on Aby Warburg's *Mnemosyne Atlas*. Known today thanks to the fundamental work of George

---

[1] Détienne, M., 2000. *Comparer l'incomparable*, Paris: Seuil.
[2] Didi-Huberman, G., 1995. *La ressemblance informe ou le gai savoir visuel selon Georges Bataille*, Paris: Macula.
  Didi-Huberman, G., 2002. *L'image survivante. Histoire de l'art et temps des fantômes selon Aby Warburg*, Paris: Minuit.
  Didi-Huberman, G., 2011. *Atlas ou le gai savoir inquiet. L'œil de l'histoire*, 3, Paris: Minuit.

Didi-Huberman, this atlas put images against black backgrounds in an ephemeral, interchangeable way. It was the source of our methodological, epistemological, and aesthetic inspiration.

The assembled maps, the questions they raise and the spatial interpretations they invite are thus put together, creating a bond of ideas and images. A montage proceeding by friction and attraction is established, creating a form of figural thinking or *thought in images.* The montage[3] decomposes and recomposes, dissolving contrasts, renewing relationships, inciting contact, and generating meaning. Born of clashes, it embodies the shock of encounter. By combining, it marks out and underlines conflicts and contrasts.[4] This kind of montage, where maps and questions enter and exit the field of vision, creates a visual kaleidoscopic and a collection of attractions and ruptures between the maps. It is less an indication of permanency than of a *relationship* expressed in clashes and repercussions. However, the map requires in-depth study and reading. At once a time lapse and time suspension, the map implies duration, a suspension of time. The images are animated by a game consisting in removing maps, replacing them, or changing their position on the plate. They are from both past and present, near and far. The plates are developed through anachronisms and analogies; it is the interval, the *in-between* that becomes the place, the centre of the reunited images, that is to say, the ephemeral relationships and cognitive, imaginary associations. This interval is an off-beat that demolishes chronology and underscores a hiatus: a perforated mesh rather than a solid fabric of history.

Thus, the montage of maps renders a refocusing around certainties or acquired notions impossible, instead demanding non-centric, transcendent, intuitive thinking. The cartographic plate becomes *thought provoking*, and its meaning emerges from something unthought of, immersed in the relationships instigated by the montage.

The emphasis on relationships and intervals, and the act of moving maps to reconfigure plates based on the corpus of maps was potentially infinite, and induced a setting-in-motion of the atlas. The notion of montage, so dear to the cinema, is also taken into account here. Expressed here in a simple, 'primitive' way, the montage – which allows the maps to be moved – replaces the maps on the plates. The images appear when they enter into the plate's field and disappear when they leave it to return

---

[3] Montage as an epistemological method was used in Mauron, Véronique, 2001. *Le signe incarné. Ombres et reflets dans l'art contemporain*, Paris: Hazan.

[4] Didi-Huberman, G., 1995, op. cit., p. 304.

later in another configuration. This 'apparition' becomes a kind of presentation. The maps are presented by the theme (itinerary plate, grid plate, body plate, etc.). While the maps together have meaning, they also create possible meanings for the plate itself. These meanings are called into question each time the maps are moved. The movement created by the destruction and reshuffling of plates is the main goal of this mutating atlas. Thus we agree with Serge Daney's *monstration,* opposed to programming and defined as an act that calls forth a world.

Experiments

Fifty-nine maps were identified, collected, and documented. The variety and diversity in terms of techniques, printing, bases, contexts, and cartographic intentions was broad. Some of the documents in our corpus (see Appendix 2) are now recognised. They have been abundantly commented on as milestones in the history of cartography and could be analysed thanks to the lengthy works of Brian Harley and David Woodward.[5] Others, nearly invisible, have been exhumed from the archives. Garrison's map – a map of the Han dynasty found in a tomb in Mawandgui; Matthew Paris' map of Britain, creations by contemporary artists, and transcriptions of a Tuareg map all stand out for the singular way they propose an original representation of space.

We will now provide a detailed explanation of our two lines of inquiry and, as a result, two types of plates. Issues relative to the itinerary and the grid were gradually disengaged from a work whose intent, we repeat, was double: to describe the issues of contemporary cartography and to create a montage using the images. The naming of the plates thus entailed uncovering the issues, not the topics.

Proposed here in an 'unstable equilibrium',[6] plates 1 and 2 are presented as variations on the theme of *itinerary.* Even though the repertory of mounted images remains the same, the positions are clearly different: images are not set in motion without serious consequences. Creating the plates involved the same compositional issues and principles as any pictorial work. As such, everything is important – size, location, the choice of details, relative position, spaces and gaps, etc. – and requires a choice which reduces all initial ambiguities. This approach generates multiple plates is because decisive, definitive

---

[5]   All three volumes of the project History of Cartography are an essential resource.
[6]   Gracq, J., 1995 [1985]. *En lisant en écrivant*, Paris: Gallimard.

statements are not easy to produce. Thus, while the two plates we propose below may 'speak' of itineraries, they 'say' whatever they have to say in different ways. From one montage to another, certain arrangements nevertheless stabilise, becoming permanent fixtures. Useful conceptual and formal collusions emerge. From these, specific affinities are affirmed with successive iterations. We find the movement of the maps inside plates thrilling. Born of a process based as much on reflection as on intuition,[7] these experiments challenge the eye. They constitute the central tool of our exploratory approach.

Itinerary: an aesthetic of passage

Maps produced from itineraries were the inspiration for one of the first plates in our experimental atlas. This is not surprising, given that itineraries have haunted cartographic production throughout the ages. Plus, itinerancy[8] is emblematic of the major orientations in contemporary art, although cartography today struggles to take omnipresent mobilities into account. The *itinerarium*, the 'travelogue', is based both on a *praxis* – namely, walking – and a space, be it simply linear, guided, or even organised. As movement, itineraries are a narrative of experience. As exploration, itineraries are a description of a course of events. This tension between spaces and representations, combining track and route, is present here.

Let us first simply note the recurrent use of lines. Lines are, in fact and without doubt, the most likely graphical way to describe a journey. Lines[9] are used in all of their forms: straight, curved, continuous, and those obtained through a succession of points. The thread that establishes and maintains the relationship between two places, between man and space, is sometimes tenuous. In *The Loser/The Winner* (Figure 50), by Francis Alÿs, the artist unknits a sweater until he is naked in the streets of Stockholm; the work presents a fragile lifeline, like the string of voices in Aboriginal *songlines* (Figure 47). However, crossings can thicken to the point of coagulation.

---

[7] Let us recall that intuition is directly related to the eye: intueri originally means 'to look'. Let us otherwise note that Henri Bergson likens intuition to mobility, which he distinguishes from intelligence without exclusion: Bergson, H., 2009 [1934]. *La Pensée et le mouvant. Essais et conférences*, Paris: PUF.

[8] In reference to the eponymous book by Buffet, L. (ed.), 2012. *Itinérances. L'art en déplacement*, Grenoble: De l'Incidence Editeur.

[9] For an in-depth analysis of this subject, see Ingold, T., 2007. *Lines: A Brief History*, Oxford: Routledge.

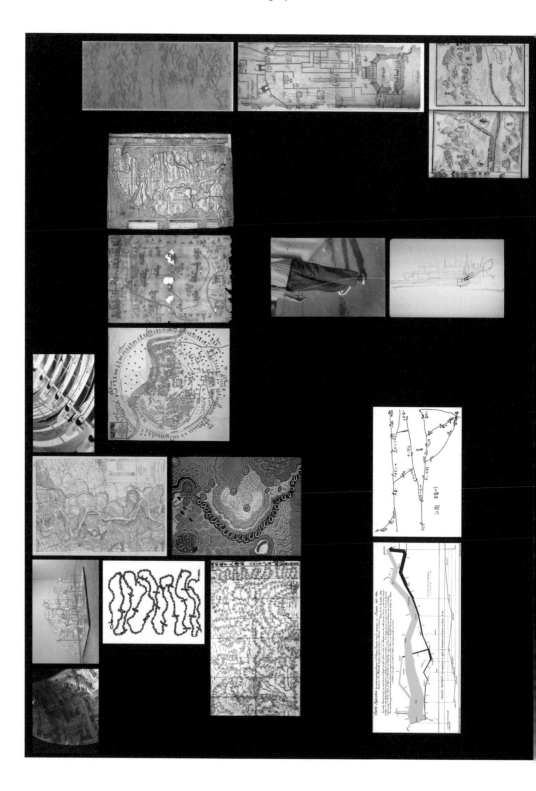

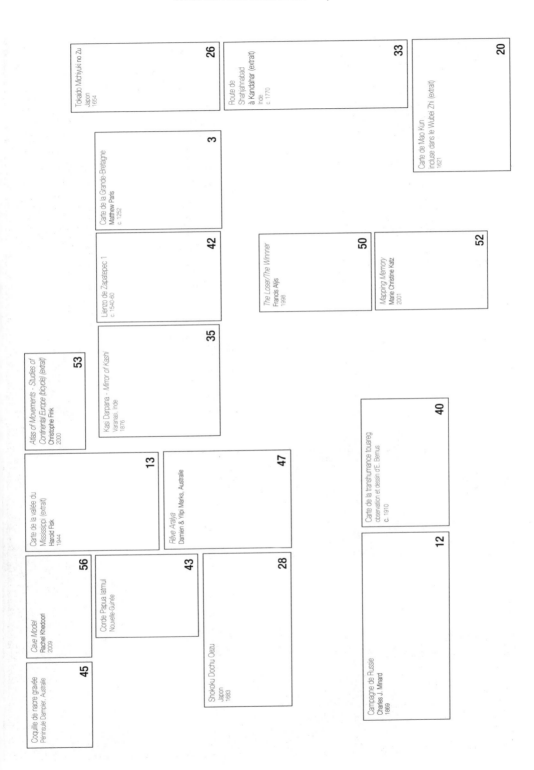

Tokaido Michiyuki no Zu
Japon
1654
26

Route de Shahjahanabad à Kandahar (extrait)
Inde
c. 1770
33

Carte de Mao Kun
incluse dans le Wubei Zhi (extrait)
1621
20

Carte de la Grande-Bretagne
Matthew Paris
c. 1252
3

Lienzo de Zapaltepec 1
c. 1540-60
42

The Loser/The Winner
Francis Alÿs
1998
50

Mapping Memory
Marie Christine Katz
2001
52

Atlas of Movements - Studies of Continental Europe (bicycle) (extrait)
Christophe Fink
2000
53

Kâsi Darpana - Mirror of Kashi
Varanasi, Inde
1876
35

Carte de la vallée du Mississippi (extrait)
Harold Fisk
1944
13

Rêve Aralya
Damien & Yilpi Marks, Australie
47

Carte de la transhumance touareg
observation et dessin d'E. Bernus
c. 1910
40

Cave Model
Rachel Khedoori
2009
56

Corde Papua latmul
Nouvelle-Guinée
43

Shikoku Dochu Oezu
Japon
1683
28

Campagne de Russie
Charles J. Minard
1869
12

Coquille de nacre gravée
Péninsule Dampier, Australie
45

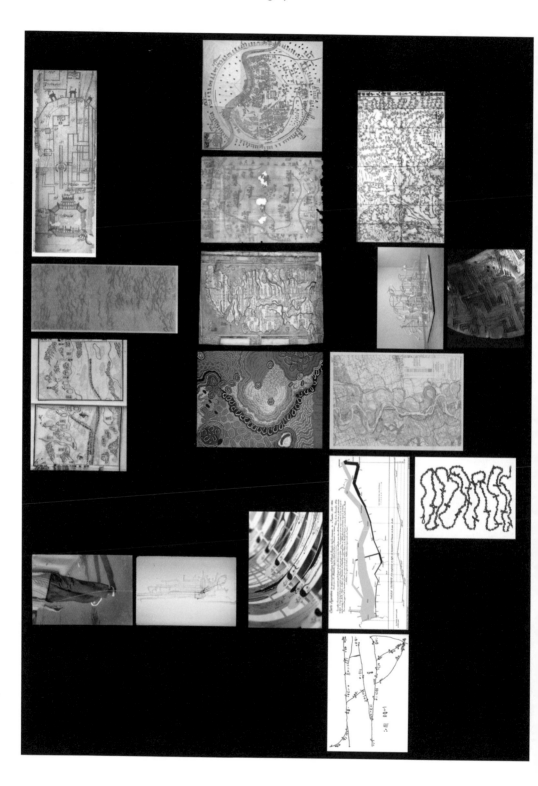

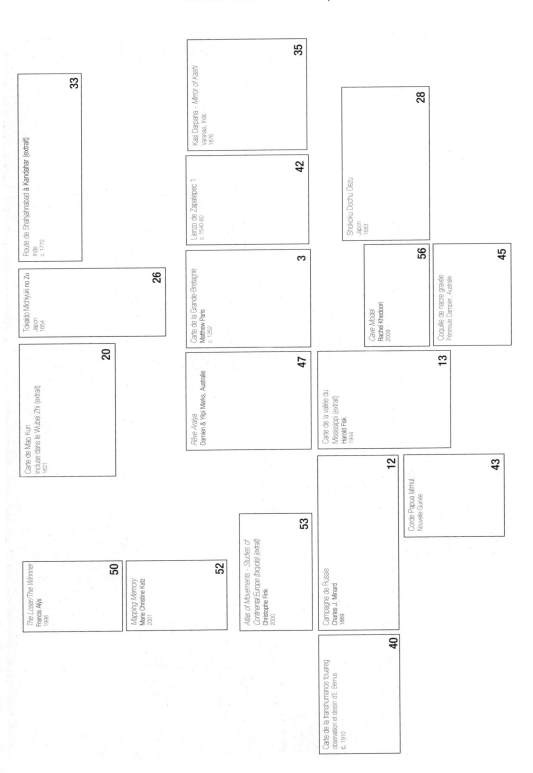

33 Route de Shahjahanabad à Kandahar (extrait)
Inde
c. 1770

35 Kasi Darpana - Mirror of Kashi
Varanasi, Inde
1876

26 Tokaido Michiyuki no Zu
Japon
1654

28 Shokoku Dochu Oezu
Japon
1683

20 Carte de Mao Kun
incluse dans le Wubei Zhi (extrait)
1621

42 Lienzo de Zapatepec 1
c. 1540-60

3 Carte de la Grande-Bretagne
Matthew Paris
c. 1252

56 Cave Model
Rachel Khedoori
2009

45 Coquille de nacre gravée
Péninsule Dampier, Australie

47 Rêve Araiya
Damien & Yilpi Marks, Australie

13 Carte de la vallée du
Mississippi (extrait)
Harold Fisk
1944

50 The Loser/The Winner
Francis Alÿs
1998

52 Mapping Memory
Marie Christine Katz
2001

53 Atlas of Movements - Studies of
Continental Europe (bicycle) (extrait)
Christophe Fink
2000

12 Campagne de Russie
Charles J. Minard
1869

43 Corde Papua Iatmul
Nouvelle-Guinée

40 Carte de la transhumance touareg
observation et dessin d'E. Bernus
c. 1910

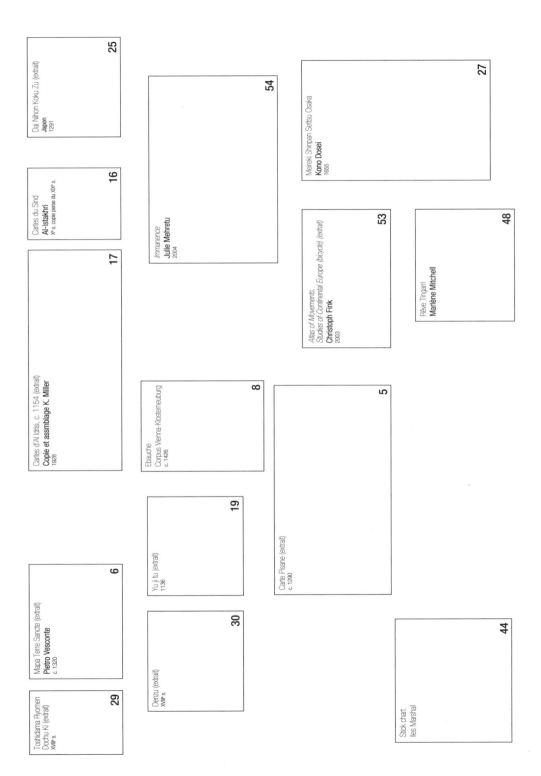

Dai Nihon Koku Zu (extrait)
Japon
1291
25

Cartes du Sind
Al-Istakhri
Xᵉ s. copie perse du XIXᵉ s.
16

Immanence
Julie Mehretu
2004
54

Mereki Shinpan Settsu Osaka
Kono Dosei
1656
27

Cartes d'Al Idrisi, c. 1154 (extrait)
Copie et assmblage K. Miller
1928
17

Atlas of Movements,
Studies of Continental Europe (bicycle) (extrait)
Christoph Fink
2003
53

Rêve Tingarri
Marlène Mitchell
48

Ebauche
Corpus Vienna-Klosterneuburg
c. 1426
8

Carte Pisane (extrait)
c. 1290
5

Yu ji tu (extrait)
1136
19

Mapa Terre Sancte (extrait)
Pietro Vesconte
c. 1320
6

Denou (extrait)
XIIIᵉ s.
30

Toshidama Ryomen
Dochu Ki (extrait)
XVIIIᵉ s.
29

Stick chart
Iles Marshal
44

Halts are marked by punctuation, lines broaden lines, and etchings are accentuated. The grain highlights inconsistencies, or, on the contrary, highlights routes that have been taken a thousand times. Hence, a palimpsest would in no way be of any value, since the traces only become tangible with accumulation or sedimentation (think of a map of the Mississippi's course, Figure 13). As if we walked in our fathers' footsteps... Emerging from the desert, the streak thickens bit by bit.[10] The map becomes a memorial process, an explicit struggle against disappearance, a noema. The space of choice is not that of passion, as Marie Christine Katz discovered (*Mapping Memory*, Figure 52). Long after September 11, 2001, the transcription of her movement through New York City turned the stigmata in the walker's body – and in the urban body, more generally – into a reality.

In all evidence, the act of representing an itinerary is indissociable from the body's movement through space. The body is an explicit actor, even the exclusive one, for certain maps in our corpus. The major issue concerning these cartographies, therefore, is translating movement into an image, and one of its apparently paradoxical modulations is a strongly narrative dimension. The narrative of Nigerian Tuareg pastoralists' seasonal migrations, retold by Edmond Bernus in the 1970s (Figure 40), is punctuated by marks traced in the sand at the same time as the chronicle is told. Gestures accompany the mention and appearance of days spent on the road (which become distances), nights (encampments), and water holes. The movement and its trace are equally ephemeral. Each element drawn lends to the narrative, which itself is cause for a drawing. The gestures of the body, upon mention of something, are translated into those of a walker during a journey in a mimed motion (no doubt mnemonic), which were long excluded from the canonical field of cartography.

In this account, the journey is more than just the starting and ending points; it is the experiences 'along the way', which are important as they put walking as a prerequisite. The cartographer is not limited to discovering the world but is *himself* invented during the journey, which is both perpetual and renewed. A 'biographical' work is created, and may be read as an affirmation of an individual in his 'territory of self'[11]. The experience

---

[10] On the opposition between streaked and smooth space, read Deleuze, G. & Guattari, F., 1980. Mille plateaux, Paris: Minuit.

[11] Lavadinho, Sonia & Winkin, Yves, 2005. 'Les territoires du moi. Aménagements matériels et symboliques de la marche urbaine', http://www.unige.ch/ses/geo/oum/articles/Lausanne_ SLYW_versionfinale.pdf

is without doubt performative. The body in pilgrimage is a measure of the world that is referred to as a space – in fact, the appropriation of a territory.

'Playing with steps shapes space. Walking weaves the basic structure of places. In this sense, the movements of pedestrians [...] cannot be pinpointed to any particular place or located, because they themselves create a space',[12] affirmed Michel de Certeau. This production of space is above all a conquest, both symbolic and cultural. We can find here identity in search of anchoring at once in an ancestral past and in a dream, which is in essence unattainable: a utopian archaism[13]. The boundaries of a mixed territory, such as the one represented by the Zacatepec *lienzo* (Figure 42), are likewise the representation of the itinerary of its founding dynasty, a vestige of its foundation.[14] However, what we also retain from this Meso-American map is the role it played in attesting to the legitimacy of a group's power over a space during territorial disputes. Hence, this document hence bears witness as much as it mobilises.

Maps whose narrative dimension has been forgotten are outlined here. The narrative of an ancient journey, the experience of a body in motion, fades. In short, the route is erased when a road appears along the same superposed strokes, that of single lines.[15] It is the power of action that orients these cartographic projects. A dissolving of the individual into the social body exists at its basis. We would almost be so bold as to think that the representations of roads signal the birth of public space. As Paul Zumthor notes in his analyses of the European Middle Ages,[16] the increasing distance between man and his body is concomitant with the emergence of a culture of roads based on specifically documented journeys.

This objectivisation of space marks a shift from a hodological space, where the space travelled becomes tangible and can be appropriated in the sensible space of perception,[17] to a referential Euclidean space that is homogenous and isotropic.

---

[12] Certeau, M., 1990 [1980]. 'Le parler des pas perdus' in *L'invention du quotidien: L'art de faire*, Paris: Gallimard, p. 147.

[13] On this point, see Chavinier, E., 2011. 'Cartes d'identité(s). Où l'on se fait une certaine idée des cartes autochtones' in Walser, Olivier et al. *Les SIG au service du développement territorial*, Lausanne: PPUR, pp. 55–62.

[14] Détienne, M., 1990. *Tracés de fondation*, Louvain, Paris: Peeters.

[15] Representations of networks are not an issue in this plate, even when their linear dimensions is particularly strong, as in Peutinger's table (Figure 4).

[16] Zumthor, P., 1993. *La mesure du monde*, Paris: Seuil.

[17] It was psychologist Kurt Lewin who, in the 1920s, developed the notion of hodological space. See also on this point Gilles Deleuze, 'Cinéma: vérité et temps', lecture given on 6 December 1984, or Gilles A. Tiberghien and Jean-Marc Besse, 'Hodologique', followed by 'Quatre notes conjointes', in *Les carnets du paysage*, 11, 2004.

However, this space of universal scope is not necessarily quadrangular in nature, and orthonormal, even less so. The journey's linearity is a model that gives shape to all of space, including that of representation. The understanding and ordering of the world first occurs through lists. As evidence proves, Umberto Eco's comparison of form and enumeration – even without hierarchizing them – is not so operative.[18] This close relationship between list and line is magnificently expressed in *Papua Iatmul* cords (Figure 43). In Melanesia, inhabitants organise a litany of road names, recalling ancestral migrations into a kind of mantra to be chanted. The mnemonic use of this gesture is known; one after another, the ties are read. The reading has significance. Here, the eye does not take in the entire image in one glance. In fact, this type of representation is much closer to the scriptural than to the pictorial system[19]. Thus, the more than 5.5-meter map of *Mao Kun* (Figure 20) shows Zhang He's expedition from Nanking to the Strait of Ormuz in an almost straight line. This impact on reading is considerably reinforced by the inclusion of a map in the book, as well as its division into about forty pages. However, the argument is not valid for the road in *Tokaido Michiyuki no Zu* (Figure 26), where the eye's movements are complex. It oscillates between the reading of a linear writing system and the temptation to survey the landscape with a vagabond eye.

This untied space can also be subtly and boldly folded. It is constrained by the line, as much as by the sheet[20], in the case of Matthew Paris' *Map of Great Britain* (Figure 3), or in the stupefying *Road from Shahjahanabad to Kandahar* (Figure 33). Variations of scale appear classically to be multiple. Like light or heavy inflections, they come from a density of information – or, where appropriate, an intensity of experience – and its representation. This process is undoubtedly less linked to anamorphosis, *per se*, than to the simple principle of economising knowledge; the more that is known, the more that is literally spread out in a place. However, this folding is even further expressed when the model of symbolic geometric shapes massively affects space. Here we can hear the whispered voices of Yves Michaud, Gilles Deleuze, and Stephane Mallarmé before them. The circle form is manifest in *Kasi Darpana* (Figure 35). As is common to world maps and

---

[18] Eco, U., 2009. *Vertige de la liste*, Paris: Flammarion, p. 18 et seq.

[19] On the close relations between the two systems, see Christi, Anne-Marie, 2011. *L'invention de la figure*, Paris: Flammarion.

[20] Matthew Paris himself directly spoke of this when he declared, 'If the page had allowed it, this whole island would have been longer'. Cited in Harvey, P.D.A., 1980. *Topographical Maps. Symbols, Pictures and Surveys.* London: Thames & Hudson.

other city plans, while *omphalos*[21] – the centre of the world and choice of place – is not immanent here, *ouroboros* is present –strongly expressesing an unending procession that consecrates the city and purifies the pilgrim. However, the king of folding is no doubt that which is expressed in the figure of the labyrinth. Paroxysm is achieved by *Shokoku Dochu Oezu* (Figure 28), a representation of main roads in the Honshu province. Paradoxically, the labyrinthine figure was best able to guide travellers who carried a copy of the image in their pockets. Leafing through draft itineraries of Christoph Fink's *Atlas of Movements* (Figure 53), or the cavernous circumventions of Rachel Khedoori in *Cave Model* (Figure 56), space is bent, playing on gaps, interstices and empty spaces. 'The in-between' links and captures the pure passing of time. Transparencies and opacities are pathways for memories and for exploring matrices. With the mother-of-pearl shell of Dampier's peninsula (Figure 45), the figure leaves the ordinary iconographic realm to enter the iconic realm without surprise, as soon as symbolic forms are touched. Amulets are passed from hand to hand, from group to group, no doubt following the voyages of mythical beings. They will be used ritually to make rain fall in the desert. 'Mastery'[22] is no longer that of man over body or form – even a sheet of paper. Instead, it is an effort to substantialise the divine, which is unrepresentable. The analogical principle is, by the same token, disqualified.

Grid: the quadrature of the circle solved

Imagine a compass and a ruler without graduations. How could a square with the same area as a given circle be drawn? It is impossible[23], given the transcendence of π.

Imagine that distances and continuities are respected. How can that which is spherical be made flat? Again: impossible. Position and mensuration are thus two irreconcilable operations; making a circle flat or folding it into a square has no advantage. However, the latter, through the intermediary of the orthogonal grid, has been imposed in an ordering of the world that is also a call to order an arbitrary set combined with praxis.

---

[21] For more information on the figure of omphalos in cartography, see Westphal, Bertrand, 2011. *Le monde plausible. Espace, lieu, carte*, Paris: Minuit.

[22] Playing on words: (maîtrise/métrise) mastery/metering (measuring).

[23] A crazy solution assumes bending a bit the value of π from 3.14 to 3.2. To do this, Edwin Goodwin made fi the transcendence of π.

As Christian Jacob notes, 'the orthogonal grid [...] betrays a will to master and to control [...] The grid generates a specific geometry based on the recurrence of the same units, on a strict horizontal and vertical alignment ruled by right angles. The Cartesian grid [...] makes clear the presence of an order of reason, imposing coherence, uniformity, and homogeneity in the space represented'.[24]

The grid even precedes the world it frames. The draft map, an element in the works of Vienna Klosterneuburg's (Figure 8), is one of the most telling examples. Several scattered places from the *Toledan Tables* take their place among the heritage of Ptolomy's works. Was this grid destined to disappear? Were these construction lines merely an addition to an enlightened cartography? It was a game of positioning and relative coordinates when Pietro Vesconte applied a grid to his map of the Holy Lands (Figure 6). The reader need only refer to the zone in the map described in Paulinus Venetus' *Chronologia Magna*. Japanese travellers move from one cell to another and from one step to another on a map. The *Toshidama Ryomen Dochu Ki* (Figure 29) shares its name with the game of backgammon. It is the measure of distances, and especially surfaces, from which the square grid of 100 Li, applied in the map *Yu ji tu* (Figure 19), is designed. The administration of a kingdom or management of a rice-growing domain require appropriate tools, such as the *Denzu* map (Figure 30) showing a *jori* grid[25]. How to make sense of the world set out on a grid or a framework stuck onto the world? We feel that there is still something like an aporia here, and that it would be easy to get lost in an impasse. The grid's transcendence and immanence do not depend on genealogy. The work of Arab cartographers could further enlighten us in this matter.

At the court of the King of Sicily, Abu Abdullah Mohammed Ibn al-Sharif al-Idrisi wrote *Kitab nuzhat al-mushtaq*,[26] seventy chapters of which each boasted a cartographic plate. This partitioning of the world arises from the seven Greek *klima* and the ten longitudinal sections. Eight centuries later, Konrad Miller proceeded to assemble these maps.

---

[24] Jacob, C., 1992. *L'empire des cartes. Approche théorique de la cartographie à travers l'histoire*, Paris: Albin Michel, p. 163.

[25] The relationship between these Japanese and Chinese maps with writing is both strong and singular. The ideograms for sea and mountain are written in one of the cells of the denzu grid, while the standardisation of Chinese writing into a square by calligrapher Wang Xizhi is contemporary to Pei Xiu's probable invention of the cartographic grid.

[26] Latin: Opus Geographicum, English: 'A Diversion for the Man Longing to Travel to Far-Off Places' as translated by John Dickie, 2008.

The very possibility of making this collage, the *Tabula Rogeriana* (Figure 17), revealed that which we were unable to see: namely that maps are tiles with lost edges. It is a transcendent grid outside the world it described, which cuts off kingdoms, mountains and roads. However, such a montage is not always possible. Al-Istakhrî, from the Al Balkhi School, described the Muslim world based on the principle of Persian *kishvars* (provinces). He described the regions in his *Book of Roads and Kingdoms* and offered a cartography of them (Figure 16). These maps, finely crafted and refined, had uncertain horizons: namely elusive, yet by no means indecisive. Al-Istakhrî in no way sought to represent one part of the world. His project, involving objects, routes, and kingdoms, resulted in an *ad hoc* grid whose cell size was variable. This immanent grid creates an inconstant world, without a possible consistency.[27]

Julie Mehretu's distortions of reference lines and blowing-up of plans and perspective in *Immanence* (Figure 54) create off-shoots which blow up an immanence and free us from it. The clean lines and tumult of quasi-Baroque whirlwind are contrasts that mystify the grid – including by multiplication. Elevation mocks the ordered stretches. The Osaka of Kono Dosei's map (Figure 27) also uses the contrast between two points of view, both of them familiar. The checkerboard plan of the city, which makes the abstract masses of the built urban area show up like a stencil, cut through a bucolic landscape where a light pen stroke – through a trick in perspective – transforms the rice fields into a motif. Everything in this scene competes to radically distinguish two spaces, two worlds: city and countryside. This difference is a matter neither of conjuncture nor of structure; it is essential.[28]

An interesting extract from the *Atlas of Movements* (Figure 53) originates from another form of misappropriation. We have already discussed how artists use folds in the cartography of ordinary movements. What is striking here is how, when an image resonates due to the adjacent images around it on the plate, the fabric and train of thought are woven together to sculpt a bottomless map. The grid model becomes a light base whose changing, crossing-points also lend to the map's theme.

---

[27] Let us attempt a hypothesis: It was the umma, the community of believers, which made the unit of the (Muslim) world for Al-Istakhri whereas at the court of King Roger of Sicily the link was another one, maybe territorial continuity. We are certainly inspired here by André Miquel's and Denis Retaillé's analyses.

[28] Can attempts at spatial variations be discerned in the mysterious footnotes of the Carta Pisana (Figure 5). No one can say…

It is natural for our reflections on the grid to find an extension in an analysis of the arrangement of base maps. Transcendent bases ensure stability, reproducibility and comparability. The topographic base has thus become a useful template. That which was merely a representation of the visible has become the basis for many other maps, with no significant link between the theme and the base. All the others have immanent bases whose creation originates from simultaneous movement towards conception and demonstration. Cartograms – inhabited anamorphoses – are of this order. It is no longer a question of whether it is a circle or a square, but it is true that resistance to the globe remains entire. Have patience. The World is a novel object.

Following the trail

Has this exploration of a heterogeneous corpus through the *atlas method* allowed us to answer any of our initial questions? Modestly, without doubt, but more so than we would have imagined – and in unexpected ways.

Itineraries, by definition, reflect a journey made by a single person. Yet, they are of general interest in at least two ways. First of all, they show the tension between a journey, i.e. action, and the environment in which the action unfolds. If a cartographer focuses on a great traveller, whose autonomy we wish to demonstrate in relation to the pre-existing world, the base-space for the voyager's movements must be transformed to make our proposition credible. This is where the different types of 'folds', of which maps are full, come from. Today, all individuals are as exceptional as these great men. There is no longer any question of 'deforming' space travelled in the name of a given ideology, but rather of *forming* it, in other words, by placing two legitimate entities (in this case, the actor and the environment) in dialogue with one another. One of the paradoxes here is that the individual has been encountered in social worlds (Medieval Europe of the great travellers, Meso-America of the migrant dynasties, China of the conquering navigators, etc.), where ordinary individuals did not really exist. While passing over (or under) statistical cartography of the 19th and 20th centuries, we reach out to these characters. Contemporary art helps us in this endeavour through its ability to establish free associations between realities that other approaches separate. The maps of social engineers reduce individuals to uninteresting cogs, letting them accumulate into aggregates possessed by their own logic whose parts can no longer be identified. The 'era of the masses' is also completed in the field of spatial practices. Now that geolocated traceability allows our journeys to be followed step by step, the question of making the actors' spatial logic compatible with the environment – which undoubtedly already existed and framed their movements – arises. However, environments can also be changed through action, possibly carried out by a single person. The semiological procedures that allow for this matching thus take on new meaning today, as the richness of new personal spaces combines with an absence of theoretical tradition to study them. The ancient maps of itineraries offer techniques for treating this proliferation.

The grid allows for a fresh look at the relationship between *base* and *theme* in a map. By definition, the base-map (the grid being a geometric variant of it), comes before the map's theme. Yet, this anteriority could be simply methodological, and not semiological. In practice, there could be interference between the two, as we can see with the 'variable geography' of the Arabo-Persian maps' *klima*. It is no mistake that the baseless maps of this school also sparked a revolution that 'Western' maps have (had) difficulty understanding and putting into use, as they saw space as a network rather than a territory. Rural territoriality and the exhaustive struggle for military control, very present in Europe from the Renaissance through the 20th century, undoubtedly carried less weight in an 'oasis' universe made up mainly of cities and links between these cities. The fact is that, ten centuries later, this semiology – so simple and yet so well adapted to today's world – has yet to be grasped. Not only because we are living more than ever in a universe of networks, but also because it proposes a vocabulary and grammar unencumbered by frills and that cuts straight to the quick, as inter-war German cartography and 'chorematics' tried to do in their own ways at the end of the 20th century. The map as a cognitive project emerged in all its purity. It is not without relevance that this was obtained by evading the base-map issue. The fact is that theme-driven metrics, of places and of links between them, including weighted points and viscous lines, would not lead to reducing the represented spaces into a single type of pre-existing phytopography, physical or historical. Thus, the question is: Given the world today, must we bypass the base entirely to map the world as if it were a subway network? Or must a minimal, flexible '*klima*-tic' grid be sought, to link us to pre-existing maps without changing the specific spatialities we want to bring out?

Very often during this exploration, the question was asked, 'Is this really a map?'. This question was first addressed regarding a space of reference to which the image in question could be linked or not. However, it also involved the transformations that the image imposed to the referent by adding new layers of meaning. In every case, we ultimately asked ourselves the question. Thus, if we did not think it useful to question the zenithal axiom, which allows for a shift towards the symbolic and gives strength to the map when faced with other spatial languages through the violent 'disfigurement' it causes, we were constantly driven by numerous hybrids of plane and elevation. The presence of figurative elements cannot only be read as a laborious by-product emerging from a two-dimensional space. Nor can it be reduced to a pedagogical access to the zenithal for lay readers. As contemporary aesthetic creations demonstrate – pushing this game to its conceptual limits – it is a question of the tension that remains even when the standard rules of a map's construction are respected, such as a song that recalls and challenges lyrics, all the while remaining music.

At the end of the day, what validates this experiment was looking elsewhere, outside of the field, for inspiration and to try and solve today's cartographic quandaries. We took our time entering into the logic of the maps analysed, only to betray them by confronting them with our questions. We thus found in our corpus elements that differed greatly from those found by art critics or cartographic historians. To conclude, we could say that by cutting up objects in a different manner than Western cartographies from the 19th and 20th centuries, these *other* cartographies invite us do the same with our objects. They blur the usual dualisms between base and theme, large and small, network and territory, fixity and movement, and prove that it is possible to, once again, spark the imagination with as much or more rigour than the classic Euclidean map. We can innovate with points, lines, and surfaces in the representation of space inhabited by the image's space, and continue to experience cartography as an open cognitive process.

Appendix 1: Worksheet on several works by Hélène Gerster

The Approach

Hélène Gerster's works (including drawings, texts, embroidery, and necklaces) often resemble maps, or alternately use the map as a model. The artist uses a corporeal approach, travelling through cities on foot or by bicycle and then transcribing the movements and spaces in two dimensions. The maps thus are a product of actual experience in situ. The artist assumed the gesture of a topographer through a primarily corporeal management of the territory.

Gerster's 'reconnaissance' approach to *place* resembles 'drift' – a kind of territorial understanding that could be called 'urban sensibility' – as described notably by Guy Debord. 'Drift' is free movement, with no particular destination or goal, from one object/place to another. For Hélène Gerster, this drift is materialised in the form of drawn lines, photographs, and narratives, 'cartographic' forms expressing a territory and, above all, an *experience* of this territory. *Drift* offers information about an encounter with the explored urban territory and about a disappearance, since she defers to the real to recreate it. Hélène Gerster puts random and oriented spatiality into words and drawing, creating less a representation of the city than a *performative operation* that immerses the individual into the object of her observation.

While drawings link thoughts and image, they render the latter opaque to the usual cartographic discursiveness; they work less on transposition than by transformation. By crisscrossing truth and falsehood, Gerster's cartographic drawing re-territorialises reality and illusion, space and time.

The map is less a logical arrangement of forms than a *praxis*, more a *gesture* than a *sign*, offering *transitions* rather than *positions*.

Movement, adventuresome exploration, casually changing places, and directions – this fluidity is not unlike the exploration of virtual spaces on the Internet. Carried out here is a *resistance test of spatial plasticity*.

Description of *Letters to Klaipeda*, 2008, book

'In the summer of 2008, Hélène Gerster was at the Klaipeda Cultural Communication Center residence during two weeks in Lithuania. The artist created an experimental book on the city. As a traveller, Hélène Gerster compared Klaipeda with other places. Hélène Gerster chose Klaipeda as a place of investigation: laptop, notebook, travel guide, letters addressed to Klaipeda, points of reference, references, comments, images...; little by little, all of these fragments were crystallised into a book-object'.[29]

In *Letters to Klaipeda*, the artist disorients readers, rather than offering them a traditional tour of the city. We do not know where we are. In zigzags and straight lines, we go from a neighbourhood to a bridge, a road to a square, a park to a building. The artist's journeys flow freely from her pen. Her body becomes a receptacle for the city. She also explores the city by bicycle, helping to better express its topography, history and ambiance. The capacity for movement, the ease and casualness with which place is changed, in short, assume the city's pulse.

Description of *Tell Me Where You Are and I'll Tell You Who You Are*, 2010–2011, canvas and cotton thread, embroidery, silver and freshwater pearls.

'"Necklace-sculptures" have been created based on some embroidered city maps, the path of roads represented by silver chains and that of water freshwater pearls. To this day, five cities have been created: Geneva, Rome, Nuremberg, Paris, and New York'.[30] Our eye follows certain features, gets lost, straying from its route, before finding its way again. The journeys are non-homogenous and multi-directional, comprised of forces and effects, and open, nomadic space, like the ephemeral Tuareg maps drawn in the sand with pebbles. With no fixed reference, this creased space challenges Euclidean space. The map itself also becomes mobile, as it can be worn as a necklace.

Description of *You Say Venice and a Bunch of Signals Light Up*, 2007, screen-printed and embroidered fabric.

'A series of 120 fabric handkerchiefs sent by post. They were screen-printed according to a city map of Geneva; then a red cross was embroidered onto them at the place where the receiver of the shipment resides'.[31]

The map embroidered onto cloths is a sign towards an interior universe, that of the home, table linens (tablecloths, napkins), as well as the body via the embroidered tissue, an intimate object worn on the body or

---

[29] Hélène Gerster's site: www.helenegerster.ch
[30] www.helenegerster.ch
[31] www.helenegerster.ch

carried in a pocket or purse. We move from the map in the library, in the atlas, on a computer's hard drive, or pinned to a wall to a map kept in a drawer or cupboard or worn on the body. The map exits the world of knowledge to enter that of private and domestic space.

The maps embroidered by Hélène Gerster recall the tapestry-maps of cartographic history, embroidered in an artisanal way, in keeping with the origin of the Italian word *mappa* meaning 'a cloth'. Alighiero e Boetti, an Italian artist of the *Arte Povera,* renewed ties with this tradition in the 1980s, creating maps of the world using the technique of embroidered Afghan rugs.

Key words
Fiction, topography, journey, city, embroidery, movement, drift

Families of maps
Body-maps
Maps of itineraries
Narrative maps

Appendix 2: The Corpus of the Cosmographies Project (by geographic area and chronological order)

Europe / Western World

1. Mosaic of Madaba, late 6th century.
2. Ebstorf's world map, c. 1239 (30 parchments, 358 x 356 cm).
3. Map of Great Britain, Matthew Paris, c. 1252 (33 x 22.9 cm).
4. Peutinger Table, copy c. 1265 (11 parchments, 682 x 34 cm).
5. *Carta Pisana*, c. 1290 (manuscript on parchment, 103 x 48 cm).
6. *Mapa Terre Sancte*, Pietro Vesconte, c. 1320 (ink and paint on vellum, 65 x 25 cm).
7. Opicinus de Canistris' Map, c. 1335.
12. Countryside of Russia, Charles J. Minard, 1869 (lithography, 62 x 30 cm).
13. Map of the Mississippi Valley, Harold Fisk, 1944 (15 hand-coloured plates).

Arab World / Persia

14. Tulsi Slamani's world map, c. 1170, copy from the 14th c. (32 x 23 cm).
15. Ibn Al Wardi's world map, 15th c.
16. Map of Sind, Al-Istakhri, 10th c. Persian copy from the 19th c.
17. Al Idrisi's Maps, c. 1154, copy and assembly K. Miller, 1928 (ink and paint on paper).

China

18. Map of the Garrison of Mawangdui, Southern China, c. 202 BC – 9 AD (28 pieces of assembled silk, 98 x 78 cm).
19. Yu ji tu, 1136 (xylographic print, 560 x 20 cm).
20. Map of Mao Kun included in the Wubei Zhi, 1621 (xylographic print, 560 x 20 cm partitioned into 40 images).

Korea

21. Kangnido from Ryûkoku, Korea, 1402 (paint on silk, 171.8 x 164 cm).
22. Ch'onhado, Korea, reproduction from the 16th – 19th c. (Ink on paper).
23. Tosongdo, Korea, 18th c. (Ink jet print, 92 x 67 cm).
24. Taedong Yojiko by Kim Chongho, Korea, 1861, reproduced in 1936 (block printing, 28 x 21.5 cm).

Japan

25. Dai Nihon Koku Zu, Japan, 1291 (black ink on paper).
26. Tokaido Michiyuki no Zu, Japan, 1654 (130.7 x 57.7 cm).
27. Meireki Shinpan Settsu Osaka, Kono Dosei, Japan, 1655 (119.4 x 77.5 cm).
28. Shokoku Dochu Oezu, Japan, 1683 (63 x 38.3 cm).
29. Toshidama Ryomen Dochu Ki, Japan, 1744 (16.5 x 7.3 cm).
30. Denzu, 18th c.

Arctic

31. Tchouktcha plates, Far-Eastern Russia (9 wooden plates, 425 cm long).
32. Map of Mandarka, Far-Eastern Russia (paint on sealskin, 119.3 x 114.3 cm).

South Asia

33. Road from Shahjahnabad to Kandahar, India, c. 1770 (paper roll, 2,000 x 25 cm).

34. Mughul Map of North-West India, copy 1795 (79 x 69 cm).
35. Kasi Darpana - *Mirror of Kashi*, Varanasi, India, 1876 (block printing on cotton, 92 x 79 cm).
36. Shrinathji Temple Complex, Nathdwara, India, late 19th c. (Paint on paper, 67 x 47 cm).
37. Ngaju Dayak Map, Indonesia Borneo, c. 1905 (black ink, pencil 138 x 69.5 cm).

Africa

38. Luba Lukasa, Republic of Congo, 17th c. (Wood plates, shells and pearls, 20–25 x 13 cm).
39. Map of the Kingdom of Bamum by King Njoya, 1912 (ink and pencil on paper, 93 x 87.5 cm).
40. Touareg Seasonal Migration Map, Kili Kilu Ag Najim, c. 1910 (observation and drawing by E. Bernus).

America

41. Khipu Inca, Chulpaca, Peru, 1425-1532 (cotton rope, 72 x 39 cm).
42. Lienzo de Zacatepec 1, c. 1540-60 (facsimile, manuscript on cloth, 325 x 225 cm).

Oceania

43. Corde Papua Iatmul, New Guinea (facsimile, original in vegetable fibre, 6–7 m).
44. Stick Chart of the Marshall Islands, Micronesia (coconut leaf fibre, wooden or bamboo sticks, shells).
45. Shell in Engraved Mother-of-Pearl, Dampier Peninsula, Australia (engraved mother-of-pearl shell).
46. Rainbow Dream Serpent with Horns, John Mawurndjul, Arnhem Land, Australia (acrylic on canvas, 176 x 72 cm).
47. Aralya's Dream, Damien and Yilpi Marks, Central Desert, Australia (acrylic on canvas, 122 x 91 cm).
48. Tingarri's Dream, Marlene Mitchell, Central Desert, Australia (acrylic on canvas, 133 x 123 cm).

Contemporary Art

49. Guillermo Kuitca, *Diarios*, 1994 (paint on canvas stretched over a round table).

50. Francis Alÿs, *The Loser / The Winner*, 1998 (performance/video).
51. Moshekwa Langa, *Stage,* 19971999 (installation, mixed techniques, objects, variable dimensions).
52. Marie Christine Katz, *Mapping Memory*, 2001 (mixed techniques).
53. Christoph Fink, *Atlas of Movements, Studies of Continental Europe (Bicycle)* – A Selection, 2000 (ink on cut paper).
54. Julie Mehretu, *Immanence*, 2004 (ink and acrylic on canvas).
55. Kim Jones, *Blueshirthorns,* 2005 (screen printing on cotton).
56. Rachel Khedoori, *Cave Model*, 2009 (plaster, aluminium, and wood, 244 x 244 x 162 cm).
57. Sohei Nishino, *Diorama of New York,* 2009 (jet ink print, 172.2 x 134 cm).
58. Cannelle Tanc, Cut Map, Paris, 2009 (recessed map, 90 x 60 cm).
59. Hélène Gerster, *Dis-moi où tu es, je te dirai qui tu es,* 2010 (silver and freshwater pearls).

Part 2
Map as Language

Chapter 5

Space for Reason

Jacques Lévy

> Alice was beginning to get very tired of sitting by her sister on the bank, and of having nothing to do: once or twice she had peeped into the book her sister was reading, but it had no pictures or conversations in it, 'and what is the use of a book', thought Alice, 'without pictures or conversations?'
> Lewis Carroll, *Alice's Adventures in Wonderland* (1865).

What is the use of images in the social sciences? More precisely, how can discourses on 'the social' incorporate logics of language, which more-or-less stray from habitual verbal structures, other than by means of 'illustration'? In the following article, I will attempt to answer these questions in three ways: by classifying the different modes of expression concerned, by characterising a condition, and by examining the contributions of language, which are themselves neither verbal nor sequential.

Classifying languages: being and time

Let us begin with an etymological curiosity. In many Indo-European languages, the word derived from the Latin *figura* means both a figurative representation (non-human, except in French) and a symbolic reality. The many social uses of the face (Latin; *os, oris*) – one of the meanings of *figure* in French – illustrates this hesitation in semantic choice. Regardless, it seems more of a paradox than a contradiction here, as if we had not yet isolated the objects well enough and identified the opposing pairs, or as if elementary distinctions remained in limbo within a fluctuating, mobile space.

Non-verbal and non-sequential

Let us then begin by trying to describe the landscape. The language we speak, often called 'natural language', and which shall be identified here as *verbal* language, has a fundamental trait: its *sequential* nature. The information contained in a statement is only a vector of communication if the rules resulting in a strict time sequencing of the message's elements are respected. Depending on the language, what is called the 'verbal chain' follows different, more-or-less normative systems at the scale of the first level of organisation of units of meaning (the sentence).

What may be possible at this first level – especially in languages with declinations, where virtual stability of meaning is maintained despite the permutation of words – becomes impossible as soon as we move to a higher level. Even in poetry, a mode of expression that by definition has the greatest freedom (with rare exceptions),[1] it is forbidden to render the position of an element in the chain irrelevant.

In the case of cognitive-objective statements,[2] eliminating polysemies that would be impossible for the reader to reconcile leads the author to choose

---

[1] To add a figurative dimension to verbal statements, Guillaume Apollinaire took up an ancient tradition, superimposing another mode of reading over classic sequentiality in his *Calligrammes*. Due to their figurative effectiveness, the objects created with words lead the reader to regard the poem as a non-sequential verbal discourse (see below). In *Cent mille millards de poèmes*, Raymond Queneau proposes 140 verses of ten sonnets. Without changing the order of each verse (1 to 14), so as to respect the regularity of the rhymes, 10^{14} virtual poems are generated. If this constraint disappears and one verse is repeated in the same poem, a number of 140^{14} is attained.

[2] Human productions, especially linguistic, can be classified according to two simple principles. The first case, which contrasts *cognitive* and *affective*, concerns the way of production with a strongly-connected horizontal network, and the second case concerns a strongly-hierarchised structure with a one-direction flow. The second principle, which contrasts *subjective* and *objective*, is the producer itself, individual or collective. It is an affirmation that links the product to the singularity of its creator; or conversely, this creator tries to step aside and make the use of the product as autonomous as possible for a third party. Through the hybridisation of these two pairs, a four-box table is obtained. In the cognitive/objective case, productions belonging in the field of reason will be found in philosophy, sciences, and techniques. (See Lévy, J., 1995. *Egogéographies*, Paris: L'Harmattan, pp. 123–126.

the *flattest* 'poetics' possible, unless expressly stated otherwise. Thus, the author does not try to pull the language tool to the limits of its technical performance. Thus, the arrangement of logical operators between propositions allows him to assess the degree of compliance with the formal rules of reasoning: the identity of discursive objects and the non-contradiction of a proposition, explicit links between several propositions according to the principle of proximity (correlation), similarity (metaphor, metonymy), causality (simple causality), or integration (systemic causality). At first glance, sequential speech indeed seems to be the rhetorical style (defined as the linguistic dimension of reason) *par excellence*, that by which works of rational construction of reality are produced and communicated.

Yet, almost immediately, it becomes clear that this is not the whole problem. Non-verbal languages play a key role in our communicational universe. Some conserve their sequential nature ('symbolic' expression in mathematics, music, etc.), while others eliminate it. Communication is, to a large degree, the domain of the *image* (except for sequences of images in painting, cinema, and comic strips). Finally, there are modes of mixed expression, such as tables and verbal-graphical 'figures', consisting of groups of words joined by symbols, in which the material is verbal but non-sequential. A first classification is presented below.

| | | Verbal | |
		Yes	No
Sequential	Yes	Verbal - oral or written - speech	Music, 'symbolic' mathematics, cinema
	No	Tables, verbal-graphic figures	Analogical mathematics, pictorial, photographic, or cinematographic images, graphs, maps

Table 1 An elementary language classification.

This table may appear overly simplistic. When Jack Goody explores the consequences of the transition from speech to writing, he insists on the process of 'de-contextualisation' and the production of stable objects that are much harder to reinterpret than the memory of speech.[3] This transformation

---

[3] Goody, J., 1977. *The Domestication of the Savage Mind*, Cambridge: Cambridge University Press.

frees units of meaning from an exclusive arrangement. The 'hand-to-hand with words' thus challenges the constraints of sequential reading. The *list* and, more clearly still, the *table* were decisive innovations. In other words, if, like speech, writing takes place in the *yes/yes* box, then it is similar, in some respects, to the non-sequential verbal. Thus, we should also imagine different types of speech in the form of a continuum (at least virtual), every position of which could be filled according to the request. Assigning a language technique to a certain position must therefore be qualified.

We also find the same ambiguities of vocabulary identified above. In French, the word *graphique*, as an adjective, originally referred to writing, but as a masculine noun refers to formalised images, such as graphs in mathematics. Like the feminine noun, it tends to refer – and more strongly in the wake of Jacques Bertin's work – not only to maps but also to all non-verbal, non-sequential scientific languages. Finally, there is a new meaning of the adjective, which, in the visual arts, refers to a stylised drawing comprised of a few key lines. This polysemy, present in other languages, reinforces the impression of cultural reluctance on these topics.

The following considerations are intended to clarify the content of the box *no/no* – that of non-verbal, non-sequential languages (NVNS), notably the one in which images are found. What is unique about non-sequential languages is that they do not require an extended reading in terms of duration. As far as non-verbal languages are concerned, the constraints of separate decryption for each unit of meaning disappear (for instance, to read a table, the verbal contents of each box nevertheless must be read sequentially), and a *spatial reading* occurs. This type of decoding is an instantaneous, global visual processing (in fact, it is a multiple and rapid scan) of the two-dimensional object, in order to create a new reality of the ocular image. Given the functioning of visual tools, this construction is global and synthetic, but it lacks information. We immediately see the difference, relative to sequential verbal language, is predominantly analytical and has unlimited semantic richness.

Between transparency and self-reference

To identify the place of NVNS in the spirit of the preceding comments, it is useful to look at the problem from another angle: all discursive practices can be placed at different points along a line. This line is bound on one side by what would be a perfect harmony between the signifier and the signified, and by ignorance of the principle of this harmony on the other. At one extreme is *transparency*, and at the other *self-reference*. We could also say that by generalising the pair commonly applied to painting: *figurative* and *abstract*. Where are the NVNSs on this line? Everywhere in fact, as the following diagram shows.

	'Figurative'	Analogical	Symbolic	'Abstract'
Examples within	Photographs	Maps	Graphs	'Abstract'
NVNS				painting

Table 2 From figurative to abstract.

Let us immediately specify that neither extreme point of the graph – pure abstract or pure figurative – is attainable. Since Saussure, linguistics has acknowledged that speech is an autonomous object that can never be reduced to what it 'represents'. Perspective, an invention historically situated in pictorial transparency, shows the vanity of naturalist and positivist approaches. Conversely, the notion of a 'pure signifier' is an oxymoron that is very much characteristic of the 'structuralist period',[4] to which the Lacanian substitution of denotation with connotation – or even of rhetoric with pun – tries to give shape.[5] However, both of these extremes clearly reveal the tension constitutive of any speech act. Thus representation, an identifiable relationship between a language object and a non-language object, is always present; speech that does not imply anything other than itself does not belong to the register of communication. Similarly, the different envelopes of the language environment of speech (the speaker and other possible speakers, different types of speech, past speeches, etc.), including elements of the speech itself, are transformed into objects that take on the status of referent, on the same basis as realities deemed non-language and that can therefore be 'represented'. This leads to the more general view that the statuses of *referred* and *referent* are relevant but cannot be defined as permanent and exclusive attributes. The same 'thing' can be approached

---

[4]   See Havelange, C., 1998. *De l'œil et du monde. Une histoire du regard au seuil de la modernité*, Paris: Fayard.

[5]   On this point, see Dosse, F., 1991. 'Le soleil noir du struturalisme', *EspacesTemps* Les Cahiers, La fabrique des sciences sociales, 47–48.

in two ways: the arrangement of an urban space *speaks* and integrates all speeches a society has about itself; and a speech on the city *acts* and produces objects within the world of objects.

Given these explanations, each 'speech act' can be placed somewhere between these two extremes. Near the figurative side we find 'realist' languages (painting and sculpture from the 15th through the 19th centuries, as well as photography and cinema). At the extreme of abstraction are, for the most part, other aesthetic productions (music, non-figurative painting), and, to a lesser degree, all of those that, through verbal language, allow for the greatest distance to their explicit referents: poetry, science, and philosophy. In-between, two poles prove structuring: the *symbolic* and the *analogical.*

The analogical and symbolic in-between

The first option is well represented by verbal language. The relationship to the referent is strong, but the logic of language itself – from sound to discourse – is profoundly detached. We see this relationship in sequential mathematic languages (where 'formulae' tend to drive verbal discourse toward the edges of the statement), or in musical *notation*'s relationship to the sound-referent (reading a score and listening to music are two distinct activities). This is also the case at the visual boundaries of text and image in tables and figures.

The second option is embodied in maps and other non-figurative expressions. Here we partially find the referent's logic in that of language, which allows for a more immediate, automatic, intuitive reading, once certain rules of construction have mastered. The map, which spatially represents a spatial object, totally assumes its specificity when it encourages a truly spatial *reading*. This is not so straightforward, as many maps (we could also use the English word *chart*, thereby recognising the semantic gap between it and the word *map*) use data – often as simple as lists or tables, organised according to objects' location. We really only have what could be called a *map* when the analogy works, in other words when the message concerns a spatial configuration, like in the space of reference, on a synchronic set of relationships between localised phenomena. In principle, it is possible to use both functions (for example, by writing place names on a map to facilitate identification). However, a cartographer can never forget that if he adds too much visual noise with this verbal input, he undermines the strictly spatial reading of the object.[6]

This classification has the advantage of making languages comparable that are too often treated as incommensurable. Yet, in doing so, we hardly illuminate the specific status of NVNS's. The world of the image finds its place in the fringes of the figurative, the analogical, the symbolic, and the abstract. At this stage, it seems difficult to make the use of images in discourses on social issues correspond to a specific cognitive posture. Hence, a hypothesis, developed below : We must approach these modes of expression first by comparing them to verbal language, and not based on their own coherency. In a second stage, we can question the contributions of different language logics to the expression of scientific statements – that is, to the enrichment of our rhetorical tools.

Different times (of communication), different customs (of discourse)

Once these first classifications have been made, we can better enter into the reality of the combinations that bring together different linguistic resources. This means we must take seriously what is meant by expressions such as 'an image explosion' or 'image civilisation' and ask ourselves whether if, in the social sciences, the balance has tilted in favour of NVNS.

Storytelling: even better with pictures

Let us first try to identify several recent changes in the life of our societies. First, in the area of fiction, there has been a shift from written narration towards audio-visual narration. This is undoubtedly the most incontestable aspect of the relative decline (i.e. in proportion to the total production of fiction) of books compared to television and cinema, and of the novel relative to the (tele-) film. The advantage of the image, which explains this

---

[6]   At another level, criticism could be made of a certain philosophical style in which the difficulty of identifying a referent in the discourse and the benefit of a cross-cutting approach among different types of objects serves as a pretext for aesthetic (cognitive-subjective), moral (affective-objective), or even 'psychological' (affective-subjective) tangents. See Bourdieu, Pierre, 1975. 'L'ontologie politique de Martin Heidegger', *Actes de la Recherche en Sciences Sociales*, 5–6.

effective competition, is twofold. As Michel Lussault (1996) shows, *demonstration* appears to be superior to description or narration in that it can fully realise what verbal discourse can only attempt to do. Furthermore, unlike reading, which always demands great attention, image consumption allows for a wider variety of sensorial and mental attitudes, from extreme concentration to total passivity. One of the major uses of the story and the novel – of being told stories – has changed,[7] in large part due to the fact that, for most people in most situations, televised images correspond better to the expectation of readers of yore: to effortlessly 'escape' and 'dream'.[8]

Given this, the current increase in the weight of images clearly goes beyond mere fiction narrative. We are now into a language universe where alternatives exist, and the idea that there is a choice between two 'forms of expression' to 'express something' has become accepted. It is easy to criticise this position by saying that, with two different languages, you cannot say exactly the same thing. We could even add that, if this competitive situation exists, it is because comparative advantages exist and because message and media tend to reflect one another. Nevertheless, the translation can be meaningful, as can different statements. However, their expression – one by a verbal chain and the other by a graph – may be judged by producers or consumers as being quite similar. There is, therefore, a 'language market' that makes the use an *intergeneric communication complex* possible, everywhere and by everyone. The 'weight of the image' is thus not only expressed by the mere impact of its eruption, but also by its opening-up – not its trivialisation. The image ceases to belong to a communicational ghetto, and instead becomes more comparable and commensurable to other languages. It can hardly be circumvented by the very people they who socially distinguish themselves through their mastery of writing.

Three stances

How does this emergence fit into the overall dynamic of languages? Let us try to identify the processes and rhythms.

---

[7] On this point, see 'Cartes: les menus' in Durand, M.F., Lévy, J., & Retaillé, D., 1993. *Le monde: espaces et systèmes*, Paris: Presses de Sciences Po/Dalloz, 2nd ed., pp. 32–35.

[8] Notably, but not only, the emergence of the social sciences also plays a role through both information and reflection by drawing a good part of their 'cognitive-objective' dimension from novels.

We can summarise language's relationships to the world via three positions which are, in the history of representation, sometimes successive and more often simultaneous.

- *Symbolisation* is a shift towards the right of the line that goes from the figurative to the abstract (Figure 2). It is a production of specific objects that are fundamentally detached from their non-language reality. In the invention of writing, the transition from a 'stylised', yet still figurative, image (pictogram) to ideograms or letters expresses aptly this fundamental *disfiguration* of the world that we find, for example, in the production of cognitive, ethical, or aesthetic abstractions.

- *Figuration* seems to go in the opposite direction: the shift is towards the left of the line. Thus, we can compare the geometric figures of Islam to Christianity, with its representation of sacred figures as identifiable men. The mid-20th century in Western Civilisation saw the completion of what seemed an immense collective project in which, as we now know, perspective in painting occupied a central role: to recreate a world both artificial and plausible that – insofar as is possible – has the same effects on the viewer as the 'real' world. Cinema and television, and, more recently, the multi-sensorial attractions of 'theme parks' give new strength to this aim, since two-dimensional mobile and sound images create a highly contextual environment to the point of creating places (the *heterotopias* of which Michel Foucault speaks). These are capable of partially blurring relationships with the rest of the world. However, at the moment it reached its peak, this 'reality effect' was denounced by Bertolt Brecht, in theatre, and Jean-Luc Godard, in cinema, as the opposite of realism – in other words, as a veil of convention depriving the spectator of his critical relationship to the outside world. One could say that, in similar terms, critical distance is at the heart of the aesthetic revolutions of the early-20th century in painting as in music. Hence, the third position.

- *De/reconstruction*, in some ways, consists in combining the other two approaches and assuming all the points along the line. The critique of figuration and its supposed mimetic transparency is the first deconstructive component. In the second, it is not necessary to remove the most figurative language objects. The ideal of authenticity tends to fade, and artificiality, which is ultimately synonymous with human action, ceases to be reviled. It is basically when societies stop claiming principles or ideals outside of themselves as the essence of their existence. The real/represented dichotomy ceases to be a partitioning of the world, but instead defines a simple point of view whose consequences must never be ignored. The abstract/concrete divide is also threatened by transversal splits between the formless and the informed, that is, between the empirical and the conceptual. The universe of representation is thus accepted as such. We cease to both mythicise it and settle our scores with it, allowing us to better exploit it. It is therefore not the sham ('simulacrum') of which advocates of postmodernism speak.

There is nothing to suggest that we have entered the era of *illusion*. Viewers of *The Muppet Show*, or other comparable satires, do not actually believe that the characters on the show are 'real'; however, consider that politicians who are presented as real differ from the puppets merely in degree but not kind.

The first approach valued the verbal-sequential, and preferably the written word; the second valued the non-verbal, essentially non-sequential. Because of this transformation and reorganisation, all language resources end up equal in principle, including those somewhere between the figurative and the symbolic that were hitherto caught up in the other two logics.

We can detect this dynamic within the temporality specific to the history of knowledge. The approaches of contemporary social sciences instead relate to the third position – that description no longer claims to be free of all theory. On the contrary, it takes its place in an even more innovative conceptual construction, since, along the way, it does not forget its study objects which, in this case, speak and act. After a period dominated by classification and linear causality, the emergence of reasoning relative to sets (individuals, societies, the world, etc.) that were irreducible to their components better valued the necessary coherence between a multitude of elements and were not content with simple juxtapositions or successions. Even the 'small patterns' of *microstoria* (sic.), *ethnomethodology* and the *sociology of objects* offer an opportunity to create large and ambitious theoretical constructions. The transition from 'great histories', still marked by the discursive religious order to the current *constructionist* approaches, therefore does not mean, as is too often said, a renunciation of the great theoretical edifices. Rather, it brings a more rigorous consideration of the necessarily contradictory implications inherent in every act of knowledge.

Hence, greater attention is required to ensure the (internal) consistency and (external) relevance of scientific propositions.[9]

These changes lead to a new order in the relationship between words and images, or, more precisely, between sequential and non-sequential expressions of statements. In this respect, as stated above, while verbal rhetoric is satisfactory in sentences and short texts, shifts in meaning, the surreptitious introduction of implicit principles, and breaches of rigour of all kinds due to weak connections between statements remain possible in vast discursive structures. This is true despite procedures (titles, abstracts, table of contents, and other complements to the main text) aimed at allowing for a quick, global reading of an article or book. These techniques can easily be subverted and widen the gap between the viewing and the implementation of rigourous requirements. Synchronic languages have the opposite advantage, and thus are used to propose a concise, synthetic expression of a complex message. The search for relevance and overall coherence obliges all to undertake a process of inventing specific objects, a *theorisation* of scientific work.

More than study topics or techniques for processing information, it is the more-or-less willing acceptance of this approach that differentiates disciplinary styles.

It is in this context that sharing, which varies according to the social science area, between classic rhetoric and non-verbal and/or non-sequential forms, must be analysed. Overall, the move towards more responsible theorisation is accompanied by increasing use of NVNS, with a tendency to mathematise when working on linear or static causality. There is likewise an interest in less strictly formal expressions when contradictory dynamics, global movements, and systems of actors are involved.

On another note, that of a technological reading of development such as proposed by Pierre Lévy,[10] a redistribution of contributions from different languages can be observed. It would probably be a false trail, in fact,

[9]   Does narration with images not strongly resonate with dreams? In Figure 1, 'cinema' figures in two boxes: at the scale of film, it is sequential, but not at that of images. Yet, dreams also possess these qualities, namely a continuous unfolding or a stop at a still shot, with two essential points in common: a) the presence of images, strictly speaking, and not description, and b) the dreamer moving in a complex way from the role of actor to that of spectator, and even to that of the author. The dreamer navigates from the 'illusion of reality' to invention by way of 'critical distancing'. Wouldn't audio-visual narratives provide a new actualisation of an essential part of our mental activity?

[10]   The two other principles are *relevance* (communication with empirical reality) and *accessibility* (communication with pre-existing culture).

to merely reduce what could be called the virtualisation of the world to a simple victory of the reality of the image ('virtual', i.e. simulated) over the (concrete) reality of action. We can indeed read the history of humanity as the production of increasingly sophisticated intermediaries between society and the material world. Nature is socialised through the establishment of constructed mediators that interface with a part of reality, one where the logics of physics and biology apply. In the social universe itself, some interactions, in fact the less complex, are delegated to machines that manage a certain number of standardised action programs. In all cases, however, the image is only one possible medium. Writing and, therefore, symbolic language are ever more present, for instance, in the use of computers or in network telematics (Internet). Various expressions of NVNS (maps, graphics, and tables) are clearly a complement to words, written or oral, whether in the audio-visual realm or disclosure literature. We are therefore rather in the total triumph of the third approach, previously termed 'de/reconstruction'. Here, representations in any language are becoming increasingly common, but without necessarily ignoring the signifier/signified tension, without which the act of language would lose its meaning – and, seriously, there is no indication that this is happening.

Social reasoning exposed at the risk of image

At this stage in the reflection, it seems difficult to avoid both a term and a debate. What about *narrative*? This word finds itself at the heart of questions on the specificities of the humanities, and more particularly of history in current epistemological works. However, this does not mean that it is always well defined. This debate concerns us. Even if expanded or removed from its most common linguistic sense, narrative has to do with the verbal-sequential expression of a diachronic reality – in other words, the opposite of the map.

Enigmatisation

Recent works, such as those of Jacques Rancière,[11] revolve around the question of the status of the narrative in history.[12] Yet the issues often seem to go beyond and blur the specific problem of narrative's status. Thus, the

---

[11] Lévy, P., 1995. *Qu'est-ce que le virtuel ?*, Paris : La Découverte.
[12] Rancière, J., 1992. *Les noms de l'histoire*, Paris : Seuil.

strong connotation of the word 'narrative' relevant to the field of fiction can sometimes strengthen the position of those who defend less theoretical attitudes of the historical discipline and, under this guise, value statements that indiscriminately combine literary prose, discourses of civic reassurance, and popular legend. This can then help deter those who, conversely, invite historians to choose between different incompatible genres. The word 'narrative' is, in fact, an extremely polysemic term, and its use cannot be reduced to a rejection of theory and the theoretical ambitions of history.[13]

Paul Ricoeur's work expresses a very different attitude. From his painstaking journey through the reflections on history, Ricoeur notably draws the idea that, to meet the requirements of scientificity, history must assume the Aristotelian *mutos*, which – in the spirit of Paul Veyne – translates as '*mise en intrigue*' (sic.) (English: 'plotting'). Through this type of formatting of empirical materials, the historian considers both the presence of intentional actors and collective or structural dynamics, which no actor completely controls. Narrative thus appears as a particular kind of statement that corresponds to a time of research work – that of *configuration*, to use Louis O. Mink's term which is broadly discussed by Ricoeur,[14] versus *classification* and *theorisation*. In this phase, indissociable from the others, says Ricoeur, we seek to weave together the strands. We must identify the specific logics of a singular object without limiting ourselves to drawing it according to external general models (this would be 'causal analysis' – I would say, the 'factorial approach', criticised by Ricoeur), but by building a specific theoretical system.

This is not a question of indulging in exceptionalism. The linking of such a configuration with larger explanatory systems (notably in the form of experimentation that analyses alternative hypotheses for events that have actually occurred) establishes a link with a broader conceptual apparatus: 'unique causal ascription'. Ricoeur refuses to propose a positive global theory himself, since his goal is not to present a 'philosophy of history' that would inevitably rival the production of knowledge with a scientific aim. For him, the issue is to show the specific constraints and openings that the object of history conceals.

The essential thing here is that Ricoeur speaks less of history than of *historicity*. He highlights a double complexity: the presence of *actors*,

[13] For a state of the art see the special issue, 'Le sens du récit', *Sciences Humaines,* 60, April 1996.
[14] Ricœur, P., 1983–1985. Te*mps et récit*, Paris: Seuil, vol. 3.

each endowed with a rich intentionality, and the existence of overall societal *dynamics* requiring a 'systemic synthesis' of the 'heterogeneous'. Yet,
these singularities are present everywhere in the entire scope of society,
and thus in the social sciences.

The time of which he is thinking is both that of individuals (the Augus-
tinian paradoxes and phenomenological approach serve as his starting
point) and the complex relationship between actors and society (hence the
use of Aristotelian mimesis which, in its course from I to III, expresses the
idea of a bridge between the logic of the object and that of its cognitive
construction). At its roots, this human temporality thus raises similar problems in all of the social sciences.

In fact, Ricoeur is not particularly interested in the diachronic dimension of this temporality. When he analyses Fernand Braudel's *La Méditerranée...*, he comes up with the existence of 'quasi-personages' (sic.)
and of '*mise en intrigue*' (stic.) about a fundamentally synchronic text and
a 'painting' (*La Méditerranée* [The Mediterranean] at the time of *Philip
II*), on which are projected the different rhythms of historical movement.
Besides, history as academic discipline largely consists of exploring the
past rather than diachrony. This is the whole question of the object of history as a study of the diachronic dimension of societies, or an 'ethnogra-
phy' of lost civilisations. The place of the concept of *narrative* in Ricoeur's
reasoning ultimately has little to do with the poetics of the social sciences
in the sense of 'scientific genres' (like literary genres).[15]

One of the main concerns of his reflection is the parallel between
social science and literary fiction. This is a subtle parallel, which does not
consist of folding the former into the latter in a subjectivist perspective, as
some are tempted to do, but rather of capitalising on certain functions that
have already been analysed in literary discourse, thanks to the notion of
character. This allows for consideration of similar processes in the social
sciences, and thus for a better understanding of how they organise the construction of objectivity. The commonalities are these complex ensembles
of actors and the encompassing realities that transcend them, along with
strategies and constraints, constructed finalities, and assumed experienced
necessities.[16]

---

[15] Mink, L.O., 1979. 'History and Fiction as Modes of Comprehension', *New Litterary History*,
1979, p. 541–558.
[16] This is noted by Ducrot, O. & Schaeffer, J.M., 1995. *Nouveau dictionnaire encyclopédique
des sciences du langage*. Paris: Seuil. On this point, see the collection, 'La fabrique des
sciences sociales', 1991. *EspacesTemps* Les Cahiers, 47–48.

While this bundle of contradictions characterises all social logics and their temporality, it is detectable both now and in the long term. Once we admit that intrigue invariably has a diachronic dimension – which, moreover, is not so self-evident – we can imagine that another, synchronic form of *mutos* exists. Furthermore, great mythological constructions provide excellent examples: the interpretive edifices of post-Neolithic civilisations have mixed discourses, made both of sequential narrations and instantaneous descriptions. The Eden of *Genesis*, however, is fundamentally situational; framed by founding events (the Creation of the World) and adventures that took place before being put aside by the continuation of the story, it plays an essential role in the composition of myth by its content, alongside the organisation and disposition of places. In many comparable constructions, a construction even more favourable to non-sequential speech can be identified: an initial chaos, a series of divine interventions and a new state similar to the present world.

Augustine, and other theologians after him, precisely addressed the issue of time with the concern of maintaining the logical possibility of a situation of non-duration. Time belongs to the divine, since it is the shift in time that elapses (that is to say, the irreversibility of the individual life and history) that distinguishes Man from God(s) more than any other trait. In short, we are quite justified in establishing the same resonance of myth with non-sequential statements as with narrations and series of events. Hence, we find in great sacred texts the idea of *enigmatisation* [*mise en énigme*], either in the form of a situational analysis (where we encounter, to use Ricoeur's terms, 'problems' and 'nodes' as resources for a drama), or in realities that are not subject to time, such as 'structural' rivalries among Greco-Roman or Hindu Gods. It may be added that images (non-verbal, and not only non-sequential) have played a fundamental role in great transcendental representations. Thanks to its reality effect, as mentioned above, the (material or quasi-material) *icon* is a privileged means of accessing the (immaterial) *image,* and thus, paradoxically, of allowing for the production of an abstract god. Marie-José Mondzain demonstrates this by establishing a filiation between Byzantine iconophiles and the current 'image civilisation'.[17] This shows how the primacy of the word may seem like a recent reconstruction that both overvalues certain aspects of our cultural heritage and devalues others.

---

[17] On these questions, see: 'Le temps réfléchi. L'histoire au risque des historiens', 1995. *EspacesTemps* Les Cahiers, 59–61.

In this spirit, one wonders if the characterisation of our times by 'post-modern' thinkers as that of the 'end of great narratives' might be unilateral. There is little doubt that the fatalist conceptions of a history that is already written and has merely to *unfold* to go from essence to existence are in decline. One can potentially predict the future, but may no longer announce it. This is not to say that the historicist *fatum* is necessarily embodied in a particular language genre. The great utopias – of which these same authors, from Plato to Fourier, show the decline – had a strong pictorial dimension, either directly or largely induced by a meticulous description of the 'ideal city', which was more spatial and synchronic, given that any duration (except eternity) was assumed to be excluded.[18] *Timaeus* or *Critias* are good examples. Conversely, the relationship our societies now maintain with time involves a more complex relationship, which more easily admits plural readings of the past and recognises the difficulty of effectively articulating different scales and different points of view for the future.

Let us summarise: The 'paradigmatic' exploration of narrative, as compared to other types of discourse, is useful in that it helps clarify some aspects of the works and findings of social science. From our point of view, it is nonetheless a detour. The term 'narrative', as Ricoeur uses it, is not perfectly consistent with our investigation, which focuses on genres, not statements. Also, I will hereafter use the word 'narrative' in the flatter, classificatory sense of sequential discourse in analogical correspondence with an object that is itself sequential: events or series of events. [19]

'Are there pictures?'

Ultimately, what can we say about NVNS's contribution in the work of the social sciences? Let us first cite these discourses of *images*, in the most child-like sense. 'Images' are what someone looks at while leafing through a book. The more scholarly, consistent and impenetrable the book, the more he or she looks at them. Defined as such, images respond to the instantaneous entry function in a statement. They may contain verbal elements, provided they are in a dominated position and incapable of imposing their sequential order on the reader. These images can occupy various

---

[18] Mondzain, M.J., 1996. *Image, icône, économie. Les sources byzantines de l'imaginaire contemporain*, Paris: Seuil.

[19] On this topic, see Marin, L., 1973. *Utopiques: jeux d'espaces*, Paris: Minuit.

roles in in the development of thought: simple 'illustration', aimed at a faithful translation of a text without further contribution, or conversely, a core of the statement. In the first case, the official function of NVNS is purely pedagogical, and even if the message's recipient maintains his or her power of interpretation, it inevitably has the effect of devaluing these complementary resources. In the second case, the contributions can be diverse. Let us try to identify them.

We can start with the terminology used by Jean-Marc Ferry to identify different modes of cognitive appropriation of speech: *narrative* (a linguistic shaping of lived experience), *interpretative* (an interpretation of reality based on pre-existing schemes), *argumentative* (a disassembly of an object on the basis of lawfully founded rationality), *reconstructive* (an understanding of reality that enhances the rational approach of the resources of the other two modes.[20]

If, overall, Ferry hierarchizes these practices based on an increasing level of reflexivity, one can also consider that the different dimensions are complementary, without being unfaithful to one's approach. What is specific to the work of reconstruction is precisely to incorporate the other approaches as part of a larger truth. If the specificity of scientific work depends on the latter two, that fact remains that the four moments play a role. Reinterpreted from the angle of the tension between the empirical and the theoretical, 'narrative' and 'interpretive' appear to be decisive elements, provided they are linked to the other polarities. Narrative can therefore be linked to description or observation, which is illusionary if it alleges to be sufficient in itself, but inseparable in its dialogue with problem solving or theory building, with two-way movement. The question one may ask then is, where are non-verbal and non-sequential discourses situated in this classification? The following table attempts to cross two of the boxes from Figure 1 to show the similarities and differences between the genres seemingly the most distant in the work of the social sciences today.

---

[20] This is the meaning understood by Oswald Ducrot and Jean-Marie Scheafer, *op. cit.* and Prost, A., 1996. *Douze leçons sur l'histoire*, Paris: Seuil.

	Verbal-sequential	Non-verbal/ non-sequential
Narrative	Story, description	[Illustration]
Interpretative	Classificatory speech	Topographic maps , tables, or classificatory graphs
Argumentative	Demonstrative rhetoric	Model-maps, graphic models
Reconstructive	Theoretical proposition	Conceptual maps, graphic and theoretical language (?)

Table 3 Types of discourse and contemporary cognitive construction.

Is there perfect symmetry between the two columns? Does each of them have its centre of gravity in the same place? Apparently so, but it is uncertain whether the discursive practices corresponding to the different boxes are equally developed. The verbal-sequential prevails at the top of the table (since any image implies a clear break with lived experience), but conversely at the bottom. The primacy of verbal-sequential undoubtedly appears, and the expressions in the last box (bottom right) can be read as much as a work program as a list of effective techniques. At a certain level of complexity, 'natural' language seems to be the only one capable of weaving together all the threads of reasoning. Even if it is apparently reduced to a commentary of symbolic mathematical statements, as in theoretical physics, it plays an essential role in linking these statements to the rest of the theory and to the culture already gained in the field. For many, the verbal-sequential must continue to serve as a cognitive *universal equivalent*, no doubt thanks to its ability to include – without limitation – nuances, determinations, distances, and contexts.

Revisiting the map

Due to the immediacy with which they are read, images keep the failings of their advantages; in this case, the limitation of information is the price paid for clarity. Herein lies a risk of overusing images (for example, by using a 'chorematic' map, a model-map based on the table of elementary *chorèmes* made up by Roger Brunet in 1980) as a self-evident theoretical discourse for the sake of brevity. We can thus unduly switch back to the interpretive, under the uncontrolled attraction of undiscussed, especially aesthetic or geometric, models. This is the problem with maps, which would require much larger legends to avoid false interpretations.

The flattening of interpretation also threatens the map in another sense. The common error is to call maps that result from a specific discursive project 'thematic maps', and to call topographic maps 'general'.

We know that the latter correspond to a slow evolution of military maps (*'état-major'*) on which the phenomena represented (e.g. altitude differences, forest areas, and communication routes) were those that might interest manoeuvring armies. Today's audiences – namely drivers and hikers – create their own themes, like those of the past. One understands why there can be no narrative moment in a map: this kind of analogical image requires such a selection of available information that the profusion of the lived experience is inevitably impoverished. 'Mental maps' themselves merely move the interpretive approach towards the individual, object of the investigation. Respondents are, in fact, asked to limit their perceptions to several basic rules of expression, creating a powerful filter outside the formatted materials. One could say that the verbal-sequential has, historically speaking, tended to dominate in every area. The present rebalancing if favour of the image (analysed above) creates *ipso facto* a counterbalance that is apparent equally at every level, once an alternative (even partial) appeared. Starting from the narrative mode, images can be a tool of reflexivity. Conversely, within a weak framework, imaged discourses prevail over reflection, and the sequentiality provided by the rhetoric facilitates a less argumentative ordering. In other words, writing is often acknowledged as the antidote to the facility of using images, for instance, when the weaknesses of a cartographic discourse founded on simple visual correlations is justly criticised. However, images can also endorse this role. They offers shortcuts through instantaneous visualisations that sanction the lack of rigour of a discourse that plays too well on the semantic slips and gaps that sequentiality allows. Thus geography, long caught in its empiricist confinement by a sterile marriage between the topographic and geological map (i.e. a strictly interpretive posture that invokes 'explanatory' resources rather than contestable ones) can play the diversified cards of analogy and make them fit the different registers of its intellectual productions. Sociology, however, which in Continental Europe stems from philosophy and is strongly marked by verbal rhetoric, is being 'Americanised' at both ends. On one hand, the 'analytical' position is pushing it to *stick* even more to the domain of words; on the other hand, synthetic concerns are leading it towards the use of graphs and figures, to the point that Pierre Bourdieu ended up taking what was merely a graphic expression of the factorial plan of his (non-spatial) model of relationships between social groups as the 'social space'.[21] The axes of 'economic capital' and 'cultural capital' soon mutate into a system of geographic coordinates to which the concrete configuration of places is asked, with the exception of a few nuances, to conform. The uncontrolled metaphor becomes a usurped analogy and ends up in the horrible expression 'physical space' to describe the spatial dimension of society – in other words, social space. Bourdieu thus gets caught up in the 'reality effects' that he himself created, thereby indicating the growing legitimacy of geographic-style imagery in sociological reasoning.

In short, the historical shift of the respective influences of the word and image creates an unstable but productive dynamic, founded on rivalries and complementarities between language genres. Can we imagine a stabilisation based on clear epistemological-linguistic rules? Certainly not yet. So let us content ourselves with a first-stage *methodological milestone.*

The different variants of non-sequential languages prove suitable for handling approaches to complex global objects, be they characterised by the idea of 'totality' or that of 'complexity', and be they considered 'systemic' or 'dialogic'. Verbal language first appeared as a tool for dismantling and unfolding this 'comprehensiveness'. It is a way of fully satisfying the analytical requirement: 'What exactly do you mean by...?'. Rather than as a universal equivalent, verbal language is a safeguard that compels new forms of expression that are designed to be part of scientific statements to parallel the pre-existing ones, with at least the same degree of intelligibility already attained without words. Translation can go both ways, but it is probably more reasonable to enrich the heritage that centuries of rhetoric have bequeathed us by incorporating it into a broader language palette, rather than by replacing it by cutting it off from its ancient privileges through new modes of expression, depending on the circumstances. For the social sciences, the epistemology of scientific genres thus goes beyond the mere acknowledgement of an active dynamic of languages. It inevitably leads toward a discussion of the standards of cohabitation and interaction between these genres, capable of strengthening consistence and the relevance of statements. [22]

---

[21] Ferry, J.M., 1991. *Les puissances de l'expérience*, Paris: Cerf, vol. 2.
[22] See especially Bourdieu, P., 1993. '*Effets de lieu*', in P. Bourdieu (ed.), *La misère du monde*, Paris: Seuil, pp. 159–167.

First published in French: 'De l'espace pour la raison', ©*EspacesTemps Les Cahiers*, 62–63, 1996, Penser/Figurer. L'espace comme langage dans les sciences sociales, pp. 19–35.

Chapter 6

Cartographic Semiosis: Reality as Representation

Emanuela Casti

Over the last ten years, a new theory in the interpretation of cartography has taken shape. In her overview of the various interpretative approaches that have contributed to the present critical approach, the author notably identifies *semiotics*. A semiotic approach, nd the theory of cartographic semiosis in particular, effectively shifts the emphasis from maps as a *mediation* of territory to maps as *agents*, whereupon the actions to be carried out in territory are determined. This perspective may be defined as cartographic hermeneutics, given that it undermines the very semiotic notion of map analysis. The study of maps does not rely on autonomous semiosis but rather on second level (or meta-semiotic) semiosis, which is deeply rooted in – and closely linked to – first-level, territorial semiosis. In particular, the author focuses on two concepts: self-reference and iconisation. *Self-reference*, which constitutes the core of cartographic communication, is used to indicate the ability of maps to make themselves accepted as such (by their mere existence) and to independently communicate the intentions of the cartographer. *Iconisation* is the communicative process that results in circumstances and contingencies being communicated as truths, thanks to the self-referential nature of maps. Hence, as a model, maps do not represent territories but rather replace them. Through the process of iconisation, direct knowledge of the world is put aside in favour of the knowledge generated by the map itself.

Society and cartography

Never has there been such a rich variety of approaches, techniques, and theories for understanding the problematic nature of the relationship between geographical maps and their social role. The theme 'Mapping the Elsewhere' of the latest International Conference on the History of Cartography, in Madrid, offered a comprehensive review of the concepts scholars are now applying in an attempt to analyse several key issues, including 1) the role of a map within the social group that produced it, 2) how maps reflects the specific historical period to which they belong, and 3) the policies or projects that potentially underlie its creation.

We have clearly moved away from those positivist histories of cartography that focused only on the technical aspects of map-building and on the clarity and evidence of its content (i.e. its supposed 'objectivity'). With the jettisoning of the idea that maps are simply mirrors of a given worldview, cartography has come to be regarded as an exercise in the intellectual appropriation of the world by a humanity aimed at mastering its surroundings. This approach has led to the 're-discovery' of the dual nature of maps, as a social product that can reveal the ways in which a given society constructs its own specific knowledge of territory, and as a means of communication that not only permits the circulation of that territorial knowledge, but also plays an independent role in the communication process, thereby functioning as an agent in its own right. The study of 'cartography' now embraces this duality, with a whole range of interpretative approaches that aim to look at both the constructive and communicative processes at work in maps. Indeed, the focus has shifted from 'how much reality is reproduced' to 'what maps communicate about a territory's reality and meaning'.

Hence, the last decade has seen the emergence of a number of different methods and theoretical/critical approaches for studying maps, all of which are essential to the history of cartography.

The aim of this article is to retrace the phases of this interpretative approach to underline its most innovative features, as well as to argue that a clear epistemological framework now exists and may be adopted in the study of maps. At the same time, I will highlight the crucial role of geographical studies in the changes that have come about. In effect, such studies have highlighted not only the problem of maps being seen as emblematic of some sort of meta-geographical discourse, but also their sophisticated, 'self-referential' nature. In this respect, semiosis – the generation of signs – plays a central role, given that a 'self-referential' system is, by definition, capable of generating meaning independent of the intentions of the person using it.

Starting from these premises, we will now explore the interpretative approaches that, to varying degrees, have contributed to the present method of critical interpretation – approaches that might be described as focusing on the study of the map-object, deconstruction, and semiotics.

Studying the map-object

Studying the map-object goes beyond the positivist approach because it looks at a map as a documentary source of knowledge, rejecting exactitude and verissimilitude as the sole criteria for interpretation of a map. What is studied, therefore, is not the clarity or evidence of the information contained therein, but the social context within which it is created. This change, which dates back to the first half of the 20th century, obviously paved the way for a revaluation of the importance and meaning of maps as records of the relationship between human beings and their surroundings.[1] It was at this time that the first, tentative steps were taken to promote maps as tools for use in various social agendas. As a documentary source, maps figure prominently in pedagogy, politics, the military, public administration, religion, and science. Ultimately, maps may be perused as territorial records, even if the main research focus is to inspect their structural aspects. In the latter case, all of the aspects involved in the construction of maps are considered: the material on which they are drawn, the graphic techniques used, the reason for their creation, the body/person that commissioned them, the cartographer's knowledge and ability to express that knowledge, their commercial distribution and, in some cases, their role as models or prototypes for other cartographic works. These studies, which focus on the rarity or purpose of a given document, also revived antiquarians' and collectors' interest in the

---

[1] These approaches are still widely practiced and are highly esteemed in the history of cartography, as well-exemplified in the various volumes of *The History of Cartography*, University of Chicago Press, Chicago, 1987–. Vol I and Vol II (books 1 and 2), edited by J .B. Harley and D. Woodward; Vol II (book 3), edited by D. Woodward and G.M. Lewis.

history of cartography,[2] with the result that well-known scholars competent in the history of cartography worked in such areas. Yet, with the exception of a few rare cases, no great contribution was made to critical reflection on the map itself.[3]

During the same period, however, certain scholars focused on the social aspects of maps, leading to significant developments in the critical discourse on cartography. In Italy, foremost amongst these was A. Almagià, who considered that the value of the map-document lay not in its metrical rendition of reality, but in the importance of its content. 'Content' here was not merely that information we nowadays refer to as 'referential'; it also included what we might call 'social' information. Hence, the importance of maps lies in the fact that they reveal the territorial praxis of a given society at a given period in its history.[4] This is why Almagià reintroduced those 'territorial images' previously denied the status of 'geographical maps' – namely administrative maps and charts – into a critical discussion of cartography. Prior to this, such works had been considered rather ingenuous sketches of territories and nothing more. How could they be described as legitimate works of cartography, being not bound by indications of scale or type of projection, and often of uncertain authorship?[5] Almagià, however, considered them the greatest expression of the territorial policies that States of the Early Modern period were developing and applying. His claim that they were indeed works of cartography led him to include them in the *Monumenta Cartographica*, one of the greatest products of the renewed interest in maps as objects

---

[2] For an overview of the dawning antiquarian interest in maps, see M. Harvey, *The island of lost maps: a true story of cartographic crime*, Broadway Books, New York, 1999; Italian edition: id., *L'isola delle mappe perdute. Una storia di cartografia e di delitti*, Rizzoli, Milan, 2000.

[3] It should, however, be reiterated that these studies analysed and shed light upon the relationship between printing and cartography. As a recent example, one need only mention D. Woodward, *Map Prints in the Italian Renaissance*, The British Library, London, 1996.

[4] Here, one need only mention his investigation of various important documents, including the 'Carta del territorio veronese detta dell'Almagià', which enabled him to date them and put them in social context. See R. Almagià, 'Un'antica carta topografica del territorio veronese', in: *Rendiconti della Regia Accademia Nazionale dei Lincei*, XXXII, 1923, fasc.5–6, pp. 61–84.

[5] In most cases, these works were produced by unknown technicians and land surveyors, who used cartography as a tool for surveying projects commissioned by public or private bodies. However, the latter were sometimes produced by great cartographers, or men who went on to become so, and in these cases the administrative maps contained important innovations at both a technical and conceptual level. For a recent discussion of this latter point, with regard to the administrative cartography of the Venetian Republic, see E. Casti, 'State, cartography and territory in the Venetian and Lombard Renaissance', in: D.Woodward, G. M. Lewis (eds), *The History of Cartography*, v. 3, The University of Chicago Press, Chicago.

of scholarly research,[6] in the first half of the twentieth century. Designed to replace the often-deficient 19th-century collections[7], these *Monumenta* were large-format works that allowed maps to be combined with texts that highlighted their importance as documentary sources. The proof of the importance of this work lies in the fact that these volumes are still widely used and consulted.[8]

The importance of maps finally recognised, people began to reflect upon how they functioned as a means of communication and the ideological implications they inevitably contained as social products. This critical evaluation of maps was first exemplified in the studies of J. B. Harley, known to cartography historians for his extensive research in this field.[9] Thus opens the second phase, with interpretation becoming deconstruction.

The deconstruction of maps

This marked an important transition, more so than the development of the previous approach, as it focused on areas that had until then been ignored. The idea that there was only one way of studying a map was abandoned in favour of focusing on multiple areas of interpretation. Maps continued to be

---

[6] He produced the two collections *Monumenta Italiae Cartographica*, Istituto Geografico Militare, Florence, 1929. Re. anast.: A. Forni, Sala bolognese, 1980; *Monumenta Cartographica Vaticana*, Biblioteca Apostolica Vaticana, Città del Vaticano, (1944–1955). A later work, written in collaboration with another scholar, is R. Almagià, M. Destombes, *Monumenta Cartographica vetustoris aevi*, N. Israel, Amsterdam, 1964.

[7] Among these, in the Italian context, G. Marinelli's *Saggio di cartografia della regione veneta*, Venezia, Naratobich, 1881 is of note. However, despite the fact that this was one of the first to take a *catalogue raisoné* approach, the absence of photographic reproductions (given the date of publication) means the book is now of little use as a reference work.

[8] These great collections, which started to appear at the end of the 19th century, cover many regions, including: Y. Kamal, S. Fauat, *Monumenta Cartographica Africae et Aegypti*, Cairo, 1926–1951, reprint.: Institut für Geschichte der Arabisch-Islamischen Wissenschaften an der Johann Wolfgang Goethe Universität, Frankfurt, 1987; C. Armando, A. Teixeira da Mota, *Portugaliae Monumenta Cartographica*, Imprensa National-Casa de Moeda, Lisbon, 1960, (reprint. 1988); U. Kazutaka, O. Takeo, M. Nobuo, N. Hiroshi, *Monumenta Cartographica Japonica*, 1972; G. A. Skrivani'c, *Monumenta Cartographica Jugoslaviae*, Istorijski Institut, Beograd, 1974; P. H. Meurer, *Monumenta Cartographica Rhenaniae*, Stadtarchiv Mönchengladbach, 1984; G. Schilder, K. Stopp, *Monumenta Cartographica Neerlandica*, Uitgeverij Canaletto/Repro, Holland Alphenaan den Rijn, 1986-2000; M. Watelet, *Monumenta Cartographica Walloniae*, Editions Racine, Brussels, 1995.

[9] He wrote 140 articles and contributed to numerous books, including 'The Map and the Development of the History of Cartography', in: J. B. Harley, D. Woodward (eds), *The History of Cartography*, The University of Chicago Press, Chicago & London, 1987, vol. 1, pp. 1–42.

interpreted as *qua* objects, so as to shed light on the implications of their mode
of construction and their significance *qua* records of the relationship between
humans and their environment.[10] They were also studied as social products
within the wider framework of reflection on modes of representation emerging in the social sciences.[11] This widening of the critical approach, however,
did bring with it new problems, for while new disciplines contributed to
the understanding of maps, they also resulted in a certain fragmentation. In
fact, as approaches to the history of cartography began straddling different
fields, their internal cohesion dissolved into the specialized realms of each
discipline. In Italy, for instance, cartographic studies seeped into the fields of
history, architecture, and urban planning, which made circulation and cross-
referencing more challenging. For that reason, cartographic interpretation
tends to be viewed as a specialised subfield shaped, at times, by the education and mind-set of the scholar addressing it, rather than as a self-contained,
independent discipline. Specific areas of study were determined either by the
specific characteristics of a certain kind of cartography (studies of historical
cartography, the modern map, etc.), or by the various disciplines involved in
reflection on maps. Nevertheless, despite this drawback, the result was the
same: the involvement of multiple critical approaches in the study of cartography – a fact that reflected an attitude Harley described most succinctly
when he said, 'maps are too important to be left to cartographers alone'.[12]

The figure who first broke new ground in this area was J. B. Harley,
whose theoretical work began in the 1980s. Analysing the communicative
power of maps, he saw the need for an approach that laid the foundations for such deconstruction, i.e. the exploration of different, even con-
flicting discourses, that could potentially raise new problems in terms of
cartographic interpretation.[13] Starting from Jacques Derrida's definition

[10] I am referring to the focus on certain aspects (filigree, heraldic devices, etc), which are
certainly important for interpreting maps but should, I feel, be left to specialists of certain
antiquarian/artistic disciplines.

[11] Among the many works on this question, see J. B. Harley, 'Maps, knowledge and power',
in: D. Cosgrove, S. Daniels (eds), *The Iconography of Landscape. Essays on the symbolic
representation, design and use of past environments*, Cambridge University Press, Cambridge,
1988, pp. 277–312.

[12] J.B. Harley, 'Deconstructing the Map', *Cartographica*, 26-2, 1989, pp.1–20, cit. p. 2; re-
published in: T. Barnes, J. Duncan (dir.), *Writing Worlds: Discourse, Text and Metaphor in
the Representation of Landscape*, Routledge, London and New York, 1992, pp. 231–247.

[13] For more about the radical position he took and his belief in his own ideas, see the debate
published in the review *Cartographica* in 1980–1982. On this point, see P. Gould, 'Une
prédisposition à la controverse', in: P. Gould, A. Bailly, *Le pouvoir des cartes. Brian Harley
et la cartographie*, Anthropos, Paris, 1995, pp. 53–58.

of deconstruction of literary text – namely, the exploration of the *aporie* (impasse) between rhetoric and thought/ideas – Harley's approach had three goals: 1) to challenge the epistemological myth (created by cartographers) which argued that there was a cumulative acquisition of objective knowledge created by striving towards greater likeness to reality, 2) to uncover the social role of maps and their power in consolidating an existing ordering of the world, and 3) to give cartography a place in interdisciplinary studies of the representation and construction of knowledge.[14]

Harley did not reject the importance of technique in the production of maps, but rather the idea that cartography could be reduced to the study of technique alone. His starting point was that technical rules were influenced by a set of social factors whose presence one should be able to read within the finished map. He argued that much of maps' power is derived from these social factors disguised within an apparently neutral science that supposedly exists outside of society, but that simultaneously serve to legitimise social order. For Harley, precision and accuracy in rendering were the new talismans of power and its exercise, and the culmination of this talismanic authority was to be seen in the modern-day use of computers to draw maps.[15]

His insistence that maps embodied a language was developed in three points, the first arising from J. Bertin's studies of the semiotics of graphics, the second from E. Panofsky's studies of iconology and the third from findings from the sociology of knowledge. These led Harley to reiterate his belief in cartographic knowledge as a social product linked to power interests, thus shedding new light on the link between cartography and ideology.[16]

However, his key contribution was his understanding of the crucial link between cartography and geography, which highlighted the inexplicable rupture that existed between the two disciplines (inexplicable in that maps must necessarily make reference to geography, given that they represent territories).

Harley hoped for the emergence of a social theory that might serve as a starting-point for reflections on the hidden implications of cartography.

---

[14] J. B. Harley, 'Deconstructing the Map'…, p. 64. The page reference is for the French edition, published in his honour, which contains a re-publication of the article. P. Gould, A. Bailly, *Le pouvoir des cartes. Brian Harley et la cartographie*….

[15] J. B. Harley, 'Deconstructing the Map…', p. 77.

[16] J. B. Harley, 'Maps, knowledge and power'…On this point see also: B. Beleya, 'Images of power: Derrida/Foucault/Harley', *Cartographica,* 29 (2), pp. 1–9.

It is here that the limitations of his approach began to emerge: How can a 'social theory' – understood in the most general terms – only produce results that are equally general and generic for map interpretation? Perhaps the weak point in his work was the failure to recognise that any such theory, while reflecting social issues, must be specifically geographical in nature. We will later discuss how one can achieve quite unexpected results using such a theory.

Harley's theory paved the way for a number of important scholars, including Jacob and Farinelli, both of whom work on the question of the language of cartography, though with different objectives[17].

Jacob's theory argues that the persuasive power of maps lies not only in socio-political factors but also in the fact that maps satisfy a fundamental need of individuals for tools to build a 'poetics of space' which show how the world might be. Through his study of the architecture and the combination of figurative codes used in cartography, he concluded that maps are less objects than functions, authorities of social mediation that lend themselves to numerous interactive situations (construction work, project design, field operations, teaching, discursive exchange, etc.), and as such are social objects, strategic instruments of power, even when their diffusion is subject to restriction or monopoly.[18] Jacob focuses on the complex dialectics at work in maps, which are not anchored in a generic 'knowledge of territory', but in the socially-consolidated knowledge that makes up 'geography'. His most important work for our purposes here is *L'Empire des Cartes*, wherein he uses a synchronic structuralist approach to the entire history of cartography, taking the subject as a whole to bring out the theoretical problems raised by maps and their graphic components. Jacob also explores the various stages in the perception and interpretation of cartographic works.

As a result of his studies, geographical maps are no longer 'obvious'. His analysis of the different stages of their history, how they are produced, and the intellectual choices behind the content and graphics makes it clear that the nature and function of 'maps' are legitimate areas of study.

Farinelli, however, follows in the footsteps of Harley, providing a basis for the critique of geographical knowledge, with a particular emphasis on

[17] The most important works by these two scholars are: C. Jacob, *L'empire des cartes. Approche théorique de la cartographie à travers l'histoire*, Albin Michel, Paris, 1992; F. Farinelli, *I segni del mondo. Immagine cartografica e discorso geografico in età moderna*, La Nuova Italia, Florence, 1992.

[18] C. Jacob, *L'empire des cartes. Approche théorique de la cartographie...*, p. 458.

the ideology of maps. He traces the development of cartography from the standpoint of ideology, arguing that the changes therein are linked to those in the political organisation of the state. Firm in his conviction that maps have been used as interpretative models for geography, Farinelli insistently examines how maps affect geographical epistemology. He likewise explores their communicative function to show that 1) what maps convey is invariably subject to ideology, 2) when received in an uncritical manner, a map's message may deeply impinge on the very notion of territory – a notion inadvertently taken up by geographers. He also argues that maps have a dangerous influence on the very concept of 'space', and through his studies of geometrical cartography demonstrates that 'bourgeois' geography only emerged when the spatial logic imposed by the cartography of the previous period had been abandoned.[19] At that point, the world became a complex made up of individual, mappable – and therefore, observable – components; the cartographic image was decisive proof of the concrete existence of an object (if it could be given a symbol and a name, its 'reality' could not be questioned). Hence, human geography as an act of knowledge is based not on concepts but on the simple act of representation.

A semiotic study of maps: the hermeneutical approach

Unlike the deconstructive perspective, the hermeneutical approach elaborates on the idea of the map as a tool for intervention between society and territories and concludes that maps, as such, play a crucial role. Hermeneutics focuses on the role of maps as agents capable of deploying self-referential information to mould human action on territories.

In other words, maps handle complex geographical spaces by reshaping them as cartographic spaces based upon which action is performed.

Before looking at the results of this approach to date, it is worth noting that it is, in fact, just one of the many forms of reflection on cartography with a common aim: using semiotic sciences to interpret maps. Of notable mention here are the studies of North American scholars Denis Wood and John Fels and, later, of A. Mac Easchren. Both approaches focus on the

---

[19] On this point, see F. Farinelli, 'Alle origini della geografia politica 'borghese'', in: C. Raffestin (ed.), *Geografia politica: teorie per un progetto sociale*, Unicopli, Milan, 1983, pp. 21–38.

semiotic functioning of maps,[20] albeit from different angles and with varying degrees of formalization. I feel strongly that their specialized field is
worth endorsing because it is currently one of the most structured, vibrant
lines of research.[21] While innovation of necessity requires testing and experimentation, one must recall that formalised results have already been produced and subjected to critical scrutiny within the scientific community.[22]

I refer here to the various discussions of cartographic semiosis that
have emerged in recent years; discussions that define this theory as 'hermeneutical' because it falls within the realm of semiotic studies while, in fact,
remaining independent.[23] Unlike other approaches, cartographic semiosis
claims that a semiotic study of maps cannot be separated from a semiotic
study of territory. Borrowing from geographical theory, the idea that a territory's social significance is to be found in its semiotics,[24] this approach holds
that maps rely on meta-semiosis (or second-level semiosis), as their language

---

[20]   D. Wood, J. Fels, 'Designs on signs: Myth and Meaning in maps', *Cartographica 23,* n. 3,
       1986, pp.54-103 reprinted in: D. Wood, *The Power of Maps,* New York, Guilford Press, 1992,
       cap. 5; A. Mac Eachren, *How Maps work. Representation, visualization and design,* New
       York, Guilford Press, 1995.

[21]   Though it brings together a limited number of researchers, the importance of this analytic
       approach to the interpretation of maps has, in some way, been officially recognised by the
       creation of the Commission on Theoretical Cartography, a working group of the International
       Cartography Association (ICA). It should also be mentioned that the heads of that
       working group have created a series of discussion papers entitled *Diskussionsbeiträge zur
       Kartosemiotik und zur Theorie der Kartographie,* published in Dresden under the editorship
       of A. Wolodtschenko and H. Schlichtmann (respectively, President and Vice-president of the
       Commission). In all, the Commission brings together roughly twenty scholars from around
       the world, see the website: _ HYPERLINK http://rcswww.urz.ut-dresden.de/-wolodt/tc-com.

[22]   Among the many contributions posted on the ICA website, I would like to mention to the
       following: A. Wolodtschenko (ed), *The Selected Problems of Theoretical Cartography, 2002,*
       ICA, Dresden, 2003.

[23]   The full discussion on which these pages are based can be found in: E. Casti, *L'ordine del
       mondo e la sua rappresentazione. Semiosi cartografica e autoreferenza,* Unicopli, Milano,
       1998, (English translation: *Reality as Representation. The Semiotics of Cartography and the
       Generation of Meaning,* Bergamo University Press, Bergamo, 2000), reviewed in: *Revista
       Bibliográfica de Geografía y Ciencias Sociales,* 185, 1999; *Rivista Geografica Italiana,* 108,
       2001; p.145–146; *The Portolan,* 53, 2002, p. 64.

[24]   More specifically, reference is made to questions of complexity. A. Turco, *Verso una teoria
       geografica della complessità,* Unicopli, Milan, 1988. It should be noted that these studies use
       findings from the fields of semiotics and linguistics, and the work of scholars like A.Greimas
       and F.De Saussure, who resist disciplinary classification. More importantly, this line of
       research touches upon the two neighbouring disciplines related to the philosophy of language,
       and especially to the research of Charles Morris. Morris' concepts were developed with a
       view to formalising a semiotic theory of territory that has proved fruitful and worth pursuing.
       See for instance: A. Turco, 'Semiotica del territorio: congetture, esplorazioni, progetti', in:
       Rivista Geografica Italiana, 101, 1994, pp. 365–383.

is based on territorial language (or first-level semiosis). Because of this, and for reasons I will discuss later, two aspects of cartographic interpretation should be mentioned. The first is that the *name* on the map is not seen as one sign among many others, but that based upon which all cartographic information is arranged. The second is that semiosis – the process whereby information is produced and transmitted – takes place via an interpreter, who functions dually as a territorial agent and one who communicates within a given society.

This theory has been tested within the specific context of maps of both European and colonial territories made in the West.[25] This is precisely the cultural milieu in which a map takes on distinctive importance both as an ideal tool of territorial conquest and an instrument of self-affirmation for colonialist policies. However, as this theory addresses the functioning of territorial symbolic systems in general, it can be applied to virtually any cultural context.

We reiterate here that the present analysis aims to deconstruct, delocate, and re-encode the theoretical coherency of geographical maps, which are considered powerful mimetic tools that go beyond their intended ends and the cultural issues that originally shaped them. We will begin by outlining the theoretical cartographic assumptions upon which cartographic semiosis is based.

Maps and the territorialisation process

To begin, this approach does not see 'territory' exclusively as an empirical given, but rather as the result of a process through which a society transforms natural spaces and imbues them with man-made pertinence and meaning. The various processes that act upon territories can be broken down schematically into three broad categories – denomination, reification and structuralisation – which together comprise the process of territorialisation.

The first involves the control of symbols – that is, those operations aimed at the intellectual modelling and appropriation of territory, i.e. the attribution of names to points on the surface of the earth that are thereby identifiable as places. Reification is the exercise of material control – that is, the physical construction and appropriation of 'territory'. Finally, 'structuralisation' involves the creation of operational contexts for the execution

---

[25] E. Casti, 'The Analogical and Digital systems in Euclidean Cartography: the colonisation and iconisation of Africa', in *Diskussionsbetraege zur Kartosemiotik und zur Theorie der Kartographie* vol. 4, 2001, pp. 15–28.

of social projects. Given its relevance in the present discourse, we wish
to reiterate that when one speaks of denomination, one is referring to the
attribution of names, which reflect the values of that society. The cultural
importance of the names used is evident in that they are called 'designators'.[26] Designators are therefore 'abbreviations of descriptions' and, in a
more or less clear-cut way, 'agglomerates of concepts' that pinpoint the cultural values upon which a society functions on a territory. Denomination is
a complex process, in which different meanings come into play depending
on the type of designator used and the types of values it conveys. Using the
categories of designation proposed by A. Turco, one might say that 'referential' designators are designed to set referential frameworks, i.e. to orien-
tate and/or move around in space (e.g. the Grand Canyon, Colorado, Fifth
Avenue). Although additional layers of meaning have formed over time,
these designators originated from the visual impact of these places or the
locations they described in a series of references. 'Symbolic' designators
convey socially-produced meanings, i.e. linked to the ideas and metaphysical values of the society that produced them. They also indicate religious
(San Francisco, Saint Laurence, and Mecca), historical (New York), political (Washington), and other values. 'Performative' designators, like the former, contain socially-generated meaning but, unlike them, are empirically
ascertainable (Mount Soufriere, Great Salt Lake, Hot Springs Mountain,
Reykjavik).[27] Following this pattern, one can see that a given designator
contains all of the qualities of the object it refers to, and that its cartographic
signification is, in fact, so condensed that it can only be understood through
an interpretation that is simultaneously denotative and connotative.[28] The

---

[26] I deal specifically with 'designators' rather than 'toponyms', because my intent is to reclaim
the social importance of names, beyond etymological-linguistic constraints. While toponymy
is the science of place-names, denomination goes back to the semiotics of territory. Namely,
denominational analysis addresses two issues: I) the symbolisation of a given place, and; II)
suggestions as to how that place ought to be perceived and experienced in society. See: A.
Turco, *Terra eburnea, il mito, il luogo, la storia in Africa*, Unicopli, Milano, 1999, pp.177–178.

[27] The word Reykjavik in Icelandic translates into English as 'Bay of smokes' or 'Bay of
steam'. Let us not forget that distinction between designators is essential to the research
on territorialisation. Analogies with the terminology developed by J. L. Austin and others
(especially J. L. Austin's *How to do Things with Words*, Oxford U.P., Oxford, 1962) as part of
their speech act theory should be avoided.

[28] In fact, designators are abbreviated descriptions of reality, a 'concentrate' of meaning that
includes all the qualities of the object identified (A. Turco, *Verso una teoria geografica della
complessità...*, pp. 79–93). With regard to *denotation* and *connotation,* I draw upon the classic
semiotic distinction between denotative or primary codification and connotative or secondary
codification (A. Turco, 'Semiotica del territorio...', pp. 372–373).

first level of interpretation is that of referential designator, which has been explicitly codified to create a referential framework, i.e. a clear but superficial meaning. The second level is necessary for symbolic and performative designators, in order to recognise the sedimentation of the cultural, technical, and 'historic' values of a given society, which can only be understood through a deeper level of investigation. Evidence of the social importance of connotation can be seen in the fact that place-names change as soon as a society or its transformative projects are altered: Saint Petersburg was renamed Leningrad after the communist party came to power in Russia; Leopoldville became Kinshasa after it gained independence and the values of the Congolese State were restored[29]; and more recently, Iraq's *Saddam Hussein* airport was renamed *Baghdad* airport by the Anglo-American coalition.[30] Ultimately, names echo social and/or political projects. Once the project or society it addresses changes, the territory is renamed. What is certain, however, is that by using performative and symbolic designators, societies imbue territory with their values.

However, what we wish to stress here is a dimension that has yet to be recognised: in such contexts, the map – far from mere intellectual appropriation of territory – plays a central role as the means of representation whereby denomination reveals itself, is strengthened, and also ratified. The crucial consequence of this is the symbiosis of denomination and cartography and thus, as we have already mentioned, the key role of names within cartographic communication.[31] Hence, maps are not just supports when one intellectually appropriates territory; they are also *denominative projections* as conveyors of the designator's meaning(s). 'As such, they accompany the designator, along with other codes (called *denominative surrogates*),

---

[29] I am referring to the current capital city of the Democratic Republic of Congo. Towards the end of the 19th century, Kinshasa became an important trading post on the Congo River, at initiative of the Anglo-American explorer Henry Morton Stanley, who named it Leopoldville in honour of the Belgian king Leopold II. In 1966, the designator Leopoldville, clearly a vehicle for European values, was replaced with the basic designator Kinshasa, corresponding to the name of the village located in that same place in the 19th century.

[30] This was done to reaffirm the coalition's resolve to liberate the country from Hussein's dictatorship and return it to the Iraqi people.

[31] In cartographic, interpretation important clues, are given not only by designative names, but by all the captions on a map that refer to the relationship between society and territory and provide information about it.

due to the communicative role they play. Such codes take on some territorial values and meanings, and communicate them as significant'.[32] The
designator *Chicago*, for instance, encompasses the meanings of the various
functions associated with the city, as a residential, political, economic and
educational space. One of these functions will be highlighted based on the
denominative surrogates that go with it. Its blueprint emphasizes its importance as a living space, the conventional symbol for a state capital marks its
political-administrative role, and so on.

In short, we argue that maps are not only products of denomination,
wherein one can see the same dynamics at work as those of designators. In
fact, maps are also a semiotic field wherein the use of codes of types and
natures different from those of the lexical code triggers a second process
of semiosis. Maps, therefore, start with geographical designators, but have
mechanisms of communication that involve the combination of these with
other codes.

One should not forget that, from a structural standpoint, maps are systems that attempt to control and order a wealth of complex information
by identifying the most relevant geographical features and arranging them
in the manner in which we perceive them. This means the use of various
linguistic codes (i.e. names, numbers, shape, and colours) and structures:
the geometrical structure of the page itself, and the symbolic structure in
which the signifiers of other codes are collected (Figure 1a).

So, even at this first level, maps are a kind of hypertext and, as such,
play a role in what they communicate in a self-referential way.[33] If we
return to our starting premise – the importance of designators – and consider the latter as elements imposing a kind of hierarchical order on the surrogates present on a map, we see the full implications of the cartographic
projection of names on reality. The designator is the crux of the process
wherein information is actually produced using a double communicative
system – analogical and digital – which will be discussed later (Figure 1b).

---

[32] A denominative surrogate can be any figure, number, color or even the position of the name
      itself on the map. This is intended to make explicit the quality of the object represented on the
      map. The term surrogate refers to the fact that a missing name is substitued for, or surrogated,
      by another. On the projection of names, see E. Casti, *Reality as Representation...*, pp. 65–96.

[33] In fact, the use of various structures facilitates the conveyance of information. The
      interrelation between different codes reveals what might otherwise remain obscured in one
      individual code. On the results on communication of the transition from a single-structural
      system to a multi-structural language, see E. Cassirer, *The Philosophy of Symbolic Forms*,
      Yale University Press, Yale, 1955, (Italian edition: id., *Filosofia delle forme simboliche*, La
      Nuova Italia, Florence, 1961, pp. 9 ff.).

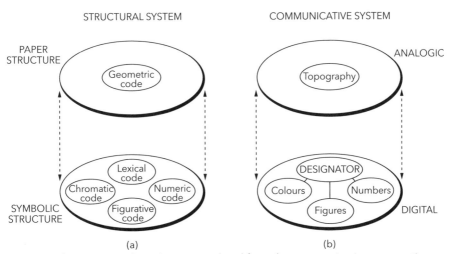

STRUCTURAL SYSTEM   COMMUNICATIVE SYSTEM

PAPER
STRUCTURE   ANALOGIC

SYMBOLIC
STRUCTURE   DIGITAL

(a)   (b)

Fig. 1 The map seen from the structural and from the communicative perspectives.

The map as a locus of semiosis

Having seen that maps can function as hypertexts, this capacity must now be seen relative to the production and communication of meaning that takes place in and through a given map. Here, one must look at the interpreter, who uses such documents to obtain information and pursue objectives. In this case, the map becomes a locus of semiosis, within which signs become *vehicles of significance.* As Charles Morris noted, signs convey something the moment their meaning is established and/or interpreted by someone.[34] In fact, focusing on the sign-as-vehicle, which in this case involves the designator combined with other signs, one sees that the former is based on three processes: I) the creation of meaning; II) the associations created due to the juxtaposition of signs; and III) the interpretation of the recipient of the information. Thus, one can consider

[34] Here I take up the model proposed by C. Morris (*Signs, Language and Behaviour*, Pertice-Hall, New York, 1946, Italian edition 1949), who moves away from an analysis of the sign itself and thus transcends the confines of logic semiotics (Charles Saunders Peirce) or linguistic semiotics (F. De Saussure). Morris adopts a functional, organic view of language geared towards pragmatics and reflects upon a sign's communicative aspect and its nature as a *sign-vehicle*; i.e. for our purposes, as a designator that incorporates information and conveys it in the presence of an interpreter. Let us not forget that cartographic semiosis proposes a study of geographical maps as symbolic operators and, as such, are not directly concerned with the analysis of the workings of the sign itself, as put forth by Mac Eachren (*How Maps Work...*). Cartographic semiosis favours a study of how the interpreter involved in the process of territorialization is affected by the study of the map itself.

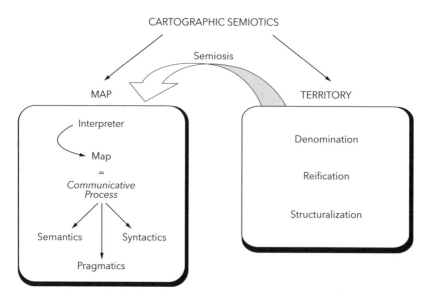

Fig. 2 The transfer of territorial semiosis and the establishment of cartographic meta-semiosis.

the areas within which to investigate the rules of cartographic semiosis, but in this case at a second level, meta-semiosis.[35] At a semantic level, meaning is produced through the encoding of signs. At a syntactic level, new meaning and pertinence is conveyed by the relationships between signs. At a pragmatic level, maps are both objects of interpretation and the framework for social praxis (Figure 2).

We will not make a detailed analysis of the specific impact of each of these domains on cartographic communication here, especially given that this information has already been widely documented elsewhere. We will simply restate the fact that maps must be seen as complex communication systems whose relevance depends not on the information contained therein, but that generated by the interpretation process.[36] It should equally be noted that, insofar as the interpreter decodes both the cartographic and the territorial language, she acts as a mediator between the two levels – geographic and linguistic – on which the semiotic approach takes place: *The hermeneutical slant of this approach consists in de-locating the geographical map in order to re-encode it in such a way as to disclose its*

---

[35] I argue here that the present analytical approach aims to investigate meta-semiosis rooted in territorial semiosis.

[36] E. Casti, *Reality as Representation...*, pp. 37–41.

complex impact on the production and spread of territorial meaning. This line of research is grounded in the awareness that the interpretation of map is territorial and thus foreshadows strategies of production, use, and mediatisation of a territory.

This approach sheds light on some fundamental aspects of cartographic representation. It is clear that by reproducing space based on analogy (i.e. the objects in the same layout and proportion as perceived in reality), maps draw on a specific topology. This topology represents a cognitive organisation of space, that is, a process that places objects in space around an observer who, in turn, is localised based on the relationship between himself and those objects.[37] All this has led to a technical and ideological reassessment of maps' compositional features (orientation, perspective, centrality) which, in turn, has provided analytical and theoretical evidence of their social relevance.[38] At the same time, it has been theoretically proven that each designator on a map is subject to certain prescriptions that, in some way, sanction its social meaning and/or significance. Attention is directed toward some aspects rather than others by processes through which surrogates neutralise excess information and prescribe certain possible interpretations based on what is included and what is excluded.[39]

Effectively, the real change of approach stems from the fact that the map is no longer seen solely as an important tool for intellectual appropriation of territory; it is also crucial in reinforcing the entire process of territorialisation. In certain social-historical contexts, the map becomes a system whereby an entire community posits its relationship to the world. Let us take, for instance, the maps drawn during the age of discovery and great explorations, where a progressive expansion of space accompanied the accretion of geographical knowledge. The Mediterranean, the sole object of 14th century maps, was gradually marginalized with respect to the ocean system, following the discovery of America. Again, frontiers are established via maps, which set

---

[37] A. J. Greimas, J. Courtés, *Sémiotique, dictionnaire raisonné de la théorie de langage*, Hachette, Paris, 1993, pp. 358–359. On the spatial organisation involved in the creation of a system of territorial reference, see A. Turco, 'Dire la terra: la costituzione referenziale del territorio in Costa d'Avorio', in: *Terra d'Africa*, Unicopli, Milan, 1994, pp. 15–58.

[38] It has been argued that the orientation of the map depends on the position of the viewer. It should also be recalled that, even though the viewer's position is ideally outside the real-world, the properties of his perceptive, self-centered space are still assimilated and conveyed through a language that hinges on a designator in its referential function.

[39] E. Casti, *Reality as Representation*..., pp. 151-173.

out, beforehand, geographical features such as rivers, to be detected in the territory later. Waterways are roughly mapped to delineate borders. When a journey into the field revealed inconsistencies, map-lines were privileged. Throughout the colonial era, maps served as mediation tools by which plans were implemented and courses of action taken, in theory, in territories that were unknown except via the maps themselves. The territorial assessment plans promoted by French colonialists in Africa was carried out based on information gathered from the thematic maps drawn specifically for that purpose.[40] Thus, cartography seems to be the product of a culture that generates a culture; it takes the cognitive patrimony of a given society and uses it to enrich territorial knowledge. It also presents itself as an autonomous form of communication and as an innovative interpretation of the world, generated by the mechanisms of territorial and social control established by the society that produces it.

The cartographic icon

A detailed investigation of how cartographic semiosis functions thus leads us to consider the relationship between maps and territories. Starting from the observation that the former is the model of the latter, one can argue that maps are an occasion to highlight certain information and play down other information (or dissimulate it altogether). As indicated earlier, technically speaking, this territorial modelling is done through the use of surrogates, combining names with certain characteristics or features. The result of this combination is what I would describe as the *cartographic icon*,[41] which plays an important role in the interpretation of maps. It takes the designator as a reference, models it, and introduces it into the communication exchange via self-productive mechanisms. The

---

[40]   E. Casti, 'Mythologies africaines dans la cartographie française au tournant du XIXe siècle', in : *Cahiers de géographie du Québec*, vol. 46, 2001, pp. 429–450.

[41]   It is worth noting that here I use the word *icon* in a way heretoforth unknown in the context of cartographic studies. *Icon* refers here to a semiotic figure that, as such, is capable of producing information and processing it in a communicative manner. The meaning of *icon* is therefore used differently, compared that used by authors who focus on the semiotic analysis of maps. Drawing upon Peirce, for instance, Mac Eachren claims that the icon is 'a sign-vehicle that refers merely by virtue of characters of its own' (*How Maps Work...*, p. 222). Dealing in his turn with the iconic code, Wood holds that 'it governs the manner in which graphic expressions correspond with geographic items, concrete or abstract, and their attendant attributes' (*The Power of Maps...*, p. 117).

result, however, is not merely the sum of meanings – those of the designators and surrogates – of which it is comprised. Rather, the icon, which functions independently of the process that produces it, transforms as well as combines. One is therefore justified in saying that *the icon takes the designator and gives it a certain content, thus establishing how it can serve in territorial praxis.*

As with the designator, one finds in the icon two levels of communication: denotative and connotative.[42] In short, once on the page, the icon acts on the designator in two ways: I) it offers a figurative representation of its location, and thus strengthens its referentiality; II) it highlights certain aspects, whose importance is determined by a particular social context (Figure 3).[43]

For instance, on a Canadian roadmap (Figure 4), the icon used to identify Ottawa enhances the city's referentiality by locating it on the right bank of the river bearing the same name, as a major node on the road network that connects it to neighbouring towns (see figure). Ottawa's political and administrative relevance as capital city is indicated both by the font dimension and by a specific token (a star). In fact, they differ from the ones used to identify Hull, or smaller towns like Plantagenet.[44] Furthermore, the icon's self-referencing data indicates that we are dealing with an important city, a political or administrative centre that can be easily reached. Hence, the icon is the key feature in the generative process of the map, which not only develops and communicates information but also produces it. To use a geographical expression, icons are the tributaries of the communication support – i.e. the map – on which they appear. Hence, they respond both to the communicative mechanisms at work in visual representations (those analysed by the semiotics of visual communication) and to the hyper-textual mechanisms

---

[42] I am thinking here of the two levels as discussed in semiotics: U. Eco, 'Denotation/Connotation', in: T.A. Sebeok (ed), *Encyclopedic Dictionary of Semiotics*, Mouton de Gruyter, Berlin, vol. 1, 1986, pp. 181–183; G. Sonneson, 'Denotation/Connotation', in: P. Bouissac (ed), *Encyclopedia of Semiotics*, Oxford University Press, Oxford, 1998, pp. 187–189.

[43] It is worth pointing out that the use of figurative processes in the creation of such icons not only develops the information communicated by the designators, but also intensifies it. These processes are: *spatial organisation*, in which topography serves to reinforce the referential nature of the map (thus working at a denotative level); *figuration* itself, in which visual codes are used to highlight the distinctive features of the referent; and *iconisation*, which combines the results of spatial organisation and figuration and imbues the designator with social implications/values. The result is that the latter becomes symbolic and/or performative, see E. Casti, *Reality as Representation...*, pp. 70 *ff.*).

[44] To underline the city's social role the color red, elsewhere missing, is used here.

ICON ⟹ SEMIOTIC FIGURE

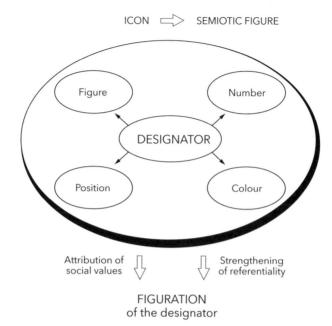

FIGURATION
of the designator

Fig. 3 Icon structure and its comunicative value.

Fig. 4 Various urban icons on a road map. Michelin road map "USA" number 761,
2004 edition. Scale 1:3,450,000. Authorization number 0411451.

whereby information is produced through self-generating processes.[45] We must therefore, at this point, take a brief look at the systems of communication at work in a map.

Systems of communication : analog and digital

In communication, the encoding of signs is either digital or analog. A third system – the iconic – is the result of the combination of the first two and can be considered as second-order (even though, as we will see later, it does give rise to operational and functional methods that are entirely specific to it and not derivative of the other two).[46]

In communication processes, the analog and digital can be used separately or together, forming poles around which a process is performed. Given that they convey the properties of an object in different ways, the same communication process might tend to favour one, and then the other.[47]

Semiotic analysis of the systems of communication used in maps also sheds light on another important aspect : contrary to popular belief, *maps are not analog models of reality, but rather systems that use both analog and digital systems in a very specific relationship to each other*. The analog system can be seen in the topography of the map (i.e. the rules establishing how the information is located on the map). The placement of objects

[45]   On the semiotics of vision, see R. Arnheim, *Art and Visual Perception*, University of California Press, Berkeley and Los Angeles, 1974. His work played a central role in research on the semiotics of vision and in promoting parallel studies in art history and art experimentation (D. Hockney, N. Stangos, *That's the Way I See It*, Chronicle Books, San Francisco, 1993). The studies of hypertextual systems inaugurated by Lotman and Greimas were followed by those from the field of art history (Panofsky, Arnheim, Gombrich), which in turn gave rise to a separate branch that is classifiable as visual communication science. The aim of this discipline is to examine communicative processes and their self-referential implications. See among others : G. Bettetini, *La simulazione visiva : inganno, finzione, poesia, computer graphics,* Bompiani, Milano, 1991 ; A. Appiano, *Comunicazione visiva. Apparenza, realtà, rappresentazione*, UTET, Torino, 1993 ; J. Fontanille, *Sémiotique du visible. Des mondes de lumière,* PUF, Paris, 1995.

[46]   The analog and digital systems can also be seen in the biological conveyance of information, which in some way may be considered as a 'primary level of communication'. However, in such biological 'communication', iconisation is totally absent, thus revealing this latter's purely cultural status (A. Wilden, 'Comunicazione', in : *Enciclopedia*, Einaudi, Turin, 1978, v. 3, 601–695 ; Id., *System and Structure*, Tavistock, New York, 1980).

[47]   F. Fileni, *Analogico e digitale. La cultura e la comunicazione*, Gangemi Ed., Rome, 1984, pp. 57–70.

and their size relative to the support itself may respond to rules of perspective and proportional reduction but are not examples of 'transformation' in the mathematical sense. In other words, no access key is needed to understand them. The map aims to show objects as they are found in the real world, understood as a continuum that is subject to certain physical laws. To do so, it uses differentiation/meaning – that one object is different from another because it is located in a specific place and has specific characteristics.[48] The digital system transmits information about a specific geographical object through various codes (colour, number, shape, etc.) to isolate certain aspects of the designator's referent. In other words, the digital system aims to create distinctions in order to express what distinguishes an object and makes it different from another.

However, the relationship between the digital and analog is clearly more than just contrastive or oppositional, even if it can be so at times.[49] For maps, the analog system is the 'context' for the operation of the digital system. Hence, an analog system cannot be seen as entirely separate from the implications of a digital system because, as we have already mentioned, the presence of both systems together can result in the emergence of a third system, the iconic system. This third system organises the information from an implicitly cultural viewpoint, as icons do not show reality as it truly is but rather as it appears in a particular theory of the world. It is through icons that what is represented becomes conceptualised and is communicated through a dynamic process that offers a particular worldview. Hence, the iconic system draws on the map's ability to transmit the cultural values of a given territory. Of course, it should be reiterated that such connotations perhaps do not belong to the territory itself, per se, but rather are the products of the map itself, as we shall see in the section on iconisation.

---

[48] On this topic, G. Bateson takes up a phrase of Korzybski's 'the map is not a territory' (A. Korzybski, *Une carte n'est pas un territoire. Prolégomènes aux systèmes non-aristotéliciens et à la sémantique générale*, L'ECLAT, Paris, 1998. Original editions 1933-1949-1950) and argues 'thus we see the map as a sort of effect which combines differences and organises information regarding differences'. See: G. Bateson, *Mind and Nature: a necessary unity*, Bantam Books, New York, 1979 (Italian edition: id., *Mente e natura*, Adelphi, Milan, 1984, p. 149).

[49] A. Turco, 'Analogique et digital en géographie', in: G. Zanetto (ed), *Les langages des représentation géographiques*, Università degli Studi, Dipartimento di Scienze Economiche, Venice, 1987, pp. 123–133.

The self-referential world of cartography

The full weight of this last statement is more obvious when one considers one of the first results of cartographic semiosis: self-reference. In this paper, I have emphasised self-referentiality as one feature of maps. Self-referentiality here means a map's ability to be accepted as such and to simultaneously communicate ideas independent of the cartographer's intent. Because of cartography's self-referentiality, names and symbols on maps do not merely replicate empirical data of a physical, natural, or anthropic nature. Rather, in accordance with their own rules, they conceal additional meanings that affect observers' very perception of the places under cognitive scrutiny. This self-referentiality results from the type of communicative systems used and the icon's role in developing denomination. Names, shapes, and colours – in short, the entire language of maps – are key in this 'self-generating' mechanism. Effectively, maps become self-referential because they prove capable of conditioning information regarding that which they depict. In other words, maps are *a system of signs endowed with life of their own; they develop independently of what preceded them and of the intent behind their original creation.*

Moreover, there is also an 'external' dimension to cartographic self-referentiality, in addition to the 'internal' one aforementioned. The interpretation of maps is likewise linked to the stratification of cartographic documents and readers' accumulated experiences over time. Such experience and stratification defines what constitutes 'a map', influences the way they are perceived, and constructs the 'memory' of those interpreting them, thereby broadening their scope of action.[50]

Indeed, the map's capacity to represent depends on its ability to regulate the complexity of the real world by applying metrics that enable us to perceive geography as cartographic space. This is how maps are able to direct multiple courses of action that are determined on the basis of this 'new reality created'. The final outcome is, as we shall see shortly, iconisation, or the ability to establish how territory should be conceived and experienced.

---

[50] Memory means that the interpreters of a document work within the codification that has already taken place. Over time, sedimentation has consolidated the various attributes of significance and meaning. Similarly, the connection between signs obeys rules of visual perception: the information conveyed is not the sum of that conveyed by each icon but rather is the result of the interaction between that information. In short, the interpretation of maps depends on recognising how maps defines themselves as such. See E. Casti, *Reality as Representation...*, pp. 140–144.

One can, in fact, reverse the claim that 'maps themselves are not territory': maps *become* territory. It is this paradox that gives maps their full self-referential capacity; they do not present themselves as territory, but as actually existing at a higher level than brute reality. For instance, let us consider the map used by Italian army officials to approach the city of Adwa during Ethiopia's colonisation. Drawn with this specific aim, this map only features that which the cartographer deemed essential for a swift approach to the city. In fact, by featuring only mountains, which were meant to be used as signposts for the approach, and neglecting survey morphology, the map propagated the misconception that plains must exist between the mountains. This self-referential information originated from the fact that the map's author used contour lines to mark mountain ranges. According to topographic convention, it was perfectly legitimate for others to infer that the absence of contour lines signified flatlands. Despite the obvious reality, army officials proceeded with the intent of reaching the supposed plains inferred by the map and launching an attack from there – despite the fact that the landscape, in fact, looked completely mountainous. The Abyssinians thus found their chance to attack and eventually managed to defeat the Italian army. Although cartographic self-referentiality in this case played into the cartographer's error, the map was nonetheless successful because it was given preference over territory.[51] To conclude, we posit that maps have the ability to turn their weak points into strong points. As models, they are unable to duplicate reality, but can, however, substitute it. The main outcome of this substitution is iconisation.

Iconisation

Iconisation is the map's pinnacle, both in terms of production and conveyance of meaning. It can be defined as *the communicative issue whereby the self-referential mechanisms of the map are used to convey conjectures as truths*.

In short, the message conveyed by a given map can replace reality. By giving meaning to the information they convey – as a veritable reflection of the characteristics of territory – maps can influence behaviours, as

---

[51] For a complete discussion of this case, see E. Casti, 'La mappa del Baratieri: la sconfitta di Adua e la vittoria dell'autoreferenza cartografica', in: *Terra d'Africa*, Unicopli, Milan, 1996, pp. 17–79.

iconisation takes the meaning created by a map and puts it in a communication circuit by exploiting its main functions: description and conceptualisation. Let us look for a moment at these two functions. As previously discussed, maps meet two basic needs for appropriating reality intellectually. First, their description aims to describe territorial features that are perceivable through direct observation. Second, they conceptualise the world, applying categories of representation (which embody an interpretation) to say how the world 'works'. It is therefore possible to identify both maps that use description as their communicative mode and maps that have a worldview that only partially adheres to established canons of real-world mimesis. Nonetheless, the important point is the relationship between this and what we have said about maps' ability to turn territory into discourse. Maps cause a shift in communication, from description to enunciation. We have shown how the set of communicative procedures used by the icon to 'show' the statement conveyed in this discourse can be traced back to maps' use of *figurative rendition*, the ultimate result of which is iconisation.[52] The latter shifts the communication from the level of description to that of conceptualisation. The message conveyed thus has a social meaning as well. Hence, regardless of whether a map intends to convey concepts or 'mere' descriptions, the very use of figuration results in the production of icons, the result being that the reliability attributed to the description is also attributed to the concept.

In other words, iconisation promotes usage of the map as a theory upon which one can rely to assess all information. It does so by activating a system wherein various pieces of information and concepts circulate endlessly, and in different forms, upon the dual plane of cartographic communication (description and conceptualisation).

This is all the more clear when the map represents a territory that has been 'removed' from the society where the map was drawn. Consider, for instance, a colonial map of Africa reflecting typical Western values that figure on the map in the form of material achievements (monuments, buildings, etc.) or in a geometrical layout (urban plan, road network, borders). Such a map fails to account for other values, namely symbolic ones that underpin African society. Consequently, insofar as they ignore the cosmological value system in which African society is rooted and organised, cartographic documents obliterate its very functioning. Iconisation has two main outcomes: I) it denies these cosmological values and

---

[52] See note 41.

thereby African territorial layout and, II) it ascribes to African territory the unfamiliar, homogenising values of the colonising culture.

Many examples of colonial cartography illustrate this point.[53] Take, for instance, the typical African village which, in the African territorial layout, relies on an internal hierarchy and a power structure dictated by the arrangement of huts. In most cases, this arrangement was neglected by colonial cartographers, who perceived it as a random, chaotic jumble, and drew maps reflecting this fact. Self-referentiality describes the African village simply as a built-up area devoid of functional order. Iconisation enforces this perception of lesser importance vis-à-vis the neatly laid-out, functional, fully-equipped colonial town. Similarly, the sacred woodland where village relations were ratified was represented as a mere feature of the natural landscape and conveyed as irrelevant by cartographic self-referentiality due to its small size. Iconisation obfuscated the woods' social importance and fed it into the circuit of colonial interests. On a final note, mountains, which Africans associated with gods, were thus excluded from any form of appropriation by the former, including naming. To Western cartographers, a mountain was simply another discovery. It was named with colonial designators and surveyed like any other territorial feature. Iconisation took over by ranking the mountain according to its elevation, in keeping with colonial appraisals. All territory was thus represented on the basis of Western criteria and managed accordingly.

Undoubtedly, iconisation can also be found in maps representing territories belonging to the society wherein they were produced. Let us consider a present-day tourist map of Death Valley, California. The valley's territorial layout is based on the road network, and on tourists and surveillance facilities, which together provide a detailed and exact representation. Self-referentiality impacts this description by extending its informational layout to the whole desert, which, despite unfavourable natural conditions, is featured as territory that has been fully appropriated both physically and intellectually.

Intellectual appropriation takes over where material, anthropic intervention ceases, and uses denomination to syntactically induce the idea of a fully anthropomorphized area. Designators scattered over the entire desert mark its complete subjection; iconisation has clearly taken over, first by using the data to convey the idea that the area is safe and then by extending

---

[53] With respect to British colonial cartography, one example can be found in C. Brambilla, 'Frontiere coloniali e identità africana: il confine orientale del Ghana e l'identità Ewe', in: *Luoghi e Identità*, Bergamo University Press, Bergamo, 2004, pp. 263–316.

its value judgement to the enterprise whereby wilderness has been turned into a social asset.

At this point, one might claim that maps are operative devices that say the world must be and function a certain way. Maps themselves are icons; in its broadest possible sense, it is a tool with which one changes the world. However, maps also embody a shift in perspectives. The fact that they are representational mechanisms capable of mimesis means they have greater communicative ability than territory alone, and thus end up replacing that territory. Maps' effectiveness as mimetic devices comes from the implicit equation map = territory – an equation that cannot possibly be defined objectively, if not as a potential tool through which coherence in the relationship between society and its territories is claimed to be attainable and is attained.

This power of mimesis, as revealed by a semiotic analysis of cartography, is what allows maps to both compromise and change the meaning of territory.

Society, cartography, and geographical sciences

The above discussion of the evolution of the theories of cartographic interpretation now brings us to one inevitable question: what skills and knowledge are needed by the person interpreting the map? This question arises from the fact that cartographic interpretation is a specialised area that, we feel, requires a certain 'expertise'. Avoiding banal description of the characteristics an interpreter should have, we will discuss only what we consider to be the most fruitful of the abovementioned approaches to cartographic interpretation: the semiotic approach. Given that the semiotic analysis of maps happens at a meta-geographical level, thus calling a second level of interpretation into play, it would seem that the starting-point is a thorough knowledge of the first level – that is, of geography itself.

Obviously, this does not mean that the interpreter must belong to one of a certain group of disciplines, i.e. geography, history, urban planning, etc., but that she must have the tools needed for cartographic analysis, namely tools resulting from knowledge of territorial theories themselves. A more radical question that emerges from the positing of territory as a complex system is whether maps are indeed capable of demonstrating that complexity. Having removed maps from the category of tools designed to register reality, can we say that maps are capable of conveying the deeper meaning of territory?

Cartographic semiosis has shown that maps not only can convey complex information, but that this information is always the product of iconisation; that it is connected with reality but cannot simply be superimposed upon it. In short, we have shown that, as a model, maps replace rather than represent territory. What is more, a study of maps reveals that the result of the communicative process they set in motion is even more radical. Ultimately, maps call into question the material significance of territory itself. Icons underline the relevance of what is created by the map itself, shifting the actual physical substance of the real world.

Here, another intriguing question – one outside the scope of the present discussion – arises: as a mechanism of mimesis, what role does the map play within the world of the Internet, which is, by definition, concerned with the creation of a non-physical world? In spite of numerous attempts to understand the role of cartography on the Web, the question appears to remain unanswered. More research and theoretical analysis is needed for an adequate reply. Perhaps, once again, the solution lies in further study of the various aspects of mimesis at work in maps.

This text was first published in: 'Towards a Theory of Interpretation: Cartographical Semiosis', in *Cartographica*, vol. 40, n° 3, 2005, pp. 1-16.

References

Almagià, R., 1923. 'Un'antica carta topografica del territorio veronese', in: *Rendiconti della Regia Accademia Nazionale dei Lincei*, XXXII, 1923, fasc. 5–6, pp. 61–84.

Almagià, R., 1929. *Monumenta Italiae Cartographica*, Istituto Geografico Militare, Florence.

Almagià, R., 1944–1955. *Monumenta Cartographica Vaticana*, Vatican City: Biblioteca Apostolica Vaticana.

Almagià, R. & Destombes, M., 1964. *Monumenta Cartographica vetustoris aevi*, Amsterdam: N. Israel.

Appiano, A., 1993. *Comunicazione visiva. Apparenza, realtà, rappresentazione*, Torino: UTET.

Armando, C. & Teixeira da Mota, A., 1960. *Portugaliae Monumenta Cartographica*, Lisbon: Imprensa Nacional-Casa da Moeda.

Arnheim, R., 1974. *Art and Visual Perception*, Berkeley, Los Angeles: University of California Press.

Austin, J.L., 1962. *How to Do Things with Words*, Oxford: Oxford University Press.

Bateson, G., 1979, *Mind and Nature: A Necessary Unity*, New York: Bantam Books.

Beleya, B., 1992. 'Images of Power: Derrida/Foucault/Harley', *Cartographica, 29* (2): 1–9.

Bettetini, B., 1991. *La simulazione visiva: inganno, finzione, poesia, computer graphics*, Milan: Bompiani.

Brambilla, C., 2004. 'Frontiere coloniali e identità africana: il confine orientale del Ghana e l'identità Ewe', in *Luoghi e Identità*, Bergamo: Bergamo University Press, pp. 263–316.

Cassirer, E., 1955. *The Philosophy of Symbolic Forms*, Yale: Yale University Press.

Casti, C., 1996. 'La mappa del Baratieri: la sconfitta di Adua e la vittoria dell'autoreferenza cartografica', in *Terra d'Africa*, Milan: Unicopli, pp. 17–79.

Casti, C., 1998. *L'ordine del mondo e la sua rappresentazione. Semiosi cartografica e autoreferenza*, Milan: Unicopli.

Casti, C., 2001. 'The Analogical and Digital systems in Euclidean Cartography: The Colonisation and Iconisation of Africa', *Diskussionsbetraege zur Kartosemiotik und zur Theorie der Kartographie* vol. 4:15–28.

Casti, C., 2001. 'Mythologies africaines dans la cartographie française au tournant du XIXe siècle', *Cahiers de Géographie du Québec*, vol. 46:429–450.

Casti, C., 'State, Cartography and Territory in the Venetian and Lombard Renaissance', in: Woodward, D. & Lewis G.M. (eds.), *The History of Cartography*, Chicago, London: The University of Chicago Press, vol. 3.

Eco, U., 1986. 'Denotation/Connotation', in T.A. Sebeok, T A (ed.), *Encyclopedic Dictionary of Semiotics*, Berlin Mouton-de Gruyter, vol. 1, pp. 181–183.

Farinelli, F., 1983. 'Alle origini della geografia politica 'borghese'', in: C. Raffestin (ed.), *Geografia politica: teorie per un progetto sociale*, Milan: Unicopli, pp. 21–38.

Farinelli, F., 1992. *I segni del mondo. Immagine cartografica e discorso geografico in età moderna*, Florence: La Nuova Italia.

Fileni, F., 1984. *Analogico e digitale. La cultura e la comunicazione*, Rome: Gangemi.

Fontanille, J, 1995. *Sémiotique du visible. Des mondes de lumière*, Paris: PUF.

Gould, P., 1995. 'Une prédisposition à la controverse', in Gould, P, Bailly A S (eds.), *Le pouvoir des cartes. Brian Harley et la cartographie*, Paris: Anthropos, pp. 53–58.

Greimas, A.J. &Courtés, J., 1993. *Sémiotique, dictionnaire raisonné de la théorie de langage*, Paris: Hachette.

Harley, J.B. & Woodward, D. (eds.), 1987. *The History of Cartography*, Chicago, London: The University of Chicago Press, vol. 1–2.

Harley, J.B., 1987. 'The Map and the Development of the History of Cartography', in Harley, J B & Woodward D (eds.), 1987, vol. 1, pp. 1–42.

Harley, J.B., 1988. 'Maps, Knowledge and Power', in Cosgrove, C, S. Daniels S (eds.), *The Iconography of Landscape. Essays on the Symbolic Representation, Design and Use of Past Environments*, Cambridge: Cambridge University Press, pp. 277–312.

Harley, J.B., 1989. 'Deconstructing the Map', *Cartographica*, 26–2: 1-20.

Harvey, M., 1999. *The island of Lost Maps: A True Story of Cartographic Crime*, New York: Broadway Books.

Hockney, D. & Stangos, N., 1993. *That's the Way I See It*, San Francisco: Chronicle Books.

Institut für Geschichte der Arabisch-Islamischen Wissenschaften, 1987. *Monumenta Cartographica Africae et Aegypti,* Frankfurt: Johann Wolfgang Goethe Universität.

Jacob, C., 1992. *L'empire des cartes. Approche théorique de la cartographie à travers l'histoire*, Paris: Albin Michel.

Kamal, Y. & Fauat, S., 1926-5. *Monumenta Cartographica Africae et Aegypti*, Cairo.

Kazutaka, U. et al., 1972. *Monumenta Cartographica Japonica*.

Korzybski, A., 1998. *Une carte n'est pas un territoire. Prolégomènes aux systèmes non-aristotéliciens et à la sémantique générale*, Paris: L'Éclat.

Marinelli, G., 1881. *Saggio di cartografia della regione veneta*, Venice: Naratobich.

Mac Eachren, A., 1995. *How Maps Work. Representation, Visualization and Design,* New York: Guilford Press.

Meurer, P.H., 1984. *Monumenta Cartographica Rhenaniae*, Stadtarchiv Mönchengladbach.

Morris, C., 1946. *Signs, Language and Behaviour*, New York: Prentice-Hall.

Schilder, G. & Stopp, K., 1986–2000. *Monumenta Cartographica Neerlandica*, Holland Alphenaan den Rijn: Uitgeverij Canaletto/Repro.

Skrivanić, G.A., 1974. *Monumenta Cartographica Jugoslaviae*, Belgrade: Istorijski Institut.

Sonneson, G., 1998. 'Denotation/Connotation', in P. Bouissac (ed.), *Encyclopedia of Semiotics*, Oxford: Oxford University Press, pp. 187–189.

Turco, 1987. 'Analogique et digital en géographie', in Zanetto, G. (ed.), *Les langages des représentations géographiques*, Venice: Università degli Studi, Dipartimento di Scienze Economiche, pp. 123–133.

Turco, A., 1988. *Verso una teoria geografica della complessità*, Milan: Unicopli.

Turco, A., 1994. 'Dire la terra: la costituzione referenziale del territorio in Costa d'Avorio', in *Terra d'Africa*, Milan: Unicopli, pp. 15–58.

Turco, A., 1994. 'Semiotica del territorio: congetture, esplorazioni, progetti', *Rivista Geografica Italiana,* 101: 365–383.

Turco, A., 1999. *Terra eburnea: il mito, il luogo, la storia in Africa,* Milan: Unicopli.

Watelet, M., 1995. *Monumenta Cartographica Walloniae*, Brussels: Racine.

Wilden, A., 1978. 'Comunicazione', in *Enciclopedia*, Turin: Einaudi, v. 3, 601–695.

Wilden, A., 1980. *System and Structure*, New York: Tavistock.

Wolodtschenko, A. (ed), 2003. *The Selected Problems of Theoretical Cartography, 2002,* Dresden: ICA.

Wood, D. & Fels, J., 1986. 'Designs on Signs: Myth and Meaning in Maps', *Cartographica* 23(3): 54–103.

Wood, D., 1992. *The Power of Maps,* New York: Guilford Press.

Woodward, D., 1996. *Map Prints in the Italian Renaissance*, London: The British Library.

Woodward, D. & Lewis, G.M. (eds.), 1998. *The History of Cartography*, Chicago, London: The University of Chicago Press, vol. 2, book 3.

Chapter 7

Doing the Right Map?
Cognitive and/or Ethical Choices

Jacques Lévy and Elsa Chavinier

A map can be seen as an issue of public debate. However, cartographers often use an implicit semiology to convey an idea or message. Is there a 'right map' that is both cognitively correct and, ipso facto, ethically just? The answer to this question is not an unequivocal 'yes'. To begin, there is not necessarily a consensus on ethical values that maps support. Secondly, cartographers limit themselves in their use of mapping tools and languages.

We will use three examples to illustrate these ideas. The first concerns the use of Euclidean base-maps, or cartograms, to represent electoral results in Switzerland. The second is a critical approach to documents produced by the French government to represent, albeit in a strange way, urbanisation processes. The third aims to show the tremendous gap between a common-sense mythology and a research-oriented approach in the historical cartography of the Jewish people.

Two Switzerlands

From 1992 onward in Switzerland, the results of federal referenda on issues related to *openness* (openness to Europe, foreigners, and otherness in sexual preferences) systematically produced the same map. What matters here are the urbanity gradients: the closer one gets to the centres of major cities, the higher the probability of a pro-openness vote. The 'popular initiative' referendum held on November 29, 2009, clearly added a new sample to the list: whether the construction of new minarets would be banned in the whole of Switzerland. The overall result was a 57.5% vote in favour of the initiative, with strong spatial disparities.

On the first Euclidean map (Figure 1), the reader gets the sense that the main contrasts are territorial – between the French-speaking Romand regions (west) and German- and/or Italian-speaking ones. This is not completely wrong: certain peri-urban municipalities in Romandie rejected the initiative, a situation that was far less common in the rest of the country. An historic 'cultural' conflict exists between French- and German-speaking Switzerland, known as '*Röstigraben*' ('rösti gap'). The temptation to detect a new expression of this supposed eternal antagonism was easily perceptible in the media.

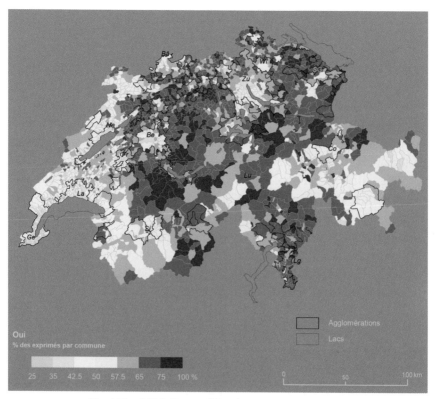

Fig. 1 The 2009 Swiss referendum on minarets: Euclidean basemap.
Map: Elsa Chavinier & Jacques Lévy/Chôros. Source: Chavinier & Lévy, 2009.

However, if we look at the second map, a population-based cartogram (Figure 2), we notice that the greatest distinction is between the country's largest city-centres (Zurich, Geneva, Basel, Bern, and Lausanne), which unanimously rejected the initiative, and other urbanity gradients (peri-urban and hypo-urban areas, centres of smaller towns). The pattern here is clearly urban network vs. rural.

This is not solely a Swiss issue. Gradients of urbanity now represent the major divide in most Western countries with regard to sexual preferences, attitudes towards ethnic/national differences, and supranational construction.

For a recent example, we can look at the 2012 elections in France (1st round, April 22) and in the United States (November 6). In the first case, we can see the manifest spatial layout for the score of the far right-populist candidate, Marine Le Pen (17.9% at the national scale). The vote was extremely strong in the outer gradients of urbanity, but the larger the urban area of

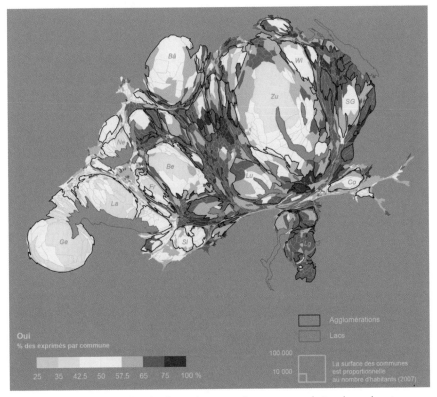

Fig. 2 The 2009 Switzerland referendum on minarets: population-based cartogram.
Map: Elsa Chavinier & Jacques Lévy/Chôros. Source: Chavinier & Lévy, 2009.

the city-centre, the weaker the vote (Figure 3). Le Pen's discourse mainly focused on the supposed threat to French identity posed by immigration, globalisation, and the European Union. In the US presidential election, the contrast between the archipelago of centres that massively supported Barack Obama and the expansive territory encompassing most of the suburban and low-density rural areas is overwhelming. In both cases, this configuration would be hardly noticeable on a Euclidean map (Figure 4).

In both countries, the classic interpretation of this kind of spatial configuration is based on a large-mesh territorial base-map: *départements* in France and states in the United States. It is often said that the Democrats

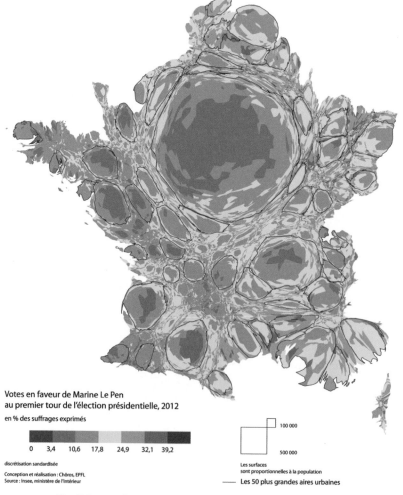

Votes en faveur de Marine Le Pen
au premier tour de l'élection présidentielle, 2012

en % des suffrages exprimés

0   3,4   10,6   17,8   24,9   32,1   39,2

discrétisation sandardisée

Conception et réalisation : Chôros, EPFL
Source : Insee, ministère de l'Intérieur

100 000

500 000

Les surfaces
sont proportionnelles à la population

—— Les 50 plus grandes aires urbaines

Fig. 3 Scores for Marine Le Pen in the 2012 French Presidential Election. Map: Elsa Chavinier, Luc Guillemot & Jacques Lévy/Chôros. Source: Lévy, 2013.

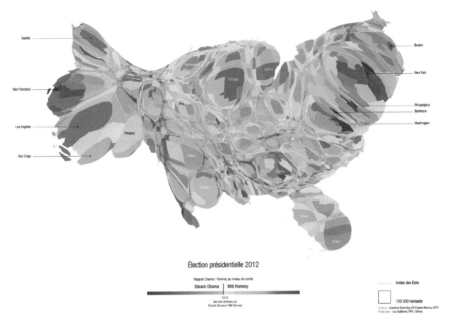

Élection présidentielle 2012

Rapport Obama / Romney au niveau du comté
Barack Obama | Mitt Romney

50 %
des voix obtenues par
Barack Obama et Mitt Romney

limites des États

100 000 habitants

Sources : Guestion Data bleg, US-Census Bureau, 2012
Réalisation : Luc Guillemot, EPFL-Chôros

Fig. 4 The US Presidential Election. Map : Luc Guillemot/Chôros.
Source : Guillemot & Lévy, 2012.

hold the 'blue states' and the Republicans, the 'red ones'. Similarly, observers of French politics say the far right scores better in the eastern part of the country. In this case, Obama won in all cities, even those in the 'red states', while Le Pen scored poorly in Strasburg, Besançon, Lyon, Grenoble, and Aix-en-Provence. However, her scores were better in the peri-urban areas surrounding these cities.

We must note, however, that exclusive use of Euclidean maps paradoxically contributes to maintaining these interpretations, since, by representing surfaces instead of people, they emphasise the inheritance of old, rural-age divisions, which, although they are increasingly less substantial, are present on almost empty surfaces.

Here, there are no lies and no liars, only distinguished colleagues who do their best to organise spatially spatial information. However, this is not an ethically neutral issue. Showing historic but gradually-vanishing contrasts or powerful emergent phenomena does not send out the same message. It could be argued that in the first case, by creating a gap between an everyday, more mythological image of the country illuminated by their maps and the actual space of the society, cartographers fail to develop awareness of their responsibilities among their fellow citizens.

The French government's war on the city

In the era of morals, the right map was defined by the geopolitical state, which fortunately controlled the official cartographic boards, who had a rigid monopoly on geographical data. The mythical layout of the national territory could be imposed, even though the reality had changed. For instance in France, as in Enver Hoxa's Albania, the official statistics' urban/ rural ratio seems to resist, even today, the landslide process of urbanisation.

When changing the standards for measuring urbanisation in 1999, the state statistical agency INSEE decided that all towns with less than 5,000 people were to be labelled 'rural'. As a result, the 10% increase in new inhabitants in peri-urban areas, i.e. urban zones that are morphologically separate from built-up areas, was compensated for with a comparable number of urbanites turned ruralites. INSEE officials could then announce that the urban/rural share was approximately a 75/25 ratio, that is to say roughly the same as the classic division that only considered morphological agglomerations and ignored peri-urban areas through a beautiful cartographic sleight of hand.

Meanwhile, the urbanisation process continued, and official French government cartographers had to be even more creative. In 2010, INSEE changed the rules. Urban areas are now divided into three sub-categories: large, medium, and small. But a strange lexical choice was made here: only large areas would be called 'urban' ('large urban areas', '*grandes aires urbaines*'), whereas the others were simply 'medium-size areas' ('moyennes aires') and 'small areas' ('petites aires').

In spite of this clear manipulation, which is now enhanced with a poetic baroque touch (viewed by the state statisticians, are medium-size and small 'areas' urban or not?), the urban nature of the French territory is more obvious everyday. But here, cartographic semiology takes the baton in the forgery. In official maps of urban areas, the greatest contrast is between 'large urban areas' and the two other types. This semiology is the same as that used during the 1999–2010 period, when the dichotomy was made between 'urban areas' and 'predominantly rural spaces' ('*espace à dominante rurale*'). Hence, now even the reference to the rural/urban divide has disappeared. The official map of 'expérienced' ('*vécus*') territories clearly expressed this dichotomy. INSEE continues to sharply contrast the different types of urban areas (Figure 5) by using chromatic discontinuities (orange/ purple/green at the same level of intensity), whereas the coherent semiological choice would have been to create a size continuum. Moreover, the

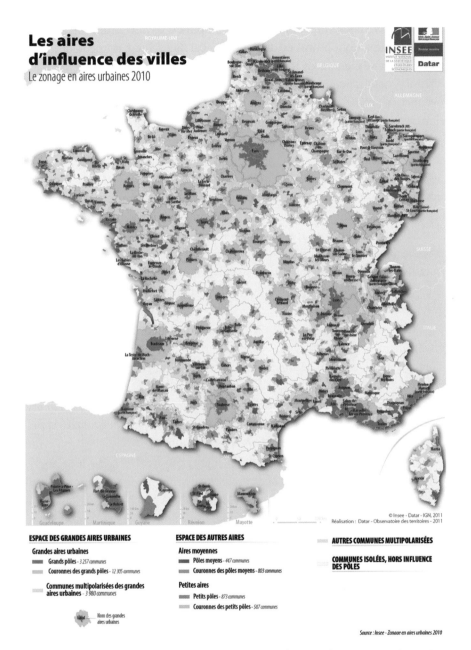

Fig. 5 Urban areas in France : the French government's version.
Source : Insee < http://www.insee.fr/fr/methodes/zonages/Fr_carteZAUER_IP2.pdf>

use of complementary colours (red for big, green for small) creates a radical contrast. The message is clear: this is not a question of gradient, but of antinomy. We chose this option for the map we drew (Figure 6). However, the cartogram option makes it unnecessary, due to our immediate visual recognition of the size of the different urban areas.

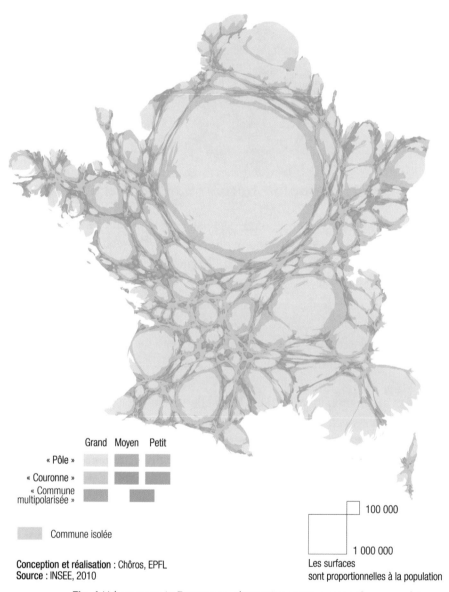

Fig. 6 Urban areas in France: an alternative version using the same data
Map: Elsa Chavinier & Luc Guillemot/Chôros. Source: Lévy, 2013.

When agrarian ideology requires it, maps can give a second life to empty territories, as if they were a human collective. There is a truth in this, and in this sense, the word 'manipulation' (used above) is not entirely accurate. The actors involved are convinced that they would be politically or even morally wrong if they placed only *actual* inhabitants on their maps. They implicitly set up a compromise between the objective state of the space they represent and their nostalgic desire for a France that is still partially rural.

State-controlled statistical institutions are among the most creative map-makers. As they have the illusion of controlling both referent and referred spaces, they do not hesitate to make fanciful cartographic representations that are supported by their eroded, yet still powerful, monopoly on data.

The 'Jewish people': between myth and history

The cartographic visualisation of 'Jewish people' is an exciting example, because the data that prove the myth to be a myth are almost universally accepted. 'Myth' is not the opposite of empirical scholarly research. Rather, it is something else.

What, then, is the 'truth regime' of the expression, the 'Jewish People'? Our approach is based on economy of thought. We are not supposed to accept an exceptionalist approach when more universal categories seem to be relevant. In the case of the Jews, mobilizing concepts of 'religion', 'community', 'state', and 'geopolitics' appears to be an effective solution, while a denomination marked by incomparability to other comparable phenomena, such as 'Jewish people' supposes a fresh construction of the entire legacy of the social sciences. This is similar to the theory of 'water memory', which, designed to justify homeopathy, requires a complete re-invention of physics.

	Mythology	**Research Propositions**
1. A Volk or a religious community?	From its origins, 'Jews' refers to, in an indivisible way, both a religious and a race-based community.	Judaism is a religion that cannot be confused in history with an ethnicity-based community. The *racialisation* of Judaism is a defensive ideology successfully promoted by one ('rabbinic') branch of Judaism in the Middle Ages and then by Zionism.
2. Judaism as a religion	The Jewish religion was founded by Abraham and deepened by Moses (18th – 13th century BC).	Jewish religion can be seen as a hybridisation between some aspects of the Babylonian religions and Hellenistic culture (6th – 1st century BC).
3. Jewish States	Jewish states have only been located in Palestine, e.g. the David-Salomon state before the destruction of the First Temple, the Judean state before the Roman conquest, and the present-day State of Israel.	Various states, some of which existed in Palestine, have chosen Judaism as an official or exclusive religion: Palestine, Yemen, Southern Volga basin area (Khazar Country), probably Ethiopia, and North Africa.
4. Diaspora or diffusion by conversion?	Jews from outside Palestine are emigrates from Palestine that were expelled after the destruction of the Second Temple, or the descendants of these emigrants; they constitute the Jewish Diaspora. The notion of Diaspora is synonymous with that of Exile.	The vast majority of Jews at the local peak of Judaism were autochthonous converts (Roman Empire) or migrants from areas outside Palestine (Khazar Empire > Yiddishland); the notion of 'Diaspora' is not suitable to characterise this population. The idea of Exile means a non-redeemable approach of existence and has no geographic significance.

	Mythology	Research Propositions
5. Who are the Palestinians?	After the destruction of the Second Temple by the Romans, the Jewish population mostly disappeared from Palestine. The local inhabitants before 19th century Jewish immigration were immigrants from elsewhere, namely the Arabian Peninsula.	As far as this notion makes sense for such a long period, modern-day Palestinians are probably the majority of descendants of the 1st century Jews of Palestine.
6. The meaning of Zionism	Zionism is a liberation movement of the Jewish people designed to reclaim a state provisionally occupied by successive invaders.	Between 1850 and 1936, the controversial debate over either an ethnic, race-based communal definition of Judaism or a voluntary, historic-cultural approach is a contemporary analogue to the debates that occurred in Germany about the definition of what a nation should be.

Table 7 Six controversial statements about the 'Jewish people'

As for the present-day, common Zionist definition of the Jewish people, it is a mix of consolidated and non-consolidated dates, of rational and non-rational logics – what the historian Shlomo Sand (2009) called 'myth-history'. In his book, Sand summarises a view gradually constructed by an important school of thought among Israeli historians since the late-1980s: the New Israeli Historians group. This group's propositions have triggered an earthquake in 'Jewish history'. The expression 'Jewish history' is written with quotation marks to differentiate between the *history of the Jews* and *Jewish history*, between the cognitive contribution to history and the construction of a state's national ideology. This opposition can be found in many corpuses of historical productions – namely in school material – in many countries throughout the world.

Following Sand's approach, we identified six controversial statements that illustrate the collision between *mythistory* and social research (Figure 7). We have drawn two different maps to get this controversy visualised. The first (Figure 8) shows a pivotal area that is supposed to represent the unchanged territory of Palestine and other locations. In this map, documented historical data are of secondary importance, as the legendary narratives constitute the core of the representational structure. The mythical land of Palestine is treated in a pervasive, hyper-realistic way. As for the rest, the available information is given much less importance, because it is seen somehow dangerous for the myth, as it might give the impression of a certain autochthony of Diaspora Jews. This information creates a *fuzzy* component because its reality does not fit the idea of Diaspora, namely that of the Falashas. Areas outside of Palestine are acceptable, albeit placed in the background, because

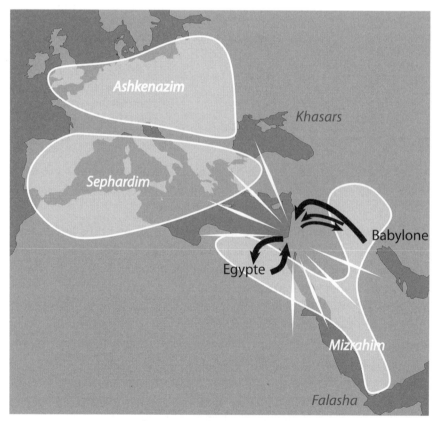

Fig. 8 Space of the myth: Chosen People, Promised Land, and Diaspora
Map: Elsa Chavinier & Jacques Lévy/Chôros. Source: Lévy, 2011.

the geographic details of so-called Exile are secondary. That is why we did not explicitly link the 'Exile' arrows to the 'Diaspora' areas.

We have included the 1920 Palestine Mandate borders because, in the Zionist imagination (as well as the contemporary one), this territory is the unchallenged reference. This illustrates the fact that mythology is structurally anachronistic. It organises a flexible combination of different temporal layers with a logical inversion: the beginning of the story is reconstructed from an idea of a desirable future.

In the second map (Figure 9), there are uncertain elements, as historians are not yet certain about some important aspects of locations and migrations. That is why we opted for a non-exhaustive legend: we show what we know and do not pretend that what we do not know does not exist, or is now as it was in the past. For example, the hypothesis of the Khazar > Yddishland migration is demographically logical but not proven.

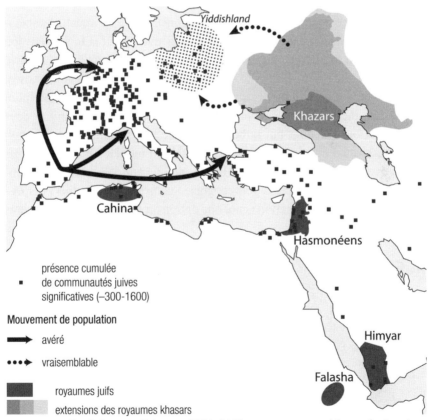

Fig. 9 Space of history, -300/+1600: states, communities and migrations
Map: Elsa Chavinier & Jacques Lévy/Chôros. Source: Lévy, 2011.

We tried to make the two maps comparable by using similar, simplified semantic tools, notably by limiting them to shades of grey. However, the comparison remains difficult, given differences in the density of data, the conception of time, 'eternal' vs. dated space, the non-spatial realities represented, ad-hoc denomination, or classic social sciences categories, etc. Despite a relatively limited vocabulary, maps reveal their limits in the cognitive integration of incompatible discourses.

That is why cartographic formalisation and visualisation of two kinds of images – the first depicting the classic myth of the 'Jewish people' and the second documented by what we more-or-less know about the actual history of the Jews – can then be useful to the public debate. It's not because maps, per se, can bring about miraculous reconciliation. Isaiah Berlin used to say that in Jewish studies, there is too much history but not enough geography. We have tried to balance our discourse by introducing space in the 'Jewish question'. In doing so, we are also incited to ask cartography new semiological questions.

These three examples invite a more reconstructive approach. As scientists, we are not supposed to *do* ideologies or myths, that is to say, our job and our social legitimacy do not consist in producing this kind of speech. Yet, we have the responsibility to explore other truth regimes than our own, and to identify their cognitive strengths and limits. This might be helpful in reconciling theoretical and empirical approaches. Our responsibility does not restrict our freedom but rather extends it. The specificity of the truth regime activated in scientific cartography should include all the others. Its distinctive feature would be its ability to include and integrate non-scientific productions as criticised yet recognised contributions. In this perspective, cartographic imagination is not one option among others – it is the law.

References

Chavinier, E. & Lévy, J., 2009. 'Minarets : malaise dans l'altérité', *EspacesTemps.net*, December 2009, <http://www.espacestemps.net/articles/minarets-malaise-dans-lrsquoalteridentite/>

Guillemot, L. & Lévy, J., 2012. 'L'espace-Obama : une victoire des réseaux sur les territoires', *EspacesTemps.net*, November 2012, <http://www.espacestemps.net/articles/lespace-obama/>

Lévy, J., 2011. *Europe : une géographie. La fabrique d'un continent*, Paris : Hachette.

Lévy, J., 2013. *Réinventer la France*, Paris : Fayard.

Sand, S., 2009. *The Invention of the Jewish People*, New York/London : Verso.

Part 3
Where Are *We* on the Map?

Chapter 8

Mapping Ethics

Jacques Lévy

We have long thought that the moral issue of cartography was how *not* to lie with maps. Monmonnier's book *How to Lie with Maps* provides not only a useful synthesis, but also summarises an overall approach to cartography. As they use an apparently realistic yet easily deceptive language, maps were naturally suspected of often reflecting a false image of the world. The split from the engineering tradition, which claimed that maps provided an accurate representation of reality due to their transparent relationship to the referred space in question and their technical precision, was complete.

Geopolitics was an obvious playground for this kind of misunderstanding. The map below (Figure 1) is technically true, but actually forged and dishonest. Moreover, it has a *perlocutory*, even performative dimension. Maps directly change the spaces they represent, as we saw with the colonial conquest of Africa: in the context of a general lack of cartographic checks and balances, drawing a map – however fanciful – staked an immediate territorial claim by the cartographer and those who worked with him.

In politics, maps can give rise to illusions about spatial justice and its opposite. Gerrymandering is often legitimated by maps, although they claim to provide an apparent spatial fairness. Paradoxically, critics of the unfairness of electoral districting use the spatial pattern of constituencies, namely their lack of compactness (Figure 2), to justify their discontent.

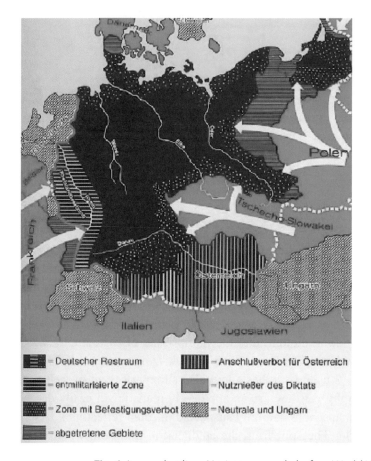

Fig. 1 A map that lies : Nazi propaganda before World War II.
Source : Werner Hilfman. *Atlas zur Deutschen geschichte*, 1986.

In cartography as elsewhere, the age of morals was characterised by a divide between supposedly universal moral law handed down from a revealed yet intangible corpus, and actual practices, which were seen as the result of an evil influence on human agency.

What does ethics offer cartography? The lazy way to answer this question would be to entertain the confusion between ethics and morals, or, worse still, between ethics and deontology. To broaden this framework, we will begin by taking the possible significance of the contemporary 'ethical turn' more seriously. We will continue with a discussion of other important events, such as the emergence of the individual actor, the increasing level of reflexivity of the society and of its constituents, and the as-yet unclear

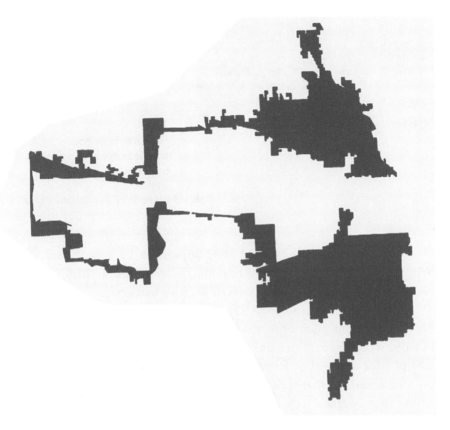

Fig. 2 A Map of geometric/geographic controversy
Source: carte d'une circonscription électorale
de Chicago. ©*New York Times/Courrier International*,
September 6–12, 2001.

perspective of a *World-society*[1]. We can define ethos – that is, the way the relationship between a society as a whole and its components is managed and arranged.

In this text, I will take for granted that ethos is part of human history like other cultural productions, such as rational discourses and practices (philosophy, science, technology, techniques), aesthetics, and other aspects of the same objective-affective box of the table: law, politics (Table 3).

---

[1] The expression 'World-society' means a full-fledged society worldwide, approached both as an historical emergence and a contemporary issue. This concept has been coined in the early 1990s. See Durand, Lévy, Retaillé, 1991 and Lévy, 2001.

	Affective	Cognitive
Subjective	Good 'Passion', intimacy, intra- and inter-personal affects, feelings, inclinations, tastes	Beautiful Art, aesthetics
Objective	Just Ethos, law, politics	True 'Reason', philosophy, sciences, technologies, techniques

Table 3 Classifying cultural productions.

In this perspective, the 'we' issue appears to be a good indicator: Where is *we* on the map? Answering this question means identifying *we*, along with having a clear awareness of the I/we tensions.

Finally, the opposition between morals and ethics has not only to do with different more-or-less honest and just means of representation, but also with the realities maps are supposed to represent. Cognitive and ethical issues are not so far away here. Ethical mapping could be based on a new realism that reflects the complexity of spaces and spatiality, as the moral stance took for granted that the issue of knowledge had nothing to do with the 'moralising' of cartography. While morals merely consisted in adding a new layer of concerns to cartographic practice, the ethical dimension, on the other hand, was much more disruptive. How much should or will an ethical turn change the concepts and productions of cartography?

What ethics changes

The first task is to define how far ethics and a potential ethical turn change the image of ethos. What can be called an 'ethical turn' is part of a larger process that encompasses the emergence of the individual as an actor, an increase in reflexivity at each level of social configuration, and globalisation.

What I will present here is a personal work based on philosophical lectures – from Baruch Spinoza to Paul Ricœur – and on an analysis of contemporary societies.

	Morals	**Ethics**
Social/Societal Relationship	Antinomy	Compatibility, convergence
Principle	Injunction	Value
Status of statements	Transcendent	Self-Organised
Creation of new statements	Dogmatic (revealed substance)	Pragmatic (constructed substance + procedure)
Epistemology	General/Particular	Singular/Universal
Relationship to truth	Concealing/Disclosing	Deconstruction/ Reconstruction
Relationship to the public	Cognitive technocracy: 'I know, you don't.'	Reflexive explicitation: 'I know, you know, we think'
Social values	Domination, equalitarianism, charity. Freedom vs. equality	Fairness, solidarity. Freedom and equality
Relationship to universalism	Universality claimed but non effective	Historically constructed universality

Table 4 Morals vs. ethics.

The ethical turn is seen here as a historical inflexion that is particularly marked in the contemporary age. This event can be defined by the emergence of ethics as a problem-solving approach, whereas morals were, and continue to be, the management of antinomies. How then can we analyse this emergence in relation to the history of cartography? At this point, we will define the scope of our discussion with two propositions that specify the scope of a potential map/ethics relationship.

1. *What ethics is not: Ethics is neither an etiquette handbook, nor a deontological behaviour guide.* Nor is it a subject that is easily addressed. It is not a set of rules but a permanent tension between certain values and their complex, questionable implementation in concrete situations.
   A good example of this is the ISO 26000 process. The new ISO 26000 (May 2010, Draft FDIS, N191) states: 'This International Standard is not a management system standard. This standard aims at offering guidance on socially responsible behaviour and possible actions; it does not contain requirements and, therefore, in contrast to ISO management system standards, is not certifiable. It is not intended or appropriate for certification purposes or regulatory or contractual use. Any offer to certify, or claims to

be certified, to ISO 26000 would be a misrepresentation of the intent and purpose and a misuse of this International Standard. As this International Standard does not contain requirements, any such certification would not be a demonstration of conformity with this International Standard'. ('ISO 26000', *Wikipedia*, <http://en.wikipedia.org/wiki/ISO_26000>). This statement also declares that ISO 26000 cannot be used as basis for audits, conformity tests, certificates, or compliance statements. As a guidance document, the ISO 26000 is a proposal and is to be used on a voluntary basis. It encourages organisations to discuss social responsibility issues and possible actions with relevant stakeholders. I suggest we approach the relationship between ethics and cartography using the same attitude.

2. *What a map is not: tracing paper.* Maps are not mere reproductions of a clearly identified 'real'. Maps are openly objected. Following Deleuze and Guattari (*A Thousand plateaus,* 2004 [1980]), as tracings ('*calques*') are based on similarities, maps are based on differences; tracings are based on closed-ness, and maps on openness. The analogy between a map and its referent allows for quick, multiple, two-way cognitive movements. Maps are translation devices. They are unique languages that have the capacity to convey novel messages. They are potentially stable, though multi-actor, constructions, though their stability is provisional – as a rational agreement. Hence, it is always possible to modify a map.

Conspiracies are constructions, albeit hidden ones, while maps are always visible. We can therefore argue that it is impossible to lie with maps, except to the people who cannot speak its language. We cannot blame maps per se, but rather the lack of a sufficient cartographic culture.

We should therefore not overlook the epistemological dimension of the ethical turn: mimetic reflection, like Alfred Hitchcock's 'Lady', vanishes on the train of history. Maps are not a question-free answer. As morals focused on the true/false and overt/covert dichotomies, ethics renders explicit. What can be hidden (and should not) is the question to which 'the map' is the answer. Being more explicit about the rules of mapmaking is the only requirement. There are no false maps, because all maps that respect an identified set of translation rules between referent and referred spaces are true.

At this point emerges the idea of truths regimes derived from Foucault, and our responsibility as scholars to identify, organise, and hierarchize different kinds of truth and their combinations. Here lies the cognitive contract we have implicitly signed with society as a whole.

The problem is determining in what way, and to what extent, they are true (see the case of the two Switzerlands in Chapter 7).

The ethical turn and cartography: cognitive significance

Let us now try to find a link between the ethical turn and cartography. My point here is that, in this connection, there is a strong cognitive component that, in part, weakens the well-recognised aspect of 'scientists' behaviour' toward the other social actors. I, of course, do not deny the latter, but would like to underline the crucial role of what happens inside the cartographer's workshop.

	Morals	Ethics
Social/ Societal Relationship	Antinomy 'True' maps/Mental maps	Compatibility, convergence Agency maps / Environmental maps
Principle	Injunction Absolutes rules	Values Justified choices
Status of statements	Transcendent Euclidean geometry (projection, metrics)	Self-Organised An open list of formalised metrics
Creation of new statements	Dogmatic (revealed substance) Euclidean maps	Pragmatic (constructed substance + procedure) Mapping
Epistemology	General/Particular Laws of space (base-map), particular places (theme)	Singular/Universal Dialogics base-map/theme
Relation to truth	Concealing/Disclosing Manipulation/Exposure	Deconstruction/Reconstruction Co-spatiality
Relation to the public	Cognitive technocracy 'I know, you don't.' Cognitive divide in cartography	Reflexive explicitation 'I know, you know, we think' Connected capabilities
Relation to universalism	Universality claimed but non effective Ahistorical metrics and configurations	Historically constructed universality Evolutionary cognitive tools for humanity

Fig. 5 What ethics does to maps.

Figure 5 seeks links between debates on ethos and cartography. It directs our reflection to two major points.

1. *A basemap is pivotal.* We cannot continue to pretend that a basemap is determined by absolute criteria, independent of the theme of the map. If we use the implicit metaphysics of a 'revealed' basemap, this means that we impose on readers a set of non-discussed, unjustified data.

2. *The issue of co-spatiality cannot be ignored.* Space is a reality that is always multi-dimensional. In this baklava-like construction, some social layers are easily separable, and others are interdependent in a 'sticky' mode. The link and the type of link between these layers cannot be postulated. They are optional. This means that any time we present a space as a single-layer map, we must say why. Conversely, if we conclude that co-spatiality does not exist between layers, we must also explain why.

The problem with classic maps is that they create a discrepancy with the emergent spatial realities they claim to visualize. Let us now consider three that pose serious problems to 'ethical cartography'.

D1. Choropleth Map ≠ Individual Spatialities

Common maps are mostly choropleth. They show bordered territories ('countries') arranged like pieces of a jigsaw puzzle. However, individual spatialities are based on multiple, intermingled networks whose nodes and links are often not compatible with country maps. This problem is all the more serious, given that mobility – and movement in general – is not valued in classic maps. Nowadays, individuals are mobile realities and individual spatialities are largely made of their mobilities. Maps have trouble representing flows coming from or going to fixed spaces, and they rarely use movement as a basic, founding space-making process. Yet, often, they should.

D2. Euclidean Metrics ≠ Generalised Urbanity

Most maps are isotropic. They show continuous and roughly similar spaces. However, the urbanisation process has generated anisotropic space, in which cities are the heavyweights. People live, and things happen here. Nevertheless, because of their limited surface areas (which is the very definition of urbanity [density + diversity]), cities appear as tiny dots buried in an empty but ubiquitous countryside.

D3. Projected Globe ≠ Human Globalisation

Finally, a map is not a globe, firstly because the principle of projection distorts the sphere to make it fit into a plan. Secondly, this is so because globalisation creates archipelagos that emphasize reticular proximities and ignore the vast salt desert of oceans.

If the ethics of knowledge have any link to the truth, and if the specific purpose of scientists is to explore a truth regime in which the tension between the empirical and theoretical dimensions is explicit, then cartographers indisputably cannot be indifferent to the cognitive effect of mapping tools.

From agency to environment, and vice versa

The history of cartography (Peutinger, Nakasendo, Wubei Zhi, and Meso-American codex maps) can be read as an evolution from agency to environment, from spatiality to space. However we can easily detect a reverse evolution. The convergence of, on the one hand, the emergence of the individual actor and, on the other hand, the birth of digital technologies makes new cartographic objects possible and necessary. These objects take individual spatialities as a relevant theme for maps.

Fig. 6 Subjective and cognitive.
Source: Daniel Belasco Rogers, The Drawing of my Life 2003-2009 London, Berlin, <http://www.planbperformance.net/index.php?id=danmapping>.

What has changed is that switching from spatiality to space is much more fluid than it used to be in societies where individuals were of little import compared to overhanging 'structures'. Spaces have effectively become environments. They encompass many other realities, but these *encompassed* spaces can alter and transform the *encompassing*. Individuals should not be seen as tiny cells submitted to overwhelming constraints, but also as active, pervasive 'foams' (a term coined by Peter Sloterdijk, 2004) whose patterns construct, deconstruct, and reconstruct society as a whole. Figure 7 shows a simple superposition of individual spatialities of people with primary residences in the same urban area (Paris). This superposition, we must admit, produces a 'wild' map of this urban space.

Where is the borderline between mapping individual/collective spatialities and mapping social spaces? If we define *inhabiting* as the spatial-ethical issue, where the compatibility between space and spatiality is in question, to what extent can this issue also be seen as a cartographic problem?

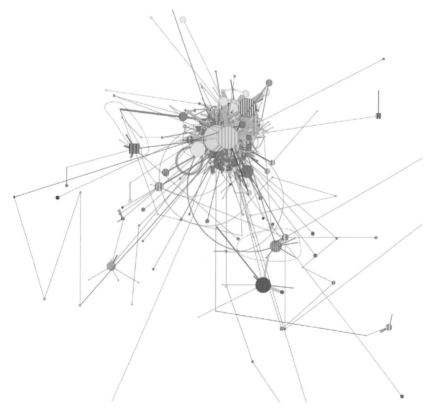

Fig. 7 Spatialities make space.
Source: Lévy, Jacques (ed.), 2008. *Échelles de l'habiter*, Paris: Puca.

An anti-ethical cartography can underestimate and undervalue the importance of non-state actors, as we have observed in the long history of official statistical cartography (see in Chapter 7, 'The French State's War on the City'). The autonomy of civil society is challenged by an official cartographic truth.

Conversely, the denial of society as a whole also creates observable cartographic discourses. Thus, gender and ethnic maps can be interpreted as an emerging awareness of the spatial dimension of gender inequality. For some authors, however, they also can be seen as a substantialized, de-historicised partition of space. Space is not public; rather, it is a partition of hostile territories on which geopolitical entities must impose strength relations before negotiating provisional truces with each other. Mapping public space, in this case, is quite different from mapping the multiple layers of communal rationales separately.

The empowerment of individuals formerly discriminated against strengthens both individuals and society, which makes this empowerment possible. In contrast, the reinforcement of communal groups as such may result in denial of the very existence of the society, and it could portray inter-group relations as a zero-sum geopolitical game. Ideologies of anti-historical culturalism combined with conspiratorial, neo-structuralist approaches attempted to impose this way of thinking in North America in the 1990s. The communalist truth regime was put forth as the only one possible. This has heavy consequences on the representation of the social world as a whole: space's multi-layered nature is challenged, and spaces are reduced to a flat expanse of territory where borders are the only issue.

After the ethical turn, no collective body is the owner of values. There is no moral privilege for the poor, as in the traditional religious habitus. Everyone is equal and expected to co-manage the undivisible freedom/responsibility duo. An actor is always part of the societal system. His/her subjective geographies and those of his/her identity groups matter, but no one can pretend to be outside an all-encompassing social environment. A social space is not the algebraic sum of the individual or communal claims. It is something else. However, Ed Soja (2010) does not seems to accept this when he defines spatial justice as the right of any 'first-occupant' group to conserve its territory, even if societal rationale is at odds, for instance if an urban project aims at giving a better social mix or more functional diversity to a neighbourhood.

In both cases (denial of civil society, denial of sociality), anti-ethical maps are strongly linked to the denegation of the existence of an autonomous society of individuals, by imposing the dictatorship of non-chosen communities – the nation being one of them.

Cartographers as actors among other actors

Finally, we can address the issue of the social/societal relationship in another way: through participatory processes. Here, the world of actors is 'densified' by the presence of cartographers themselves.

Ethical maps make sense in a process of knowledge democratisation, but, as we know, accumulated knowledge is not easily accessible to illiterate people. How can we imagine participatory cartography? We know that urban projects have little chance of success without the effective involvement of ordinary citizens. In other words, the project must be at least partially co-produced by politicians, practitioners, *and* inhabitants. The term 'urbanism' tends to replace 'urban planning' because city-making is no longer a 'planned' activity; rather, it is a multi-actor mix of discourse and action. This *dialogics* is impossible without maps, which serve as a legal authority as well as a basis for discussion at the different stages of the process. However, generations of cartographers have expressed their conviction that mapping was such a complicated and esoteric skill that it would be technically impossible and socially dangerous to reveal the 'company secrets' to the non-initiated. Urbanism reveals that cartographers are merely actors among others, who, though they may deploy other skills and rationales than theirs, fundamentally belong to the same category: individuals in a social environment, endowed with strategic capabilities.

Today we can see that ordinary citizens are not only able to decipher and challenge maps of power, but also to use their imperfect knowledge for the purposes of critique. Thus, the 3D GIS of municipalities or other territorial authorities can be easily used in political controversies or judicial cases because of their figurative dimension and the hyper-realistic image of urban materiality they propose. This weapon can also be utilised by these GIS professionals as strong support for supporters of the status quo. This 'it-was-better-before' party (a close cousin of the NIMBY movement) can then be diagnosed as a by-product of cartographic skills that have not been completely assimilated by those who are victims of this 'reality effect'.

Fig. 8 Any there is a here, too.
Source: Dessin de Chapatte. ©*Le Temps/Courrier International*,
March 7-13, 2002.

In short, the problem is not only avoiding the exclusion of otherness, but also promoting its integration into something larger. The ethical turn implies a clear switch from communality to sociality, and from geopolitics to politics, which means the emergence of an 'us' without 'them'. Living in a world where everybody is human and no one is an enemy complicates the definition of this *we*. However, by and large, we now have the task of showing the state of the union – that is, the complex ways in which social realities make or do not make society together – on our cognitive dashboard. Thus, we should not ignore that a social space is not a collection of spatialities, but a public good that must be co-constructed by all actors.

Norbert Elias has rightly associated his concept of a society of individuals with a new relationship between *I* and *we*. This *we* is not a community (*Gemeinschaft*). In the society of individuals described by Elias, groups are a collection of *I*'s. The *we* is societal, and the question is: in what conditions can a map become something more than an individual contribution, in other words, a legitimate environment? The (possible) consensus on a political map as a set of territorial jurisdictions or constituencies is an example of the emergence of a more complex *we*. The ethical *we* is not a

collection of *I*'s, but more a combination of different constructions of the I/
we relationship, with strong spatial significance at each level and in cross-
level nesting combinations.

As we can see, science's contribution to ethics often consists in playing the bad guy by proposing changes in the spontaneous arrangement of
truth regimes. However, the cognitive strength of a map can help citizen-
map-readers and map-makers to reconsider spaces in all their complexity,
and to make this complexity compatible with their mobile and moving
identities (Figure 8).

Inhabiting maps

Maps are not about space. They *are* spaces. How could these spaces be
affected by the ethical turn? Space, at once, belongs to everyone and no
one. And this is true for the spaces of the map as well. What matters is not
only where *I* am on the map but also how *we* – the subject pronoun of a
society that redefines its values and goals at every major turning point –
will create its new space. During European explorations, maps made travel
possible because they showed an often-fictive but pre-existing space. As
an extra space, maps can be environments at the project stage as well as at
the agency stage. In short, combining cartography and ethics is not about
telling us how we should love our neighbour through cartography: it just
aims to make maps contemporary.

Another goal is to reconcile, within a clearly cognitive approach, subjective and objective contributions. To do this, we must be fully aware of
the muddled, though dramatic, weakening of various *us/them* communal
oppositions (including at the national level), as global issues increasingly
invite themselves to the map table.

This involves less disclosure and more reconstruction, which, in cartography, means more co-spatiality. The issue is not so much how not to
lie, but how, within a specific project, to select the most efficient truth
regime. Mapping the un/inhabitable, making maps inhabitable, and making the world less uninhabitable can then be seen as a single cartographic/
ethical operation.

Where are *we* on the map? Of course the content quality of the map
depends upon the nature of the *we*. If it is an ethical one, the answer could
be the following: it is precisely *where* it is possible to say 'I have been
there', or 'I wish I were there', and 'We are here together' at the same time.

Fig. 9 'Actually, the World looks like this'.
Source: Photo Luc Guillemot, 2010.

References

Deleuze, G. & Guattari, F., 2004 (1980). *A Thousand Plateaus*, London: Continuum.

Durand, M.-F, Lévy, J. & Retaillé, D., 1991. *Le Monde: espaces et systèmes*, Paris: Presses de Sciences Po.

Lévy, J. (ed.), 2001. *From Geopolitics to Global Politics: A French Connection*, London: Frank Cass.

Sloterdijk, P., 2004. *Sphären, III Schäume*, Berlin: Suhrkamp.

Soja, E., 2010. *Seeking Spatial Justice*, Minneapolis: University of Minnesota Press.

Chapter 9

A Reappraisal of the Ecological Fallacy

Hervé Le Bras

Let us begin with an example of an ecological fallacy in the 2012 French presidential contest. The regions where Francois Hollande, the candidate for the left, won were largely situated in western and southwest France, regions mainly populated by the elderly and the retired, and less so by working people. Effectively, the former voted in large majority left and the latter right. To solve this archetypical case of ecological fallacy, we must turn to other phenomena, often referred to as *third variable effects*. However, in this case, the third variable was to be found in an anthropological layer, rather than a demographic or economic one. Anthropology connects us to ethics, in the oldest sense of the word. This geographic layer is characterised by a rural-urban difference between left and right, as is the case in many advanced countries.

The 2012 French presidential election

Map 1 shows the percentage of votes for Hollande at the local level (36,570 units). Even unsmoothed, the meaning of the map is clear, with large continuous areas of red and brown (votes for Hollande more frequent than at the national level) and blue and dark blue (votes for Sarkozy more frequent than at the national level). The smoothed map (Map 2) conserves the global aspect of the map but emphasises the role of large cities versus rural areas. Before discussing these maps, we wish to consider a third one, which reflects the first vote (the presidential election process involves two separate votes, two weeks apart. The first ballot is open to multiple candidates; the second only to the two who received the most votes in the first round). We compared the ballots for Sarkozy and Hollande, ignoring the ballots for the other candidates (in other words, 45 % of all the ballots). Map 3 shows the percent of ballots in favour of Hollande out of the total number of votes for Hollande or Sarkozy in the first round. As one can see, the smoothed map is identical to the smoothed map (Map 2) of the final result of the second vote (at the *département* level, the correlation is 0.983). It seems as though the result of the second vote was strictly encapsuled in the result of the first one. In other words, the 45 % of people who voted for neither Sarkozy nor Hollande in the first round voted – fifteen days later, in the second round – in exactly the same proportion as those who voted for Sarkozy or Hollande in the first round. This means that the left/right border is very stable; the first round is a good, unbiased sample for the second. It also means that other strong factors underlie these results, either demographic (age structure) or economic (occupational structure). Let us observe the spatial distribution of these factors.

The young, the old, the clerks, the workers

If the results were based solely on socio-economic determinants, then knowing the proportion of the social classes in each ward (*commune* in French) and the proportion of Hollande supporters in each social class would make mapping the results according to this hypothesis easy. The proportion of social classes at the local level is provided by the last census and sample surveys made on the election day. They give the proportion of voters for Hollande in each social class. For example, IFOP gave the following proportions :

Social category	% votes for Hollande
Craftsmen, shopkeepers	30%
Executive, professional	52%
Technicians, associate professionals	61%
Clerks	57%
Workers	58%
Pensioners	43%

The map corresponding to this socio-economic hypothesis is provided in Figure 4. It is nearly opposite that showing the votes in favour of Hollande. A completely different result could have been expected. According to social class preferences, Hollande should have won the smallest percentage of votes in the north and east – quite the opposite of the real result.

Is age responsible for this anomaly? We can perform the same calculation with age as with social class. We are aware of the age-pyramid at the local level, and the sample surveys on election day asking the people their age allow us to determine the percentage that voted for Hollande for each age group. The IFOP proportions are as follows:

Age	% votes for Hollande
18–24 years	59%
25–34 years	55%
35–49 years	49%
50–59 years	60%
over 60 years	46%

If age were the sole determinant of the vote, then these data would allow us to know the results of the election. The map in Figure 5 reflects these data. As for socio-economic structure, the result is the exact opposite of the actual results. The best results for Hollande should have been in the north and east of France, where the young are proportionally more numerous than the old. However, the opposite, in fact, occurred. One may argue that age and socio-economic status are interdependent. Yet, they are actually very close, as one can see in Maps 4 and 5 (correlation at the departement level is 0.962). Any linear combination of these two factors will result in same pattern, and always in diametrical opposition to the actual result.

Urban vs. rural areas

A more thorough exploration of the maps reveals a major gap between large urban areas and the rest of France. Except for certain cities in the northeast, Hollande performs always better in urban areas than in rural ones. Does this explain the discrepancy between the distribution of age and socio-economic status, on one hand, and votes for Hollande, on the other? This question can be answered by analysing the crossed results by area and city size. We considered 9 groups of cities according to their population, from less than 1,000 voters to more than 2,000,000 (Paris). We took two groups of departements, the 21 where Hollande received more than 57% of the vote, and the 30 in which he did not obtain the majority. The percentages of votes for Hollande are shown in Table 1.

Number of voters	Hollande *dépts.*	Sarkozy *dépts.*	All *dépts.*
less than 1000	58.3	43.7	49.5
1000–2500	58.0	41.8	48.7
2500–5000	58.0	43.0	49.5
5000–10,000	57.9	44.1	51.2
10,000–25,000	57.9	46.4	52.3
25,000–50,000	58.1	46.1	54.2
50,000–100,000	60.4	47.3	55.2
100,000–1,000,000	61.9	51.5	55.9
Paris			55.6

Table 1 % votes for Hollande according to city size and overall results of the *départements*.

The differences according to city size were not surprising: the more populated the city, the greater the number of votes for Hollande. However, this pattern, if not identical, was similar for each group of *départements*.

Thus, it does not explain why the distribution of votes was the opposite of that which one would expect given the ages and social statuses of voters. The distribution of votes by city size, obtainable if we assume the hypothesis of an effect of the sole age or the sole social status, confirms that view. Table 2 shows the effect of age:

Number of voters	Hollande *dépts.*	Sarkozy *dépts.*	All *dépts.*
less than 1000	49.8	51.3	50.8
1000–2500	50.7	51.5	51.2
2500–5000	50.9	51.4	51.3
5000–10,000	51.1	51.6	51.5
10,000–25,000	51.2	51.6	51.5
25,000–50,000	51.3	51.9	52.2
50,000–100,000	51.8	51.5	52.3
100,000–1,000,000	51.8	51.5	52.3
Paris			52.0

Table 2 % of votes forHolland according to city size and the overall results of the *départements*, in the case where only the socio-economic status explains the results.

The percentages of votes for Hollande were higher in *départements* that were hostile to him, and lower in those friendly to him, with the exception of large cities. These percentages grow with the size of the city, but at a very slow rate. On the whole, one notes that the percentages in the Table 2 are much closer to the national average than those in Table 1. This fact is important. While the differences between the 'young' and 'old' votes and between the age structures in the two selected groups of departements are notable, the combination of these two orders of differences generates a minimal impact. Let us take a simple example: suppose the southeast is comprised of 40% younger people and 60% older people, and the northeast of 60% younger people and 40% olderer people. This difference can be expressed another way: there are 1.5 older people for each young person in the southwest, and 0.66 older people for each young person in the northeast – less than half. Suppose that 60% of young people and 40% of older people vote for Hollande. In the southwest, the overall result would be:

$$60\% \times 40\% + 40\% \times 60\% = 48\% \text{ for Hollande}$$

and in the North-East:

$$60\% \times 60\% + 40\% \times 40\% = 52\% \text{ for Hollande}$$

The results are quite close with regard to differences in age structure and political orientation. Moreover, these numbers closely reflect the reality: a major difference in age structures and in the propensity to vote results in a small gap between the two regions.

That conclusion is one of great consequence: Because the difference in voting behaviours between the two regions considered here is rather significant, as reflected in Table 1, there is another cause, that is neither socio-economic nor demographic. But what is it?

Anthropological and historical differences

Historians are well aware of two major differences in customs in French regions. One was documented by Marc Bloch in a beautiful book on the origin of rural history in France: the comparison between '*assolement tri-ennal*' (three-year crop cycle) and the open field, and between '*assolement biennal*' and '*bocage*' (enclosure). The first is characterized by clusters of populations in small villages and the second by a sparse population. The border between the two landscapes and the two societies runs from Normandy to Burgundy, then south, along the Saone and Rhone Rivers, and finally expands along the Mediterranean coast. In previous works, we have shown the propensity to vote National Front (the northeast and the Méditerranean coast) in these areas. The second key difference in traditionnal customs concerns household structure. In the southwest, the 'stem' family and unequal inheritance dominated for over a century. In much of the northeast (except for Alsace) and along the Mediterranean coast, the nuclear family and egalitarian inheritance were the rule, schematically speaking.

Even now, the vestiges of these differences remain, both in statistics and in the population's spatial distribution. Map 6, for example, shows the percentage of people aged 80 and over living in extended or multiple households ('complex' families) in 2009. Though the percentage is relatively small, the difference between the southwest and northeast is remarkable. The geographies of the socialist vote and complex household structures coincide almost perfectly. Even western Brittany goes with both complex household structure and the socialist dominant vote areas.

As is often said and written, comparison does not make for reason. As a factor linking family structure and leftist voting tendencies, we put forth the common interest in solidarity between family members as between members of state, or, to quote Jean Jaurès, the *'communisme rudimentaire'* shared by the ideology of the complex family and of the welfare state. Reinforcing this view is the fact that, paradoxically, inegalitarian inheritance has favored a society of more or less egalitarian smallholders. Conversely, egalitarian inheritance has led to great differences in terms of property and an unequal number of inheritors, generation after generation, building a society of peasants deprived of land and of owners endowed with large tracts of land.

Family and inheritance rules

When inheritance law was more or less promulgated in 1806 (the *code civil*), the equal rights of inheritors was recognised, independent of wills. From then on, the fertility rate in Southwest France steadily fell, with small landholders fearing the division of their property. As anthropologist Georges Augustins stated: in the north, one inherits a name; in the south, a home. A name can be shared by many children, but a home can only belong to one. In some departements along the Garonne river, from as early as 1860, the net reproduction rate fell to under one. At that time, the Catholic *départements* south of Loire maintained a high fertility rate. With the decline of the Catholic influence following World War II, these departements joined those secularized long before. Nowadays, as Map 7 shows, the entire southwest region has the lowest fertility rate. Low fertility rates and low long-distance immigration and emigration means an aging population. Effectively, the population of this region is the oldest, as Map 8 (voters over 18 years of age) shows. Finally, we can understand the ecological fallacy: the aging population of the southwest and the socialist vote are not directly related. Both are, in fact, the consequence of a third variable: the anthropology of the household and the family. They developped independently.

If we accept this explanation, what about socio-economic differences? In what way are they related to household structure? The geographic history of industry in France provides some clues. Due to the low fertility, little manpower could be mobilized at the dawn of the industrial era. Similarly, small landholders were reluctant to leave the land. Instead, in the northeast, servants and labourers were lured by high industry wages, compared to agricultural salaries. Large factories and mines developped in the north and east. Conversely, those children who abandoned the land in the southwest entered small businesses or became craftsmen in small shops. The most talented specialised in law, becoming lawyers or entering the public service. Northeastern France became a place of industry and hired manpower, as can be seen in Map 9. The southwest remained mainly in the hands of small businesses and administrations. As such, the contradiction between the socio-economic structure and the socialist vote can be explained in the same way as the contradiction between age structure and the socialist vote: early on, there were major differences in family structure, life cycle and, consequently, property ownership.

Dormant behaviours

In France today, two institutions are in decline: the welfare state, which is less and less able to obtain funds, and the Catholic church, which has been deserted by the younger generations. (According to a recent survey, only 1 % of the 18–24 age group surveyed regularly attended mass.) State protection and church protection are dwindling. With high unemployment rates, many people seek help from their families, neighbours (if they have roots in a place), and community, in every sense of the word (ethnic group, religious sect, etc.). In this respect, old customs and behaviours are re-emerging. They were not eradicated by modernity, but were only dormant. This re-emergence attests to the strength and antiquity of social organisation and, as such, can be called ethics.

Chapter 10

Mapping Otherness

Emanuela Casti

Participatory mapping has been used widely in Western Africa to promote social equity in territorial planning. However, it has become clear that, whenever the use of tools for territorial governance is at stake, the competencies of the actors involved are asymmetrical and unequal. Such an imbalance is not so much the result of technical inadequacy, but rather is inherent to the cultural diversity of the space in question, i.e. in the different representations the actors involved have in mind. One should not forget that spatiality, i.e. how given society relates to space, is largely based on specific cultural assumptions. Moreover, participatory systems are part of a communicative process that involves actors from different cultural contexts who therefore inevitably have different positions and interests with regard to territory and the environment.

The present chapter discusses the possibility of producing equitable participatory maps aimed at settling disputes. To accomplish this, these maps must account for the different spatial representations developed by each culture. This issue is highly relevant because participatory mapping plays a crucial political role. More specifically, I) participatory maps provide an arena wherein ideas are shaped and compared, and thus have strong social impact for both local inhabitants and external actors operating in the territory; and

II) cartographic information circulates between or within societies, which have embraced *diversity* (be it in terms of identity, culture, or ideology) as a value, and have adopted *governance* as a democratic option in territorial government. Governance implies not only the exercise of the law, but also the acceptance of 'bottom-up legitimacy' devised by local populations.

Cartography and social equity

The discussion will not be limited to participatory mapping. Awareness to the broader issues encountered in map building will also be essential. One obviously needs to pore over the territorial data provided in a given map. However, assessing its assumptions in terms of metrics and graphics (looking at the different roles of the actors involved and considering the self-referential nature of the map) will be equally crucial. In short, the entire cartographic semiotic process must be considered. In the present case, we must ask whether the use of topographic metrics is, in fact, apt to represent the territory of the Other, or whether other metrics must be used.

After all, topographic metrics is allegedly only one of many, but not necessarily the best. Topographic metrics, in fact, have often depleted the social meaning of territory both in the West and, to an even higher degree, in the colonies. It has also been proven that they are a powerful social *operator*, able to *iconise* the world by advancing their own materialistic interpretation of it, which eventually prevails upon territorial practices (Casti, 2000, 2005a).

Before turning to the issue of topographic metrics – which I deem unfit to express social equity in cartography – I will consider cultural views about nature in various societies, which give rise to different ways of representing space. To conclude, I will propose a number of experimental maps that express the multiple perspectives established in situations of social inequality resulting from an environmental planning project in Burkina Faso.

Spatial concepts and the nature/culture debate

Cartography was long based on the assumption that, to understand space used by individuals, it was necessary and sufficient to focus on a set of material features related to topographic metrics. Nowadays, on the other hand, we debate about how maps should reflect the cultural values specific communities have developed as they shaped their world. Practically speaking, this means devising a new type of cartographic metrics that can render a community's territoriality by taking into account the values expressed in *landscape*.[1] Employing the notion of *landscape* in cartography means highlighting the cultural essence of *territory*, thereby dispelling the erroneous illusion that topographic and social spaces are one and the same.[2] Adopting these new metrics entails an open declaration of intent: our goal is less to make landscape a universally-acknowledged absolute value than to appraise the many concepts of landscape. Our underlying assumption is that the idea of *landscape* is derived from the idea of *nature* and the relationship a given society has with it.

Augustin Berque has convincingly shown that the meaning of landscape in different societies and the values that go with them, in fact, come from a primal cultural choice made regarding nature. He has pointed out how this choice has given rise to two diametrically opposed approaches: one whereby man and nature are symbiotically conceived of as part of a cosmic sphere (*cosmogonisation*) or, alternatively, one in which such a symbiotic relationship has been severed. This rupture, which has occurred in a number of cultures including Western culture, is called *decosmogonisation*, and consists in having more or less neatly separated *land* and *cosmos* (Berque, 2008). The presence or the absence of such disjunction gave rise to different social values ascribed to nature and a different meaning of *landscape*. Berque claims that Western modernity is characterised by the loss of a unitary, axiological order in the human/universe relationship. Such loss inevitably mars our relationship with places, which are now seen as a mere base for the development of human activities. All of this is based on the fact that the meaning of the word *cosmos* has changed over time, becoming synonymous with *universe*. The original Greek sense of *kosmos* and Latin sense of *mundus*, both now lost, evoked the notion of a full-scale order where human beings occupied a crucial place. Participatory policies such as those promoted today presumably have been developed to remedy the imbalance Berque describes. Landscape is now seen as an arena where subjects meet to measure and to record knowledge acquired through their contact with nature. In time, this knowledge comes to convey the values expressed in the landscape.

[1]   We are thinking mainly here of the meaning ascribed to landscape in the field of geography, namely the one discussed by: J. Lévy, M. Lussault, 2003.

[2]   The notion of landscape is the one better suited to provide a visual representation of territory in cartography. Like a map, landscape is a form of representation that conveys an idea of territory as perceived and elaborated by an interpreter.

Hence, we must consider the landscape of Otherness not only by taking stock of its cultural features, but also by looking at the ever-changing configuration of spatial-temporal relationships between societies. Only then can the original relationship with the *kosmos* possibly be restored, after being lost by most civilisations, often at the hands of Westerners and their colonial endeavours.

Legal levels of governance

Colonialism de facto created an imbalance that previously did not exist in these conquered areas. The idea of legality based on the state was pitted against the notion of legitimacy based on territory. The latter – the product of a set of pre-colonial policies – is implemented through the criteria of *praxis* and *topos*, i.e. by regulating the 'doing' that occurs in a 'place' based on traditional rules. These rules are the result of a cosmic view of the world, which considers nature *not* as a product of creation, but as the very deity to which humans relate for their survival. Territorial configuration, social hierarchy, and the hypostatisation of power all result from this view, which validates the legitimate claim of local inhabitants to use the place they live as their own territory. This view attests to the positive relationship communities must have had with the gods, whose generosity they acknowledged (Berdoulay, Turco, 2001).

Colonisation ignores such views, instead imposing a model whereby legality and legitimacy are dictated by the state without regard for local communities. Heterocentric geography is responsible for the imposed logic of colonial territorialisation, whose aim was to establish a geography that benefitted those who did not live in those countries, while drawing from them the resources they needed to live and thrive (Berdoulay, Soubeyran, 2000). In Africa, for instance, national borders, as we know them today, are the result of colonial endeavours that disregarded the territorial legitimacy of borderland peoples. Likewise, we could also discuss the agrarian development and environmental protection projects carried out in territories considered free from legal bonds. This latter assumption was based on descriptions and representations, which colonial powers produced and topographic cartography perpetuated.

It is well known that Europe's territorial conquest was based on the peculiar notion that Africa was devoid of territorial meaning. This conception of the 'Dark Continent', shared by all colonial endeavours, was enhanced by a number of ad hoc representations: the public has come to know Africa through stereotypes inspired by Western values handed down from explorers, travellers, geographers, soldiers, painters, and photographers.

The study of the relationship between representations and colonialism, and more specifically of how a geography came to be, has enabled scholars to highlight geographers' and geographical map-makers' roles (topographical, educational, thematic etc.) in legitimising colonial and imperial expansion. Moreover, this study has critically assessed the outcomes of such representations, identifying their specific responsibilities and establishing their communicative action. What has emerged is that the role played by geographical maps (and presumably by the cartographers or agencies who produced them) was quite unique. By posing as neutral, objective representations of Africa, geographical maps turned out to be highly instrumental to expansionism, providing scientific grounds for its assumptions. Cartographic documents therefore give us invaluable tools for understanding how Africa's territorial essence, based on the cosmogonic relationship local communities had established with nature, was ultimately disregarded (Casti, 2001, 2004). Maps attest to the fact that such denial was the very cause of the tragic outcome of colonisation: the replacement of the sacred essence of African territory, from which traditional legitimacy was derived, with materialistic, instrumental meaning. Today, this substitution continues to invalidate the relationship between public administration and political authorities in villages, and between the North and South of the world.

The juxtaposition between legality and legitimacy came clearly to the fore when African States, using the logic of European politics, triggered conflict between state actors and social actors. In the words of Angelo Turco, the logic of legality in African states is based on colonial assumptions (at least as far as management is concerned). These assumptions disregard local issues and thereby ignore the traditional legitimacy that has always existed and has, over time, given rise to the hypostatisation of power in villages (Turco, 2000).

Until recently, the relationship between legality and legitimacy in Africa saw a state that claimed to be self-legitimised through appeal to the law, largely ignoring local legitimacy. However, things are changing. In international cooperation projects aimed at sustainability, states are called to take heed of the involvement of local people in the face of foreign intervention, which often has far-reaching goals (social, environmental, economic, and financial). In fact, the principle of sustainable development calls for forms of territorial legitimation that can only be achieved by involving local inhabitants in projects.

In recent years, African States have revisited their relationship to local communities and adopted decentralisation policies. The latter, however, seemingly fail to guarantee true participation, since they merely replace ancient, legitimacy-based structures with law-based, European-type structures. Ultimately, the imbalance between legality and legitimacy remains unsolved, and affects large portions of Africa, namely sub-Saharan Africa. However, it does give scholars an interesting opportunity to experiment with rehabilitating territorial legitimacy in local communities through participatory systems.

Of course, a similar need is perceived in the West, where local communities increasingly voice the right to be considered 'different' and demand the attention of capable administrators to implement participatory and shared governance. Under the circumstances, it is crucial to find actors who are willing to sit at the negotiating table. On the one hand, effective governance calls for strong interaction between social groups and the actors involved, so as to combine various interests and devise common strategies regarding institutional actors. On the other hand, it is likewise essential to consider territorial features not so much as items for localisation, but as instances of territorialisation. Participatory mapping addresses both issues.[3]

---

3 It comprises: 1) Participatory mapping, produced by local communities at the request of an external interlocutor, who establishes and guides the issues at stake. Such cartography is used at negotiating tables between various actors involved in territorial planning. While subject to variation, the scale used is primarily local, i.e. linked to the area where the resources used by local communities for various symbolic/productive activities are allotted. 2) Community Integrated GIS – CIGIS. These are GIS-produced maps that contain or combine information derived from local communities and input into the system by an external actor. They are generally intended for those responsible for understanding an area (research institutions, national or international organisations, etc.). However, these maps may be used effectively at negotiating tables to solve different local or national disputes. 3) Public Participation GIS – PPGIS, produced directly by local communities in their ongoing dialogue with administrators or a supervising body. PPGIS were initially conceived as tools for local communities, i.e. 'grassroots communities' capable of actively negotiating with administrative bodies and local institutions for limited areas of intervention. Nowadays, PPGIS address the wider scope of opportunities resulting from globalisation. They are also based on information provided by local communities and are produced by either internal or external actors belonging to the institutions involved in solving problems. See the website: http://www.ncgia.ucsb.edu/. The IAPAD website (Integrated Approaches to Participatory Development) is almost entirely devoted to developing participatory cartographic systems and hosts a mailing list (www.ppgis. net – *Open Forum on Participatory Geographic Information Systems and Technologies*).

Changing course: toward chorographic metrics

There is no doubt that the metrics used in topographical maps[4] must be abandoned, even in participatory mapping. Were we to try to give voice to empowered local communities in their tussle with the State by adopting topographical metrics, we would end up reducing real places to abstract space. Cartesian logic, which favours the visual and material features of territory, irreparably strayed from the idea of landscape as an experience of place, and turned maps into instruments for representing territory as essentially removed from any type of social interpretation.

Participatory maps built on such criteria can contextualise geo-referential projects successfully, but only in strictly material terms. The symbolic, cultural, or possibly sacred aspects of human action are ignored. Topographic metrics ultimately disregards any record of cultural features that local inhabitants may have built into the landscape. The effectiveness of topographic representation, rooted as it is in Cartesian logic, rests upon a very simple system of signs, which disregards the substance of objects and instead uses analogical distance to reflect the relationship between them. This system reflects a very specific, very limited aspect of territory – classically defined as *topos* – based on a self-legitimising idea of space. Conversely, the cultural role of place is expressed by the term *chora*. In the words of Augustin Berque, *chora* relies on the notion of space (*écoumène*) as a quintessentially social unit that expresses common goods, values, and interests originating 'from the bottom up' and clearly shown in landscape (Berque, 2000). Landscape is therefore both subjective – as it is framed by a specific view – and collective, insofar as it condenses and expresses socially produced values.

Following this line of argument, we must adopt cartographic metrics that are closely attuned both to collective mapping (the sum of all skills, knowledge, and policies linked to the use of territory) and to the visual form of landscape that relies on a subjective observer.

---

[4] Metric criteria are, in this case, based on a Euclidean idea of space and a Cartesian logic that is graphically rendered from a zenith point of observation, a standard reduction scale, and codified, abstract language.

Technically speaking, we can meet our goals using fine-tuned GIS systems to transcend – at least theoretically – the boundaries of cartographic topography. GIS systems can produce a three-dimensional rendering of places over a flat two-dimensional map and can supplement selected information and the scale reduction required by overlapping multiple layers.

Theoretically, such a change implies abandoning Cartesian logic and topographical metrics in favour of a 'landscape' logic and new, 'chora'-based metrics. The word 'chorographic', lost to the cause of positivism, may thus be legitimately reinstated, and the word 'chorography' be used to describe this *new type of metrics, which calls for a rehabilitation of the cultural meaning of territory as originally configured by local subjects in the form of landscape*. This metrics will primarily focus on the qualitative features of landscape, and is intended to give voice and shape to a topological space that has invariably been excluded from topographical space (Lévy, Lussault, 2003)

Only by abandoning the myth of a descriptive map can we create a cartographic universe wherein a given message is inseparable from an explicit endeavour. This means giving up any pretence of objectivity or impartiality and acknowledging that our viewpoint is itself a product of interpretation and, as such, based on conjecture. In the case of chorography, this position seems tenable, since it values openness and sets out to produce maps that state their goals and enable readers to make critical sense of what they see on them. In doing so, these maps avoid iconising prescriptions[5]. A tendency to iconise is, after all, ever present, especially when maps are used uncritically as instruments for making sense of objective reality. If, however, map-readers are aware that maps are biased and must be interpreted, the iconising tendency of maps subsides.

Our goal is to develop ways of mastering iconisation and use it to noble ends. This means shifting our focus from the features of 'reality' a map reproduces to the social meaning of the territory we wish to act upon, with the aim of enhancing its qualities (Casti, 2005). To conclude, by enhancing awareness that the communicative effect of a map can be mastered, we can create a testing ground where we can rethink maps by tweaking their constitutive features to chorographic metrics.

---

[5] For a discussion of iconisation see: Casti, 2005.

Chorographic metrics:
spatialisation and symbolisation

I begin from the assumption that a map is a semiotic field comprised of two structures: *spatialisation*, which is aimed at reproducing phenomena on a map's surface so that their layout on the map corresponds with their place in the real world, and *symbolisation*, which is comprised of a cluster of language codes [illustrations, colours, names] to represent the cultural substance of those phenomena. (Casti, 2000). It is crucial that such structures be preserved, as they convey the properties of objects in different ways: by invoking either the rule of difference or the rule of distinction, they either dissolve or produce the very identity of what they show and thereby add to the communicative thrust of denotation or connotation (Wilden, 1980).

In a communicative perspective – and contrary to commonly held views of what maps are and how they ought to work – a map is not simply an analogical model of reality. Rather, it combines both the analogical and the digital system of the world in an altogether unique manner.[6] The analogical mechanism is used in spatialisation; the layout of objects and their relevance as regards the medium used obviously abide by the rules of reduction, proportion, and perspective. Yet, such operations are not actually a form of transformation (in the mathematical sense of the word); understanding them requires no interpretative rule. The map aims to portray objects as they are in 'real life', which may be conceived as a continuum based on physical laws gleaned through differentiation (one object differs from another because it is located at a given point and its features are different from those of other objects). The digital system, on the other hand, is based on symbolisation, as it aims to convey information about a given territorial feature by identifying and handing down several distinctive features of its name. Thus, it aims for specificity by highlighting those elements that make up the holistic substance of a given phenomenon.

We should nonetheless keep in mind that the analogical system of maps provides the 'context' necessary for the digital system. The two work together to produce a third system – the *iconising system* – which is specific to maps. Iconisation arranges information in a novel way: It *iconises*

---

6 An analogical system communicates via continuity, whereby we pay heed to the realm of difference (of magnitude, frequency, distribution and arrangement). Conversely, a digital system is based on distinction, according to criteria of opposition, identity, contradiction or paradox. Unlike the analogical system, the digital system inevitably entails some form of access code to be decoded (knowledge of the alphabet, of numbers, etc.).

the world, presenting it not as it really is but as a given theory portrays it. Iconisation helps us conceptualise what we set out to depict and to present this depiction as a truth. Ultimately, the iconising system addresses the connotative aspect of communication. Most important to our purposes, the values we communicate iconically are not necessarily those of the territory. Rather, they are the ones self-referentially produced by the map itself (Casti, 2005). We need to focus on how the production of information occurs, as it may well allow us to meddle with it and direct its communicative thrust to our own participatory goals.

Scholars are not unanimous on this point. Some have voiced scepticism. Concerning geographic spatialisation, Franco Farinelli sees the 'plate' as a major obstacle to reflecting the world's social substance. He claims that spatialising information along one plane produces a sort of mould whereby the substance of real places is turned into mere quantification, and space is made homogeneous.[7] Farinelli warns that this has devastating communicative consequences, since an abstract, two-dimensional image is substituted for the pliability of the world. Such perspectives prevail in topography, where we are given a perpendicular, top-down view of the world below. The underlying assumption is that the exact positioning of the object and its dimensions ensure a truthful, impartial representation. Zenithal projection, the most abstract way of rendering the world, in compliance with Euclidean geometry, is ultimately to blame for excluding the subject. Such projections eliminate the human perspective and, consequently, the hierarchy maintained by a perspective view. Iconic significance is lost to mere description. Since Zenithal projection establishes an exact observation point perpendicular to a territory, it uses several points of observation – as many as the objects to be represented[8] – rather than just one (Figure 1).

---

[7]   Farinelli traced the problem back to the advent of modern perspective and subsequent reduction of 'the whole face of Earth to a gigantic, Euclidean expanse'. He asserts that the revolution brought about by Brunelleschi as he took on a linear, Florentine perspective that calculated the dimensions of objects with regard to their distance from an observer, ultimately imposed a spatial set of rules that subjected human beings ('being subjects') to a quantitative and thus spatial worldview (Farinelli, 2009)

[8]   For the sake of completeness, it should be noted that the representation of Earth as observed from a plane and satellite imaging do not, in fact, use Zenithal projection, since they only use one observation point which, while far from the Earth, still assumes the presence of an observer. Yet, the transformation achieved by assembling several photographs into one cartographic product ultimately conceals the presence of a unique observation point – which undoubtedly existed in the survey process – to the benefit of a zenith point, which includes multiple observation points.

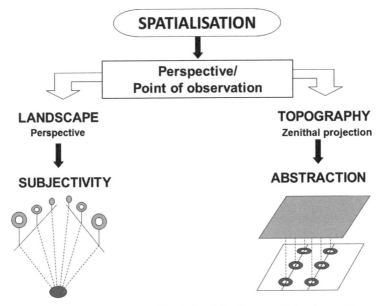

Fig. 1 Spatialisation: multiple observation points.

The type of perspective used in Renaissance cartography may well have been a sketchy, inaccurate way of rendering territory. However, it acknowledged the presence of human subjects, as does our experience of landscape. Zenithal projection, on the contrary, 1) rules out the informative ranking of *far* and *near*; 2) excludes altimetry, 3) disregards the three-dimensional nature of objects, and finally, 4) flattens volume by adopting a perpendicular perspective.

Nonetheless, following Farinelli's argument, digitisation and 3D technology now enable us to render pliability, meaning we already have the technical tools needed to overcome the limits of the 'plate'. What perhaps lacks still is a conceptual framework that can adequately render a world made up not only of shapes but also of 'societal' features. Such features demand that we consider spatialisation in its mutual relationship with symbolisation. In participatory mapping, the mutual relationship between these two dimensions is crucial in accounting for the societal features of territory and for living subjects who represent their own landscape.[9]

---

[9] On the 'societal' concept as a social feature, see J. Lévy, 2008, who claims society must be investigated in its spatial dynamics based on criteria of topology (which examine how the distance between phenomena is conceptualised); scaling (as a discontinuity threshold for measuring distance and assessing phenomena); and substance (the value given to a phenomenon).

In the case of spatialisation, it is very much a matter of finding an observation point[10] that allows us to show the convergence between landscape and map. Undoubtedly, as far as landscape is concerned, the world is seen by an observer who is placed in a given location. This location may be part of the landscape observed and therefore *within* it. However, it may take the form of an elevation – a mountain, hill, or precipice – from which our gaze can sweep the horizon. These are perspective views, since they all rely on one observation point that coincides with that of the observer. The observer's position inevitably determines not only what is far and near in a given representation, but also – by virtue of the changing distance perceived between objects – whence the image proceeds. On the other hand, the rise of Renaissance perspective, which, for Farinelli, marks the exclusion of substance from the world, puts forward an abstract space model that hints at the presence of a subject in order to enhance depth. However, it is ultimately detached from and unaffected by this subject. Whichever perspective we assume –natural, central, or vertical – we establish a geometric system of rendering that art typically calls 'view', or possibly 'panorama', when expanded to include both landscape and map.[11]

Today, we are fully aware that perspective is radically different from the volumetric rendering done by the human eye. We know that we should not be misled into accepting perspective as a faithful rendering of landscape. Yet, perspective has long been central to figurative and semiotic research on vision, so much so that concerted tests along the same lines have yielded astonishing results. As one of the primary *modes*[12] of visual communication, perspective has been acknowledged as a powerful generative tool for processing information in a specific way. David Hockney's work is remarkable in this respect. His representation of landscape, which recreates the emotions the artist felt as he viewed a place firsthand, is rooted in the mechanisms whereby the eye perceives and processes

---

[10] For the present purposes, I would rather use the word 'observation point' than the frequently used expression 'point of view'. The latter is used for technical purposes, often to highlight the role of the observer-interpreter.

[11] The quantity of bibliographical data available on the notion of perspective in art and other disciplines well exceeds our current scope. It should be noted that the term 'panorama', along with its widely accepted sense of sweeping view, was also used across the 18th and 19th centuries to refer to a circular room yielding a 360-degree view of a drawing along its walls, giving the viewer the impression of a real landscape surrounding him/her.

[12] Colour and shape must also be addressed.

images.[13] His aim is double. On one hand, he stresses the need to find technical models able to render the functioning of the human eye. On the other hand, he assumes that the way a human eye processes visual information is not merely a sensory mechanism, and that we should therefore strive to render 'visual thought', i.e. the way landscape is conceptualised. His underlying assumption is that if we are rooted in the optical experience of distance – and *then* in a perspective elaborated by a subject – we have the chance to render the conceptualisation of landscape, which obviously depends on perception. However, it is also impacted by the subject's social values, which inform his or her interpretation of the landscape. This is the line of research currently pursued by cartographers as they are called upon to build participatory maps. The examples that follow undermine assumptions based on the topographic map-ground, in order to make room for features drawn from topology. The aim is to restore a third dimension and reproduce both the visual aspect of landscape and its social significance as an inhabited place.

As we move on to consider symbolisation, we note that topographic maps represent a single, specific feature of territory, namely *topos*, and thereby value the sensory aspect of phenomena by highlighting dimensions. What is lost, however, is their social significance. Our aim here is to use the *chora,* which, as we have argued, entails shifting our focus from maps as truthful representations of reality to maps as conveyors of social significance. This, in turn, implies affecting the final communicative effect of a map, i.e. iconisation. We will proceed by freeing the semantic features of the map from topographic conventions and opening maps to other symbolic systems based on multiple languages. Information technology is also essential here, as the use of multimedia fosters novel forms of interactions between the cartographer and the people s/he is addressing. Obviously, IT skills must be adequate to render the *chora*, which means that data fed into the map should come from participation-based research in the field.

Ultimately, social equity requires a complete overhaul of symbolisation itself, from the type of data involved to their cartographic rendering.

---

[13] Hockney works from the assumption that perspective view, as the sole vanishing point, is completely different from the image produced by the eye, where multiple perspectives with multiple vanishing points overlap in a very limited time span. Hockney experiments with a painting technique reminiscent of photography though clearly different from it: he starts by overlapping partial photographic images and then recreates the eye's movement as it processes images by overlapping them. Recently, he successfully bypassed photography by using an i-Pad to build his picture during real-time observation. Hockney, 1998.

To this end, researchers at the Diathesis Laboratory at the University of Bergamo (Italy) have devised a participatory research method called SIGAP (*Sistemi Informativi Geografici per le Azioni Partecipate* (or Geographic Information Systems for Participatory Action) which addresses the whole process of cartographic construction by using TIG (participatory mapping and CIGIS).[14] SIGAP aims to restore the territorial dynamics of local communities and to identify involved agents. This in turns paves the way to an analysis of habitation as a context, which yields relevant clusters of information relative to landscape.[15] The emphasis here is restoring the symbolic value of communities (myth, traditions, and beliefs), which inevitably affects how the cultural actions of subjects relate to nature.

Our final goal here is to restore the relevance of social values as the foundation of territoriality. We have repeatedly stated that the relationship between territory and landscape is manifest at the level of communication. Territory is the product of a process of spatial transformation brought about by a social agent and rooted in multiple actions that are not always made manifest. Landscape, however, is the empirical manifestation an observer conveys through representation and, as such, takes into account a cultural dimension, upon which participatory mapping is based (Figure 2).

The creation of participatory maps requires an analysis of territory – carried out during a long stay in the field – designed to explore the layout of territory and understand how a given society relates to its natural resources. Such an understanding will aid in the process of mediation between the interests of the many actors involved. More specifically, with reference to contingent goals, SIGAP is performed in module-like phases, with the aim of providing knowledge-tools to the actors involved in the participation. The research consists of four phases:

– The first aims to set up a database of territorial systems based on a survey and sketch drawings by local residents.
– The second entails cartographic modelling of this data, with a focus on the issue and using participation to validate procedures.
– The third pinpoints controversial issues that call for consultative operational proposals.

[14] See the website: http://www.sigaponlus.org.
[15] On this participatory methodology, see: E. Casti, 'A Reflexive Cartography to Tackle Poverty: A Model of Participatory Zoning', in: *Policy Matters. Community empowerment for conservation*, IUCN, (2005); www.iapad.org/publications/ppgis/Casti_IUCNa.pdf; www.comminit.com/strategicthinking/st2005/thinking-1414.html - 44k.

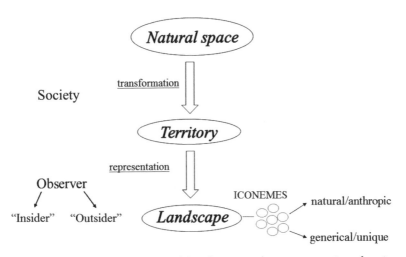

Fig. 2 Landscape as the representation of territory.

– The fourth addresses the designing and setting up of a system of capitalisation and cartographic processing for the whole procedure, becoming a tool for fostering participation that is made available online (Multimap).[16]

We shall examine some of these phases in the context of experiments currently being carried out in a traditional West-African community, the Gourmanche, who have a mythological view of nature.

The sacredness of landscape and environmental conflicts at the Gobnangou Cliffs

In a concerted inter-university effort between 2iE (*Institut International de l'Ingénierie de l'Eau et de l'Environnement*) in Ouagadougou and the University of Bergamo, research was done on the outskirts of Arly National Park over a three-year period, using the SIGAP strategy (Figure 3). SIGAP has enabled researchers to make an initial estimate of the human impact on the protected area and identify the sacred significance of landscape. It has shown that eruptions of conflict between the local population and Arly Park management for the use of natural resources has largely been due to the latter's disregard for the symbolic import of landscape.

---

[16]   An example of an interactive and multimedia system may be found at www.multimap-parcw.org.

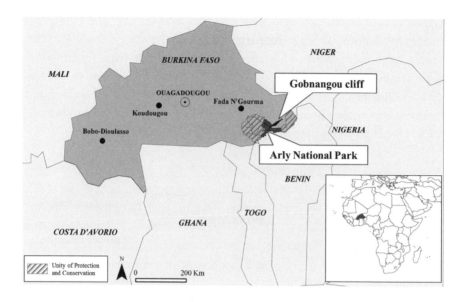

Fig. 3 Location of the Gobnangou Cliffs and Arly Park.

At the local scale, research sounded out the social setup and territorial functioning by tracing them back to the significance of landscape and local communities' relationship to natural resources. Regarding the qualitative aspect of the research, we used participatory models based on evidence provided by members of the rural community along with data collection. Data collection was carried out in accordance with a set form, which allowed us to gather relevant information, including: 1) knowledge of the physical/morphological features of the area; 2) perceived localisation of the village with respect to other villages and estimated distance from the protected area; 3) the cultural roots of the various villages, the history of their founding and the historical record we have of them; 4) social structure and organisation, i.e. the status and role of social members (sex, age groups, genealogy, and guilds); 5) exploration of the relationship between genealogies, assets, and liabilities, and of the criteria legitimising authority; 6) policies of territorial appropriation and utilisation via symbolic or physical schemes that regulate collective life and ensure social reproduction; 7) potential conflicts with park management and possible causes; 8) mutual interests and psychological/behavioural attitudes on which peaceful partnership between the agents involved would be based. The goal was to shed light on the values and issues that could potentially affect, enhance, or threaten the identity of Gourmanche society. The emergence of security values, which ensure a balanced relationship with nature, convinced the outside agents of the need to involve locals who, for centuries, had overseen the preservation of Arly and of its surroundings, in the conservation project. The persistence of a traditional system has been shown to have great potential, insofar as it can successfully steer changes brought about by external projects.

At a later stage, the rendering and cartographic visualisation of territorial data yielded information quite unlike that culled through observation and inquiry. On a regional scale, they promoted the dimensioning and cultural modelling of regional territorial phenomena. On a local scale, they promoted the emergence of values and aspects of local knowledge that highlight the importance of specific competency in terms of place management (Figure 4).

The most important finding in our research was arguably that spatiality, i.e. the way a given society relates to space, is a conceptual frame developed mainly from a set of sacral assumptions. This should be considered in more detail.

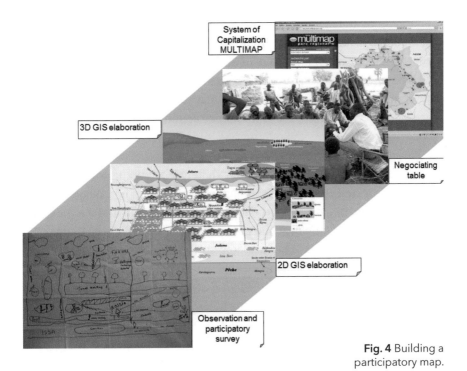

Fig. 4 Building a participatory map.

The importance of myth in social regulation led us to assess the territorial process of the Gourmanche people by considering the sacred value of the Cliff. Research has, in fact, shown that in the construction of territory as well as in the attribution of meaning to a given environment, this people sees spirituality as both the moral and the logical foundation of life and social reproduction. The principles used to sanction the natural order come from the values the society has maintained in its own metaphysical sphere. These are conveyed by myths, i.e. a narration that translates such principles into norms, whereby community life and its actions are ensured, especially in the construction of territory (Claval, 1980).

It is impossible for us to consider all the manifestations of the Gourmanche territorial process here. We can, however, look in greater detail at the persistence and centrality of myth as a narrative model among this people. On a descriptive level, myth informs principles. On a normative level, it prescribes rules whereby the territorial process must be fulfilled. Myth first intimates the presence of a supernatural entity that has made the people's settlement possible. It then ensures the legitimacy of territorial action in accordance with this supernatural link. In myth-based societies, the relationship established with the world is the expression of the relationship the society has with the deity: one cannot do as one wishes with regard to the Earth. Rather, there is an ongoing process of transformation that is compatible with the representational system of the myth. Consequently, territorial action takes on a sort of double meaning. On one hand, it is a sign of divine goodwill granting its fulfilment; on the other hand, it is an invitation to act responsibly and in harmony with nature. In fact, myth is based on the fact that a given geographic layout has intrinsic properties: it is a frame for human action, which fully exercises its autonomy by observing and interpreting divine will. As such, myth ensures the transition from a mythical to a historical universe. The territorialisation process ratifies the shift from an acknowledgment of divine munificence to an ethical view of human responsibility towards nature. Ultimately, being a lawful inhabitant of a place depends not only on the original pact sealed with the gods, but also on human action performed in accordance with divine will. Similarly, even the Cliffs are considered on the basis of myth. Their natural meaning shifts from the level of denotation to that of cultural connotation through their designation (Turco, 1999). Restoring the social meaning of the Cliffs – in which Gourmanche territory lies – as a landscape thus depends on how the mythical value is represented. Gobnangou is the place where the spirits of the place reside. The Cliffs' vegetation and steep walls are home to several sacred places: Utanfalu (the mysterious cave), Pundougou (the falls

used in initiation rites), Tanfoldjaga (the place for the endowing of mysti-
cal powers), Aguanda (the rock hidden by vegetation) and Kuoli (the stone
struck during sacrificial rites). The Cliffs are a place of myth and rite *par
excellence*, and few are entitled access. Although the cliff is plainly visible
to everyone, only select persons may access its secret meaning: the village authorities, those with religious power (*perkiamo* and/or *parkiamo*) or
political power (*bado* and/or *nikpelo*). These individuals may maintain an
ongoing relationship with it and request advice for human action. The symbolic role of Gobnangou may be traced back to the territorial action following the founding of the villages. Tilled lands criss-crossed by a network
of paths providing access to each settlement are the result of a territorial
action, which clearly set the anthropic area apart from the one preserved
in its original state. It is thus clear that, by way of of a communicative act,
landscape results from a specific set of skills and values – both physical
and metaphysical – inherent to a given society. Gobnangou is a powerful
factor of identity and may be read on two levels: 1) that of external cohesion, as the Cliffs represent the distinctive feature of the ethnic group that
inhabits the Gulmu; and 2) that of internal distinction, since the Cliffs hark
back to founding myths (and the granting of partial use of the cliff-side
for ritual practices of a single village). More specifically, each village has
a unique relationship with the Cliff that, at the same time, strengthens the
broader relationship across the whole Gobnangou area (Figure 5).

Fig. 5 A village at the foot of the Gobnangou Cliffs.

Obviously, cartographic information on such a landscape must attempt to restore the sacred features of the Cliffs and the cultural aspects of territory. We will not focus here on regional features that have been investigated elsewhere (Casti, Yonkeu, 2009). As for local features, one relevant example of the methodology we used is the Yirini village (Figure 6). We began by mapping prevalent traditional features and their hierarchical distribution in the layout of built-up areas. The types of compounds and their distribution in blocks marked by natural features such as riverbeds and vegetation underlines the presence of different genealogies, which the map indicates with different colours for each concession.

The distribution and location of production (mainly agricultural) underlines a set of basic skills and competences regarding the land. Those relative to the tilling of fields necessary for subsistence (millet, sorghum, and corn) are based on the make-up of soils and their different hygroscopic power: sandy-clay soil (*timboanli*) is found along the lower slopes; muddy-clay soil (*kuboalgu*) and clay soil (*lilubili*) are found in depressions. The locations of land for other types of farming depend on the status of the land and the role played by each member within the group. The fields belonging the village chief (*kiankianli*), a distinctive mark of his status, occupy the area facing the entrance to his concession. Inside each concession, in addition to vegetable gardens, are women's fields (*manloli*), situated at the back of the concession (*dapuoli*), along with those for private use by other members. Remote fields, be they communal (*kwa-kiam*) or private (*sual-kwanu*) property, are subject to crop rotation, whose usage rights are established by the chief of the land. The map also provides information about recently introduced, modern facilities (schools, places of worship, dispensaries, mills, cotton market, drinking water wells, etc.), which attests to an ongoing process of transformation that must be managed, with an eye to traditional values.

Nonetheless, if we wish to represent the landscape features of such settlements, we must restore the visual shape of the village and its relationship with the Cliffs (Figure 7). Thus, in order to avoid photographic reproduction, which would quite indistinctly exhibit all its visual features, we propose a modelling of landscape based on the sacred places, which gives us a hierarchy of cultural values. Such modelling reflects the relevance given to landscape by the villagers and thus highlights their cultural values with regard to the Cliffs and the layout of the village. Technically, we used a three-dimensional rendering of both to highlight their visual shape and to highlight key territorial features in which the identities of these peoples are rooted.

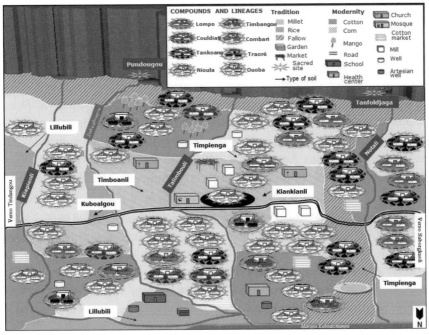

Fig. 6 Yirini.

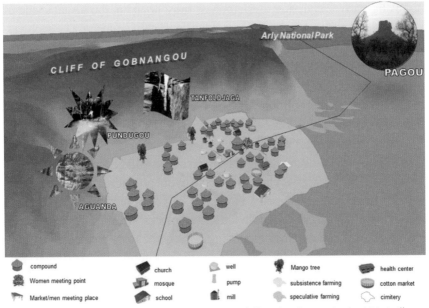

Fig. 7 Modelling landscape in the Yirini village.

The word Yirini – which in the Gourmanche language means 'top' (alluding to the provenance of its founders) – dates back to the 19th century. The narration, passed down through the 'griot', says that the founders originally came from the Cliffs led by a panther (*gambo*), which showed them the way and rescued them from enemy attacks.[17] The concessions provide a sort of pattern that gives us a fixed record of the clan history for the village, and of the varying degrees of importance each of its eight founding genealogies. Laid out in blocks, concessions are the places from which the links to the Cliffs originate. At its point of entry, each compound has an area that is used for propitiatory practices meant to protect the family. However, it is not used for divination, which can only be carried out in the holy places jealously guarded along the slopes of the Gobnangou: *Pundougou* (the sacred falls), *Tanfoldjaga* (the sacred cave), and *Aguanda* (the sacred stone hidden in the bush). Such sacred places do not all serve the same function and are not subject to the same proscription. There are those that all can approach to ask for personal/family favours; others are only accessible to the village chief, who is vested with political and/or religious powers. Only specific sacrificial areas, where the *parkiamo* invokes divine intervention to resolve the issues that threaten the village community, are forbidden. It is therefore a landscape that must be respected and is guarded jealously, as a way not only of honouring the local people but also of preserving a culture whose ways of relating to nature are quite unlike those of the West.

A figurative rendering of sacredness must abandon the visual shape of lands and use abstract icons to convey the connotative meaning of such values. It is the kind of abstract iconisation found in Figure 8, where the Cliff is stylised. Concessions are shown as spheres scaled relative to the their specific social role, and abstract forms mark sacred places. Everything underlines a sacred dimension of nature, seen as the ordaining principle of territoriality. In short, the mapping of sacred lands in the Yirini village reflects a semantics of landscape and creates a set of rules for showing the links between the Cliffs and the village. The role of the former in safeguarding the social order of the latter is thereby enhanced. By considering such places as systems that endow landscape with meaning, we note that, as they show the link between the village and the Cliffs, they also inform our reading of the village because they provide a social hierarchy of compounds. The village

---

[17] The group was followed by a cat who covered their tracks and prevented enemies from chasing them. As a token of gratitude, the clan members totemised the cat, the panther, and all other animals of the feline family.

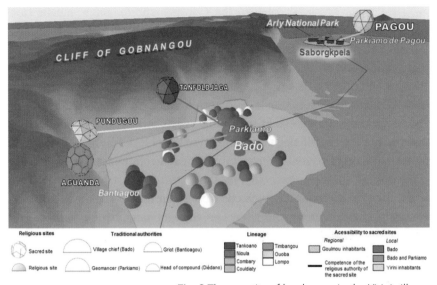

Fig. 8 The sanctity of landscape in the Yirini village.

chief's compound is naturally the most important, as he alone has exclusive access to *Tanfoldjaga* and shares the religious chief's right to access *Pundougou*. The *parkiamo*'s dwelling is important for different reasons. Most notably, it is the dwelling of he who – albeit without power over land or the community – acts as an intermediary between man and god, thereby ensuring a constant exchange with the cosmogonic world. The religious chief also has exclusive access to *Aguanda*. The concession of the *Bantiagou*, the *griot* in charge of handing down myths in the form of public narration, also plays a key social role in the village, although subordinate to the roles of the *bado* and the *parkiamo*, by virtue of their link to sacred places.

Finally, the map projects onto the *Pagou* backdrop yet another sacred place, one that is of importance not only to village dwellers but to all the Gourmanche people of Western Africa. Its function is to convey a sense of belonging to the ethnic group as a whole.

The map marks the sanctity of the Gourmanche landscape, not only by virtue of its tie with nature, but also as an ordering principle of the *médiance,* which Berque considers vital to substantiating places (Berque, 2000). Visually speaking, a landscape does not betray its social relevance. It is only by making sense of the mythical values attached to the Cliffs that one can devise a plotline or story that presents what we have discussed. Of course, we are dealing with experimental methods being gradually defined. Yet such tests pave the ways to new modes of cartographic representation.

Coming full circle

We set out with the assumption that chorographic metrics, based on topology, require that we consider the idea of space underlying them. This has entailed clearing the ground of *spatialism*, based on the idea of space as a self-contained unit to be dealt with according to universal rules. Spatialism de facto disregards the cultural import of space and supports the idea that the materiality of phenomena determines the development of social practices. In reconstructing the changing meanings of 'space' in geography and retracing their philosophical implications, Jacques Lévy and Michel Lussault see topology as the spatial feature that may finally overcome the constraints of Euclidean geometry. Topology advocates for a new concept of space based on relationships between individuals, versus the idea of empty space as an abstract container of phenomena.

Embracing this new idea of space in cartography means enjoying its advantages, both operational and heuristic. As it is open to other types of metrics, this new space paves the way for a radical overhaul of spatialisation and symbolisation in maps. In addition, as it rejects Euclidean rigidity, such a concept of space embraces relationality as the key to rehabilitating individuals, and it paves the way for the chorographic metrics that answer our initial question. We advocate for participatory maps capable of handling controversy and of respecting the place of others. However, such a place should not be set up squarely against the 'place' of the West. It is for us to show that the two places are complementary and mutually enriching.

References

Berdoulay, V. & Soubeyran, O. eds., 2000. *Milieu, colonisation et développement durable*, Paris: L'Harmattan.

Berdoulay, V. & Turco, A., 2001. 'Mythe et géographie. De l'opposition aux complémentarités', *Cahiers de Géographie du Québec*, 45(124): 339–345.

Berque, A., 19900. *Médiance. De milieux en paysages,* Montpellier: Reclus.

Berque, A., 2008. Trouver place humaine dans le cosmos', *Echogéo*, 5, 2008. <http://Echogeo.Revues.Org/3093>

Berque, A., 2000. *Ecoumène. Introduction à l'étude des milieux humains*, Paris: Belin.

Casti, E., 2000. *Reality as Representation: The Semiotics of Cartography and the Generation of Meaning,* Bergamo: Bergamo University Press.

Casti, E., 2001. 'Mythologies africaines dans la cartographie française au tournant du XIXe siècle', *Cahiers de Géographie du Québec*, vol. 45: 429–450.

Casti, E., 2005a. 'Towards a Theory of Interpretation: Cartographical Semiosis', *Cartographica*, 40(3): 1-16.

Casti, E., 2005b. 'A Reflexive Cartography to Tackle Poverty: A Model for a Participatory Zoning', in *Policy Matters. Community Empowerment For Conservation*, IUCN <www.iapad.org/publications/ppgis/casti_iucn>.

Casti, E. & Yonkeu, S. (eds.), 2009. *Le Parc national d'Arly et la falaise du Gobnangou (Burkina Faso)*, Paris: L'Harmattan.

Claval, P., 1980. *Les mythes fondateurs des sciences sociales*, Paris: PUF.

Farinelli, F., 2009. *De la raison cartographique*, Paris: CTHS.

Hockney, D., 1999. *Ma Façon De Voir,* London: Thames & Hudson.

Lévy, J. (ed.), 2008. *L'invention du Monde. Une géographie de la mondialisation,* Paris: Presses de Sciences Po.

Lévy, J. & Lussault, M (eds.), 2013. *Dictionnaire de la géographie et de l'espace des sociétés*, 2nd edition, Paris: Belin.

Turco, A., 1999. *Terra Eburnea. Il mito, il luogo, la Storia in Africa*, Milan: Unicopli.

Turco, A., 2000. 'Colonisation et après: légitimité territoriale et développement durable en Afrique Subsaharienne', in Berdoulay, V & Soubeyran O (eds.), 2000. *Milieu, colonisation et développement durable*, Paris: L'Harmattan, pp. 175–184.

Wilden, A., 1980. *System and Structure*, New York: Tavistock.

Chapter 11

Mapping the Global Mobile Space
The Nomadic Space as Sample

Denis Retaillé

Mapping the space of nomadic peoples is a fallacy, so long as these spaces represented are stationary. Synchronic, single-scale maps cannot express 'mobile' space-time when places were initially created through movement. Stationary representational space represents two place attributes: location and character. With such fixed references, nomadic mobility is a limited adaptation of local values, where space remains open. Where is this open space? It is located on the fringes of the sedentary settlements beyond the *oekoumene*. If nomadic peoples move beyond the world's reach, then attempts to understand their motives and capacities for mobility is in vain. Nomadic people simply disappear.

However, I argue that mobility is a major spatial factor, and perhaps even *the* major spatial operator in the world. I furthermore argue that the space of nomadic peoples could be useful for understanding contemporary mobility and its spaces. What is more, mapping nomadic mobility is a way of criticising the power of maps. Although Brian Harley observed and criticised the power of mapping, his criticism was not based on an assumption of sedentariness, which would necessitate a stationary space of representation. The real power of space lies in controlling movement, and in a vertical ontology based on a hierarchizing of places that is only possible through a zenithal view. Therefore, before nomadism disappears entirely, it might be useful to learn mapping nomadic mobility through a mobile representational space that is based on a 'flat ontology with multiple scalar entry points' (Jessop, Brenner, & Jones, 2008). We must then transfer this knowledge from anthropological space (the nomadic one) to a methodological one. Yet, from ontological choices come epistemological consequences.

Mapping the spaces of nomadic peoples

Nomadic peoples principally move through large, marginal areas whose resources were poor even before exploitation by underground mining operations. The new resources unearthed from these operations do not directly benefit the nomads, even when the latter claim to be the veritable owners of the land/resources in question. However, industrial development and regional integration have sedentarized nomadic populations around 'offshore' operations, with the territory of the state as a rigid framework. While transportation infrastructure supplanted old convoys, the new regional integration brought new jobs, and cities flourished in the desert.

Regardless of whether nomads become sedentary, the representational space of nomadic peoples is essentially mobile. The social bonds maintained despite of the dispersion are such that mobility allows them to follow opportunity. New patterns of nomadic movement and new patterns of general circulation, including what we call 'migration', reproduce cultural representations of space. Yet, we now know that these patterns have nothing to do with the adaptation of poor, prehistoric societies. The samples for our study, from the Sahara region and arid zones of the Middle East and Central Asia, allowed us to confirm this.

Nomadism and aridity seem to be linked – nomadism being a response to drought and to the impossibility of agricultural cultivation without irrigation. Rare waterholes and isolated oases are only linked to the world by nomadic trails. Finally, nomadic peoples often lord over oasis settlers. However, this very typical picture overlooks an important fact: oases are also cities. This is easier to prove in the Middle East and Central Asia than in the Sahara. Yet, the fact remains. Saharan cities are smaller and do not have monumental buildings. While there are some very old cities, such as Timbuktu, Gao, Chinghetti, Oualata, Agadez and Murzuk; others such as Koumbi Saleh in the Ghanian Empire, Azugi and Sidjilmassa in the

Almoravid Empire, have since disappeared. New places, such as Tamanrasset, Akjoujt, Atar, Adrar, and Sebha, have likewise appeared.

Why are there cities in the desert? The answer, in fact, lies in the question. According to traditional geographical and historical arguments, cities came to exist after the Neolithic Era, as did the development of agriculture and exploitation of rural land (Mumford, 1961; Bairoch, 1985). Cities have existed for a long time and were first founded in semi-arid zones along major rivers like the Indus, Tigris, and Euphrates. Our understanding of oases and desert cities is largely based on the meaning that sedentary and agricultural societies gave them, and totally disregards nomadism, which was seen as a relic of a prehistoric past. Thus, the uncomfortable question of 'why' becomes that of 'where', because cities do exist. The answer then is 'wherever water can be found'. The land with its resources becomes the reference. The primary resource is agricultural land, since a desert per se cannot be occupied by people. Only isolated oases with water resources can welcome settlements. Poor nomads and their livestock of camels and sheep can live in stationary spaces, but must move to find grazing land. This archetype comes from the geographical paradigm of sedentary peoples, where movement is considered a disease or even a punishment. A map of nomadic space is a map of oasis locations; a map of oasis locations is a map of water sources. Oases can be classified into categories, such as mountainous, riverine, near springs, wells and forages, with or without water galleries (*qanat, foggara*), and so on. Nomadic peoples roam the desert in search of oases, and they rely upon grass and wells along the trails.

However, nomadic peoples often lord over oasis settlers. Nomads often purchase houses in oasis cities, or even houses in several oasis cities. Nomadism and urbanity are not antithetical (Retaillé, 1989).

Based on this, I proposed another map – not one of the oasis and water, but of roads and the oasis, based on nomadic uses. Nomadic peoples once belonged to vast empires that occupied extensive spaces; empires were based on trade routes, and nomadic tribes were their vectors. In Arabic, which, in part, inherits a nomadic conception of the world, the concept of *mamlaka* could be translated as 'route empire'. It includes the prevailing dynasty, which is always in movement, according to Ibn Khaldoun, with nomadic tribes travelling along routes toward the outskirts. The extensive projects of empires combined with nomads' capacity to travel great distances could provide the answer to why there are cities in the desert and explain their locations. Cities are typically found along such routes, especially at crossroads. Thus, mapping nomadic spaces must be intellectually dissociated from the definition by delineations of arid regions and their constraints. In some respects, a positive image of mobility must be established before veiled references to aridity and negative adaptations are made. Nomadism is not a life of roving through the desert; it is a highly-ordered lifestyle that offers a multitude of possibilities. That is why space itself is mobile, according to its nomadic usage. There are lessons to be learned here: the question 'where' leads to the question 'how'.

Oases and nomadic trails create 'routes', which form the structure for one of the first 'globalised' worlds (Figures 1-3). What was initially a projection becomes reality through nomadic trails. 'Route empires' (*mamlaka* can also be translated as 'empire of wealth') derived their wealth from them, as the power lies in the hands of those who control movement. The Mongol Empire, in reality, only existed for 30 years, even though its system of mobility influenced the Old World for thousands of years. Successive Arabian Empires disappeared and were divided into territorialised, fixed provinces. 'Trade routes' were abandoned in favour of borders and confines, and nomadic peoples were rejected and expulsed. Walls such as the Roman limes and Great Wall of China were built (Figures 4-5).

Why did settlement and sedentariness triumph? It could be that nomadic space knows only one limit: the horizon. With such a broad limit, time is the only regulator, and nomadic time is also unlimited. It is cyclical, like the seasons, and held fast in the present. Unlike sedentary societies, the accumulation of neither goods nor territory are the goals of nomadic societies, but rather the possibility to be at home everywhere.

Space with time

Nomadic space is not a static, synchronic space. Because of movement and calendric cycles, time is factored into the distances between different places. What is more, Evans Pritchard (1939) said that it was necessary to take into account other types of distances than merely metric ones. Among these, Jean Gallais took Prichard's 'structural distance', a hierarchical territoriality, and combined it with an 'ecological' distance, which he himself noticed between different peoples along the Niger River. Both types of distances required a time element, such as seasons or other periods of uncertainty into the structural spaces of distances, because nomadic societies and their spaces are ordered as such. Mobility's meaning here is specific; nomadic society is mobile because both space *and* time (of uncertainty and

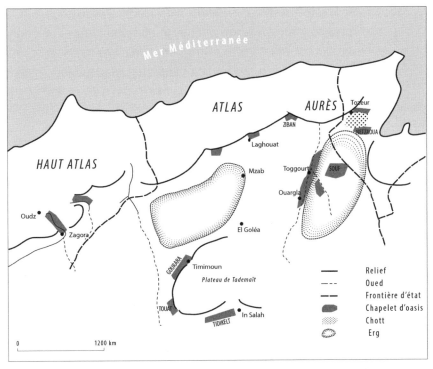

Fig. 1 Where are oases located? Where there is water.
Source: author.

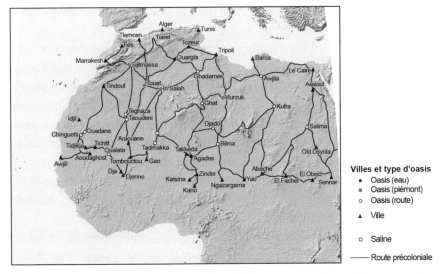

Fig. 2 Where are oases found? At crossroads.
Source: author.

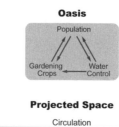

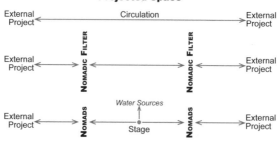

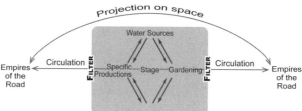

Fig. 3 Oases, outskirts, and nomadic links.
Source: author.

places) are mobile. This mobile space-time is that of a stratified society whose nomadic lords master distance and where the sedentary are forced to reside in stopping places along roads. The time and spaces are those of a hierarchical society anchored in certain places by roads. It lies below those of sedentary societies and above those of nomadic ones. After the element of time is introduced, the constraint of aridity can be considered only once plans for crossing the desert and the many options of mobile space-time have been accepted. Only *masters of distance* may make choices; sedentary dependants can only comply. Masters of distances can do this; their dependents must follow them.

This time-space (Figure 6) expresses a cultural conception of space, which is necessary for the definition of mobile space. However, it is also a hierarchical social space, which we must keep in mind. All time-spaces are not so transparent for everyone; from mobile societies to sedentary

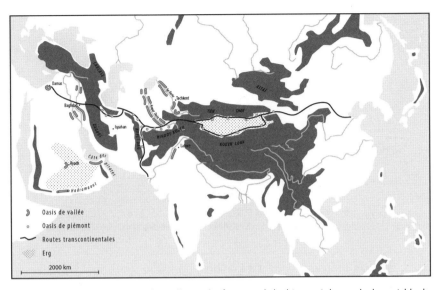

Fig. 4 The 'silk roads' form a global 'route' through the arid belt.
Source: author.

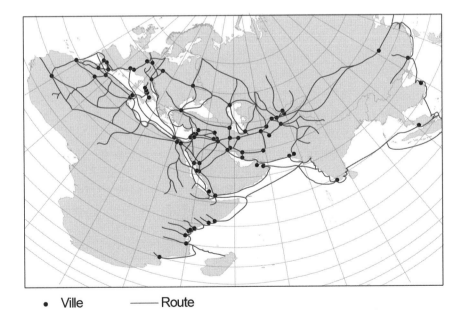

Fig. 5 The *mamlaka*, an empire of routes in the mid-11ᵗʰ century.
Source: author.

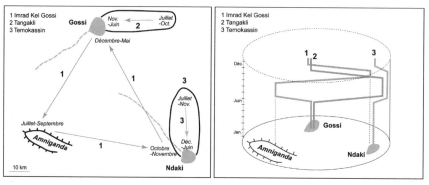

Fig. 6 Nomadic space as time-space.
Source: Jean Gallais (1975), Hägerstrand (1967, 1970), adapted using
O. Walther and D. Retaillé's 'Time Geography' (2012, unpublished).

ones, degrees indicate social rank. Thus, nomadic space includes stationary spaces in which nomadic peoples are present and therefore must be mapped in a mobile space of representation. In other words, they mustn't be mapped in a reverse fashion, as nomadic spaces in a stationary space of representation.

Introducing time into space is a step forward. However, as can be seen in this first example from the Malian Gourma region, places are determined by two attributes: location and character. Mobility mapped with time underlines social hierarchy. The lords, the Kel Gossi, occupy the best places at the best times, i.e. when lake water is plentiful, or when grazing land is abundant in the plains. Other Tuareg groups, who are socially 'inferior' to the Kel Gossi, may only use water sources and grazing lands several weeks or months after the lords. The lords – because they are lords – occupy the best places at the time that suits them best. Only they may choose. Lower groups are naturally less free and are bound by the calendar of their lords.

A second and larger example makes it possible to change scales in the continuity of space. The last trails and nomadic area of the Kel Ahaggar tribe, a tribe of Tuareg warriors, as P. Rognon described them (1963) in the late fifties, and as I described them in 1984–1987 (1989), open up nomadic spaces to a broader horizon. From January to March, the Kel Ahaggar live in the oases around their mountain. Lords and convoys leave in April for Amadror, where salt mines are exploited by quasi-slaves. From May until August, convoys loaded with salt travel south to allow for grazing in new, green pastures belonging to dependent tribes of the Kel Ahaggar who are free. In September, salt, livestock, and millet are exchanged before returning to Hoggar Mountain, where wheat and dates are collected. A final convoy travels to Tidikelt in Salah, Algeria, to buy manufactured products from Arab merchants from Gardhaïa. The circumambulatory territory of the Kel Ahaggar is a segment of a larger space, a memory of the 'route empires' as only the concept of *mamlaka* can express. Every place is a crossroads and, from this standpoint, a key place for a certain period of time. This is a characteristic of the mobile space of nomadic society. However, one place can be more significant than another. The convoys did not move everyone. Social distinction within Tuareg society determined both the time of year certain populations could occupy key places and what trails they could use. These 'periods' took place over the course of a year, but in fact the journeys took place more than once a month. The routes were a permanent travel support system, and livestock was moved from place to place along them. Using only the time-space of livestock grazing, we could make an analysis of nomadic space within a stationary framework. However, the spontaneous geography of resources always returns, and introducing time into space is not an easy task. Which time or, more specifically, which temporality? If the horizon is the limit, the continuous time of the present is necessary – not the timeless present of a synchronic map, but the immediacy of places in movement. Routes demonstrate this point better than do water sources or anything similar such as oases, lakes, or even rivers. They are resources on the condition of routes and crossing.

The different maps used in this chapter were created at different scales. The main routes with their various offshoots or meanderings were used for several centuries. The Sahara and Middle East were historically crisscrossed using these 'routes'. The map of *mamlaka* during the Abbassid Dynasty shows how nomadic space long provided a link between different parts of the world, even after the Empire disappeared. The 'route' survives, as long as it is kept alive, whatever its origin or location.

The maps above (Figures 1, 2, 4, 5) do not represent territories; the Empire was not a State with boundaries and borders. It was a 'rhizome', which is why many dynasties succeeded each other there, managing space with the nomadic spirit of the *assabiyya* that Ibn Khaldoun described. After generations of sedentary life, he showed how a new nomadic people took possession of the Empire and its cities for a new cycle. Mobile spaces and 'empires of routes' also have capital cities and centres of power that can move. The same is true in the continuous scale: the space of mobility extends over distances. If structural and ecological space-times now ensure the link, then the ontological question becomes who controls the distance, which is not space as an area but as an interval. The question of why,

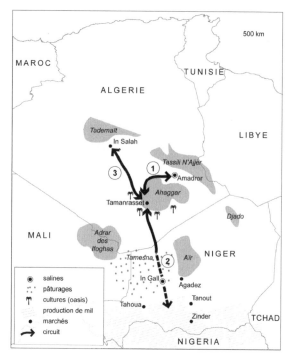

Fig. 7 The Kel Ahaggar territory until the 1980s.
Source: author.

where, or how these oases and cities and the nomadic routes linking these places were built shifts to: by whom? The answer may be nomadic peoples.

All time-space scales are linked to the general frame of nomadic movement (Figure 7). The seasonal travels of the Ahaggar people are regional; the local movement of the Gossi and their dependents over a continuous space are always guided by mobility. Different scales underline a hierarchy – one that is not spatial but social. Places change in the social hierarchy according to who is occupying them. Some sites go unoccupied or are occupied by farmers exploiting seasonal resources. Sometimes the masters of distance, simply passing through or staying for a while before moving to another site or locality, move the high place with them. Areas of nomadic space that are heavily travelled gain in importance, and are places in the strictest sense. A moving centrality is somewhere between the permanent territorialised concentration as a centre and a mobile space of impermanent crossing. The hierarchy between permanent settlements can also change according to the traffic on the routes. Hence, successive empires crossed the Sahara on a single main road, or rather successive roads that together formed the 'route'. During both times of security and insecurity, the road moved from the western, to the central, and the eastern Sahara. The same route has always existed. Even now, various migratory trails of people coming from Sub-Saharan Africa to North Africa and faraway Europe (for a minority) move according to circumstances. Time becomes part of space, and mobile space is ever-present, unlike synchrony. The synchrony of a static map in a stationary representation of space makes time timeless, where all time is condensed onto the earth in a single point. This topographical point is then mapped. This, however, does not represent the immediate nature of mobile space, whose movement mobilises it when points of crossing are mobile themselves.

Mapping mobile space

Mapping time and space together with routes means more than just superimposing, if we are to avoid a synchrony of places. Sites and localities can be represented synchronously, but not places produced by the crossing of movements. Lessons from nomadic peoples are useful here.

We showed above that mapping nomadic space means mapping places linked by nomadic travel patterns. Oases can only survive if linked to the world; one cannot live in the desert merely from the latter's resources. Two ontological possibilities requiring epistemological choices are also represented: a vertical aspect and a horizontal aspect. The former inquires and answers the question, 'Where are oases located, and why? Where and because there is water'. The horizontal aspect asks, 'Where are oases and what are they like? They follow movements of crossing and seasonal stages'. Finally, the continuity of scales is represented, which is not so much levels but extension. Mobility is the reason for this extension; routes and constant movement create a moving and moveable centrality. This is what must be mapped. Only then can the horizontal ontology of the space of mobility – which is both phenomenological and constructed – be mapped through spatial polymorphy, different from a stationary or fixed representation of space. To integrate polymorphy, we must first represent movement. In previous papers, since 2005, I have proposed three types of movements without fixed references: convergence, divergence, and crossing, which are self-referenced. Several papers published with Olivier Walther since 2011 attempt to strengthen this idea by applying this hypothesis to different empirical cases. This was the goal in moving from an anthropological representation of space (nomadic space) to a methodological model (mobile space). A mobility map that uses movement to highlight differences – and that is not the result of a previously differentiated space – may be more difficult to produce, but it offers an opportunity for progress.

It began like a contest. The systematic summary of spatial analysis I proposed in 1986 presented the structure of geographical expertise (Retaillé, 1987). Since that time, I have identified this implicit structure as 'spontaneous geography'. Points, lines, surfaces (on a map) for geographical locations, distances, and areas allow us to highlight processes of spatial production. This is also accomplished by polarisation into points, locations, and places, organisation as distribution and hierarchy, and delimitation into regions and territories.

Then, I contested this initial idea of movement and places as with the notion of *consequences*. Movements of convergence, divergence, and crossing were first identified as expansion, contraction, and exchange. I may have been influenced by a geopolitical point-of-view for the rest. Nevertheless, I wanted to argue that places are loci of exchange, but not only mercantile. Convergence, divergence, and crossing do not carry an assumption of space. Rather, space is the result and thus avoids an assumption of exchange. Before exchanges can be made, distances must be overcome through convergence and crossing.

The following representations attempt to present such a paradigm of 'mobile space'. Instead of identifying structural elements and then trying to consider how these elements can take new forms as flows intensify, I start by considering the three main forms resulting from a state of permanent movement. As indicated on the first line of the figure 8, these are identified, respectively, as divergence, convergence, and crossing movements.

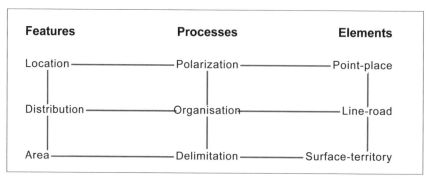

Fig. 8 The structure of stationary spatial representation.
Source: author.

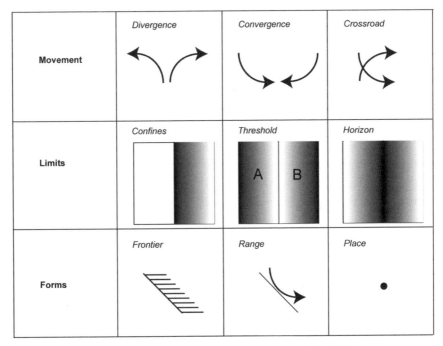

Fig. 9 The representation of mobile space: an essay.
Source: author with Olivier Walther.

Movement can lead to *divergence* when it stems from its place of departure, *convergence* when guided to what will become a centre, and generalised *crossing* when it occurs in a centrifugal or centripetal direction (Figure 9).

Every movement produces a particular type of limit. These confines, for example, constitute the limits of divergence, thresholds form the limits of a convergence, and the horizon is the only limit that can be formed from a globalised, crisscrossing exchange of flows. Confines are defined as a type of boundary with a single edge – the inner one. Beyond it, uniformity opens up the possibility of exploration, or conquest, and is a reminder of the threat of invasion. Similarly, thresholds are defined as limits with two distinct sides: one facing inwards (the boundary) and the other facing outwards (the border). The horizon is different from both in that it represents a limit with no edge, neither inner nor outer. Mobility is at the heart of the definition of horizon, since the position of a social actor can change without him having to move (for example, when he is part of a constant flow of information). Despite movement, the horizon is unattainable and cannot be reached by moving forwards, as it simultaneously extends backwards.

Within the space of movement, the most basic forms are also in motion. A line limiting expansion is a frontier, the area of movement is a range, and the crossing of movements is a place. The dominant stationary paradigm does not tolerate blank spots on maps. Thus, the aim of historic cartographic exploration has been to erase the unknown and name and claim things upon the Earth. The mobile paradigm is free from this imperative. When movement comes first, expansion pushes boundaries back to the confines: this is where the frontier can be found. The encounter with another frontier produces a crystallised boundary, referring back to the centre of emission. This is what we call 'social and spatial convergence', which is increased attachment to identity and territory. Finally, crossing any kind of border results in a multitude of possible exchanges, which we call 'places'. The principal difference between our approach and previous attempts at characterising mobility is that our main focus is not a localised stock (of people, foreign investment, etc.) characterised by their x and y co-ordinates, but by the flow itself, which we try to understand through its intensity and interactions with other flows.

This approach invites us to reconsider how divergence, convergence, or the crossing of flows lead to the creation of various kinds of frontiers, ranges, and places, giving rise to the question: What new types of limits may arise from these processes?

The nature of place, which has long been thought of as rooted in site and location, is now being challenged by the ubiquity of movement. Some authors have argued that, in fact, two types of places exist: authentic places, which allow memory to take root, and non-places, which are ephemeral products resulting from the intersection of contemporary flows, and are associated with movement and intersections (synonymous with confusion, conflict, and dispersion) (Augé, 1995). However, the complexity of places produced by mobile spaces calls for a re-examination of the aforementioned dichotomy and a conception of place that can account for mobility. In classical geography, place was defined by its fixity, its 'genius', and its natural quality, which enable identity-building. Depriving place of this symbolic feature results in 'sites'. Starting in the 1980s, the field of geography nevertheless recast the notion of *place* as an ephemeral spatial object produced by individuals, in which they gathered. Massey (1991) wrote that this place was not only comprised of its internal attributes but was above all a product of its relationships to the outer world. Place has since been increasingly perceived as a locus for action and practices, locations of social relationships, and sites with meaning. Because places are not only produced by the 'local social world' but also by the characteristics of location and meaning attached thereto, geography has successively seen societies not as existing 'in' or 'on' space, but rather 'with' space (Retaillé, 1997). Places ought not to be defined according to a particular scale but by their ability to abolish distance: in certain places, the distance between social actors approaches zero. Hence, the fundamental question geography should ask is, 'Does distance exist?'.

Such characteristics allow for a clearer distinction between places, sites, and localities: places are principally conceived as ephemeral re-compositions resulting from the intersecting of contemporary social networks; whereas sites refer to a location where enduring infrastructure is associated with localities, such as cities or markets. Put differently, localities are sites with a name and a limit, whereas places are geographical locales of various size and temporal configuration. At the root of 'place' lies movement, rather than fixity. This is the lesson to be learned from contemporary globalisation. Goods, people, capital, services, and knowledge move according to their own rhythm, amplitude, and direction: fast or slow, strong or weak, reversible or irreversible. The state boundaries of the international system slow down or speed up this movement depending on whether they function as filters or interfaces. Places in a globalised world thus take on new meaning. They are no longer fixed but mobile, animated by waves and born from their intersection and interference

When movement is constant, spatial differentiation between places is constantly at work. The space of flows ceases to be an abstraction crossed by immaterial flows of capital or information. Rather it is real space, in which individuals bestow meaning upon places and go about their daily activities. This change has been theorised as a shift from the world as the *sum* of all places to its *essence as world* and the possible relationship of each place with all others through their proliferation created by movement. Cities, for example, which were considered like small worlds unto themselves due to the fact that they concentrate a fraction of the world's economic and cultural wealth, have become integrated into the world (Lévy, 2000).

The temporary clusters spontaneously formed during international fairs are one of the most obvious examples of the ability of places to be defined as ephemeral intersections of the continual movement constantly animating the world. Scholarly discussion of the importance of these events to the global political economy supports the idea that fairs have several features in common with the Sahel, as described earlier: trans-local links, intensive exchanges, the construction and maintenance of social networks, confrontation, the exchanging of ideas and knowledge, and the identification of, selection of, and interaction with new partners (Bathelt, 2006; Maskell et al., 2006; Glückler, 2007). What these events show in particular is that permanent geographical proximity is not an absolute criterion for contemporary firms. Indeed, they may favour ephemeral meetings during which information crucial to the development of new products is exchanged. These places depend on a system of central nodes which allows a connection to 'the global political economy and provide participating firms with access to new technologies, market trends, and potential partners' (Bathelt and Schuldt, 2008: 855). Firms gather in a small space for a limited time, enabling a connection to world markets, and they benefit from a high density of local partners.

This theoretical proposition of a mobile space derived from a Saharo-Sahelian nomadic society most notably addresses the notion of place. What is a place? The confusion between site, locality, and place requires distinction so that *place* may refer exclusively to a localised event, be it ephemeral or ongoing. It should also be noted that the true particularity of place is that it erases distance, thus creating the conditions for unity but also precluding the possibility of conferring dimensions on it. Hence, in order to designate a 'place', it is first necessary to identify the link, and thus the movement, which first created it. In this respect, it is difficult to consider scale an object. As a matter of fact, within a stationary paradigm, scale is a defining tool or, at best, an attribute. With mobile space, the definition of a relevant scale and nesting levels is no longer a necessary methodological stage. We argue that scale is no longer a miraculous tool for describing spatial organisation. In our view, places can be seen principally in terms of locales where the local and global can be observed simultaneously. Most notably, we argue that if the Earth limits global scale, this is not the case for local scale, whose extent can vary greatly, from the size of a room to that of a cultural area, or a political and ideological 'territory'.

Bibliography

Augé, M., 1995. *Non lieux, introduction à une anthropologie de la surmodernité,* Paris: Seuil.

Bairoch, P., 1985. *De Jericho à Mexico,* Paris: Gallimard.

Bathelt, H. & Schuldt, N., 2008. 'Between Luminaires and Meat Grinders: International Trade Fairs as Temporary Clusters', *Regional Studies* 42: 853–68.

Bathelt, H., 2006. 'Geographies of Production: Growth Regimes in Spatial Perspective 3 – Toward a Relational View of Economic Action and Policy', *Progress in Human Geography* 30: 223–36.

Evans-Pritchard, E., 1939. *The Nuer: A Description of the Modes of Livelihood and Political Institutions of a Nilotic People*, Oxford: Clarendon Press.

Gallais J., 1975. *Pasteurs et paysans du Gourma. La condition sahélienne*, Bordeaux: CEGET-CNRS.

Glückler, J., 2007. 'Economic Geography and the Evolution of Networks', *Journal of Economic Geography* 7: 619–34.

Hägerstrand, T., 1967. *Innovation Diffusion as a Spatial Process*, Chicago: University of Chicago Press.

Hägerstrand, T., 1970. 'What About People in Regional Science?', *Papers of the Regional Science Association*, 24: 1–12.

Jessop, B., Brenner N., & Jones, M., 2008. 'Theorizing Sociospatial Relations', *Environment and Planning D: Society and Space*, 26: 389–401.

Khaldoun, Ibn (1375–1377), 2002. *Muqaddima [The Book of Examples]*, Paris: Gallimard, 'La Pléiade'.

Lévy, J., 2000. 'A User's Guide to World-spaces', *Geopolitics* 5 (2): 67–84.

Maskell, P., Bathelt, H. & Malmberg, A., 2006. 'Building Global Knowledge Pipelines: The Role of Temporary Clusters, *European Planning Studies* 14: 997–1013.

Massey, D., 1991. 'A Global Sense of Place', *Marxism Today*, June: 24–29.

Mumford, L., 1961. *The City in History,* New York: Harcout, Brace & World.

Retaillé, D., 1987. 'Les éléments constitutifs de l'espace géographique' in AFDG, *Actes de l'université d'été 1986*, Lyon: AFDG, pp. 25–28.

Retaillé, D., 1989. 'La conception nomade de la ville', *URBAMA,* 20, Le nomade, l'oasis et la ville, pp. 21–34.

Retaillé, D., 1989. 'Le destin du pastoralisme nomade en Afrique', *L'Information Géographique*, 3: 103–115.

Retaillé, D., 2005. 'L'espace mobile', in Antheaume B, Giraut, F (eds.), *Le territoire est mort. Vive les territoires!* Paris: IRD, pp. 175–202.

Retaillé, D., 2009. 'Malaise dans la géographie, l'espace est mobile', in Vanier M (ed.) *Territoires, territorialité, territorialisation*, Rennes: Presses Universitaires de Rennes, pp. 97–114.

Retaillé, D., 2013. 'From Nomadic to Mobile Space: A Theoretical Experiment (1976–2012)', in. Miggelbrink, J., Habeck, O.J. & Koch, P. (eds.), *Nomadic and Indigenous Spaces,* Farnham: Ashgate, pp. 54–75.

Retaillé, D. & Walther, O., 2011a. 'Spaces of Uncertainty: A Model of Mobile Space in the Sahel', *Singapore Journal of Tropical Geography*, 1 (32): 85–101.

Retaillé, D. & Walther, O (2011b). 'Guerre et terrorisme au Sahara-Sahel: la reconversion des savoirs nomads'. *L'Information Géographique*, 3 (76): 51–68.

Retaillé, D. & Walther, O. (2012). 'New Ways of Conceptualizing Space and Mobility: Lessons from the Sahel to the Globalized World'. Luxembourg: *CEPS/INSTEAD Working Papers*, n° 24.

Rognon, P., 1963. 'La confédération des nomades Kel Ahhagar', in Bataillon, C, *Nomades et nomadisme au Sahara,* Paris: UNESCO, pp. 63–79.

Part 4
Who is the Author of this Map?

Chapter 12

'My' Maps?
On Maps and their Authors

Patrick Poncet

'How do I make my maps?' In this question, the operative word is 'my'. Is that surprising? Can a map have an owner? An intelligent owner? In fact, an author? Aren't maps just well-made or poorly-made objects that are true or false, just or 'unjust'? My answer is 'no'.

I would simply like to present a vision of cartography here. This vision leans towards a theory of maps based on how they are made and questions the role of the mapmaker. Is he or she a technician, an author, or a layman?

It is also a lesson in cartography that attempts to consider all that comprises cartographic work, to give a form to this heterogeneous mass and arrive at universal recommendations for simple implementation free of technical esotericism.

The itinerary is as follows: We will begin by studying what makes a map, in order to establish a general definition. We will then address specific differences, as well as different kinds of cartographies. Finally, we will propose ways to make cartography something for everyone.

What makes a map

Beyond the formal definition of a map proposed by Jacques Lévy (2003), with which we all essentially agree, this article proposes a modulation – another way of saying that what makes a map has to do with the function of this type of representation.

A specific speech tool

Maps are often (and erroneously) thought to be mere illustrations that can be interpreted in their most basic sense: as image elements intended to enrich a publication, complementing a text.

What all maps have in common is that they are a means of expression like any other, which is reinforced by the fact that many maps – such as navigation maps – have no text at all. And yet, it is difficult to establish a universal hierarchy between texts and maps that would make either a map an appendix to a text (or another work) or text a secondary element within a map.

This quandary can be avoided by considering what distinguishes cartographic expression from other means of expression. We can conclude that what makes a map a map is its capacity to 'talk about' certain spatial 'facts' with greater accuracy than a text. The goal then, as in all forms of discursive production, is simply to make maps better at saying what they have to say than texts, and texts better at saying what they have to say than maps.

Euclidean irreducibility and non-cartography

Another question within the academic cartographic community is, *Is a map a flat object*? For example, saying that the planar aspect of maps is a defining element, and that globes as such are not maps, would exclude many representations of space that may act or serve as maps. This, of course, is the crux of the teachings of classic cartography, which anchors its discourse in the technical certitudes found in introductory courses on geodesy, projections, and their adaptation to such-or-such use.

Cartography enjoys flattening the Earth. Not content with this, it has also flattened buildings, sometimes casting a disdainful eye on medieval maps, like those that replicate drawings of the urban Jerusalemite landscape in plan view. Yet, if we consider all these 'views of space' (in both senses of the term) that propose a top-down view of the world as maps, we can better understand the common nature of a map, albeit excluding all representations that structure the image in successive maps.

Even though contemplating a globe at some distance uses perspective and distorts the map at the edges of the visible disc, this is only an effect of classic projection. Upon closer examination, we understand that the globe is a quasi-planar map. However in both cases, and contrary to 'landscape', a 'perspective view' is not *de facto* an instrument of cartographic semiology. No view hierarchises information. At best, centring a map and its periphery can establish order, but doing so depends on the drawing of the map itself. This flaw in maps is dealt with by trying to reduce its effect.

This does not mean perspective effects cannot be used in maps. However, they must not visually modify the content of the message (a phenomenon's intensity, for example) based on maps' geographical position. In the case of so-called 'proportional symbols' maps, the basemap can be a perspective view, but the symbols must not be significantly affected. This is a generalisation of the projection principle, which is typically centred, and therefore offers nothing more than perspective views of the Earth.

The map is fundamentally a Euclidean object, meaning it can only use Euclidean means to show that which is or is not Euclidean in the space of societies. Whether planar, convex, or a more curious shape, a spatial representation is only a map if it proposes the irreducibly Euclidean use of an image without planes.

This means that maps are not always the best tools for geography – far from it. Sometimes, they can't even be used at all.

Local reading, visual objects, cartographic totality

The final aspect that seems to define a 'common genus' (following the Aristotelian method to defining things) for mapping has to do with how we read cartographic images. To set aside the alternative of 'maps for looking at' and 'maps for reading' (Bertin, 1977, 147), one can image how to use the map as a simple visual game, with zoom-in/zoom-out and/or forward/backward effects that pause each time the viewer 'grabs' a visual object. The ultimate goal of the cartographer therefore is simply to create an image that features 'visual stops' in this game, guiding viewers as they 'find' the various visual objects the map contains, and which the legend will allow him to link to geographic objects (social, natural, etc.). Thus do these visual objects become places through this 'local' reading, and hence bearer of the map's messages.

Perhaps a cartographer's work is similar to that of a classical painter, who also seeks to lead the eye with colour, or a draftsman who avails himself of lines. Yet, cartography is distinct in that it leads the eye less by way of form – which is often figurative – than by scale, which allows us to identify objects without knowing their forms a priori.

It is on this last point that cartographic art reveals its requirements. To work well, a map must be based on a total processing of the image which, to not be reduced to a convoluted mass of more-or-less geometric shapes, must have a complex apparatus of attributes that build meaning. This includes the background, perimeter, typography, titles, legend, masthead, orientation, format, style, visual and editorial environment, media, and potential damage. In short, knowing how to optimally accommodate this cumbersome expressive paraphernalia is an art of controlling interpretation.

Differences in mapping

If we accept that a common mapping exists – in other words, several things that allow us to classify such-or-such representation of space in the vast category of maps – we must nonetheless acknowledge the diversity of the unit this formed. While no two maps are alike, some greatly resemble each other. In other words, subsets exist, and understanding their specifics is a way of learning to map, a practice akin to imitating styles in art.

Information and communication

One of the worst methods of differentiating maps is based on the distinction between information and communication. In this approach, there would be maps that inform, which are objective, just, and true. Conversely, they would be communicative maps, which operate like ads whose good intentions are a priori suspect. Jacques Lévy explains how this distinction may appear irrelevant and outdated today (see the chapter, 'Mapping Ethics'). However, unscrupulous cartographers have always served the propaganda of power. A map is merely a means to serve intentions, be they good or bad.

However, the idea that information precludes communication doesn't hold up under scrutiny. Information and communication are either the same thing, in their broadest sense, or the former is part of the latter, technically speaking. 'Information' goes in one direction only, either by diffusion or reception. 'Communication' goes both ways, as well as in a loop, and also applies to communication with itself. There is no information exchange without intent to communicate assumptions or choice. This last point is often a cliché in introductory cartography courses, but then we attempt to limit the choices. The choice then is no choice.

Mapping is, and has always been, synonymous with communicating (with itself first and foremost). A map is an interrogation. The act of mapping therefore is not a revelation. If it is only the act of producing a discourse about space in specific graphical terms, then the difference between maps is probably to be found the differences between 'mappers' – a difference that highlights other, deeper distinctions.

Cartographer, Author, Layman

To the question, 'Who makes maps?', one is nowadays forced to answer 'Everyone!' Some lament this fact, saying that cartography should be left to professionals. Yet, pirates have routinely forgotten their treasure maps in the smoky taverns of the Port of Amsterdam for a long time now, and they weren't even cartographers! Just yesterday, my neighbour was scribbling a map to the hardware store from the Alouettes roundabout in a notebook. All these usurpers are enough to drive so-called 'real' cartographers crazy. They can also irritate those who draw spaces from above with a touch of creativity and who, since a 1943 French decree, may register as cartographers at the *Maison des artistes* in France.

There are at least three species of cartographers: those whose job is to map territories – 'cartographers'; those whose paid avocation is to give a visual form to an often quite abstract space – authors who sign their maps, 'designer'; and those who, one day, thinking that a good sketch is better than a long explanation, try to talk about a 'where' by drawing on a checkered tablecloth in the local pub – or for whom GoogleMaps® is second nature.

These are, of course, ideal-types. Often, makers of real maps straddle two or three of these categories, at least partially.

Data, spaces, and spatialities

So, if there are at least three types of cartographers, then there are also at least three types of maps: data maps, space maps, and maps of spatiality.

The first are those most often produced by 'cartographers'. For them, data is legitimate by definition; they encode legitimate answers to no-less legitimate questions. For example, where do most elderly people live in France? Age distribution is available by county. Thus, a map with a visual representation of 'old' age is possible once the choice has been made.

Map designers address the issue as a problem by inverting: how old are places in France? This means looking for any legitimate way – and possibly the same statistical sources – to give a clear shape to the map of the population distribution by age. Ultimately, they will probably choose a map that very clearly shows a well-formed space whose content, in terms of age, somehow defines the 'age' of old age. And if nothing comes up, they won't make the map.

Finally, there are those who, generally speaking, never take up a pen to map seniors but who more often describe their spatial skills with words, spread their spatiality before their peers, and only occasionally give shape to them by sketching a map – *Homo habitans*' ultimate demonstration of his mastery of space.

Instrument, object, and media

We measure the immense scope of the cartographic spectrum. Using data to build a tracking device or using one's own personal experience of space to keep everyday conversation alive are completely different things. And making beautiful spaces appear as if by magic, like the aurora borealis, is another thing altogether.

A third way to distinguish between maps is to look at their specific function. They can be tools for measuring, evaluating, or navigating; or objects that we show and contemplate that are, for the most part, separable from the context of their production. They are somehow cognitively self-supporting. Like 'coffee table' books, they condense ideas and end up being messages in themselves. The countless world maps gracing entrance halls and executive offices of large corporations are just this. And in homes, the most curious atlases adorn both bourgeois' and *bobos'* end tables, bathrooms, and shelves. Yet today, maps are increasingly media, that is to say instruments of communication. They are used to discuss, share information, establish one's presence, acknowledge affiliation, maintain spatial skills, and explore 'elsewheres', but especially to explore 'here'. Maps have, in this way, always contributed to social links.

Encoding, tongues and language

A final distinction is based on the nature of the medium of exchange, namely encoding, language in the cultural sense, or language as a means of communication. While the choice of these three terms is certainly debatable, it is their differences that concern us here.

There are maps whose basic principle is a form of encoding based on a code or coding that is intended to be unambiguous, precise, and to favour a 'local' reading, even if its structured nature can also produce an interesting overall image. This is the emblematic case of geological maps, topographic maps, and, of course, simple thematic maps. Due to their systematic nature and theoretical underpinnings, these maps are often produced automatically, thus diluting the notion of 'author'.

Other maps borrow their form of expression from the 'tongues' category. This implies an aesthetic and cartographic culture of reference as well as references (often-implicit) to other maps, connoted colours, or known forms. There is also a certain creativity of expression, the invention of new visual forms to marry and best render the spatial reality one wishes to represent. For some, such maps have much in common with art. At the very least, they are subject to a 'design,' that is a thoughtful, interactive, and balanced combination of drawing, form, plan, and project.

Finally, some maps are the product of the banality of language, of efficient and spontaneous expression, and of the rules of composition whose relevance depends greatly on the context and interlocutors it links. Whether scrawled on a bit of paper or 'webmapped', they comply with norms only as necessary. These norms are often brought about by the technical tools used to create them, and these norms can becomenormative shackles, especially if they are recent. Otherwise, the language used in particular circumstances is a matter of negotiation between actors.

Cartography, 'mapdesign', and 'carto'

The following table summarizes and identifies three key distinctions in cartographic practice: cartography, *mapdesign*, and *carto*. These result in three cartographic types: maps, cartographies, and cartos.

The word 'carto' should be understood as the equivalent of the word 'photo', meaning a complex technique that has become a popular art and, today, a medium. Thanks to applications like Instagram®, essentially anyone can upload pictures taken with their mobile phone to online publications comparable to those of Facebook® or Twitter®.

Of course these pure forms are, in practise, never totally separate. In other words, they result from rather different approaches and skillsets that are sometimes difficult to combine and often require different kinds of expertise.

'Occupations' Aspects	Cartography	Mapdesign	Carto
Things	maps	cartographies	cartos
People	cartographer	author	anyone
Functions	instrument	object	media
Information	data	spaces	spatialities
Means	code	tongue	language

Table 1 The three kinds of cartographic 'occupations'.

Making a difference

Differences in the mapping world are the product of different ways of imagining and realising cartographic work. As a map design specialist, I would like to sketch out the vision and practices that give 'classic' cartographers an opportunity to experiment with novel avenues of expression. This is not meant as a critique of classic cartography but rather as an invitation to extend the cartographer's 'flight areas', to use a metaphor from aeronautical engineering.

The limits of Bertin's cartography and the logic of image

Freeing ourselves from the logics of Jacques Bertin's 'semiotic graphics' is not vain. In fact, it is necessary for those who wish to go beyond classic cartography, despite the persistent debate over whether to teach the powerful principles of free cartography directly or to begin by inculcating 'simplified' bases so that students can grasp the limits and surpass them.

But let's be clear: Bertinian principles are not completely without merit. They are even quite successful as regards graphics in general (Bertin, 1977). Their extrapolation in the field of cartography, however, raises a problem. Most notably we criticise the fact that they offer a false cartographic theory, since they only work in laboratories and textbook cases specifically designed to demonstrate that they work. Moreover, they are not attached to any cartographic, aesthetic, or artistic tradition, which reinforces their abstract, inapplicable nature. In any case, it's simple: nearly all of the professional cartographers I have met during my career recognise the need to apply these rules 'intelligently'. To be honest, if these cartographic rules cause practical problems, it is simply because they are not geographical.

Let us take the clearest example of this: Bertin's position that shape 'has no selectivity' (Bertin, 1977, p. 225). The evidence he provides is twofold. To begin, he forms the letters UNESCO and UNESCU with small identical shapes on a background of different small shapes. It's true that it is difficult to read the words, and more importantly, to differentiate them. He then shows an ethnic map of an African region wherein each village is identified by a symbol whose shape corresponds to a specific ethnic group. It's true that nothing is very clear from this map. Yet, Bertin is right on one point: while it works, and we can indeed use different shapes to map a spatial structure, it does not work every time. Herein lies the difficulty. Every map is unique because of the space and phenomenon it represents. However, it may be that in certain spatial configurations, form can be a variable used by the cartographer to distinguish two zones, as shown in the two cases below, where letters (forms) are used to map zones. In the map on the left, space is divided into zones, so this works. However, in the map on the right, it does not. It is in this sense that only the 'logic of the image' does or does not validate a mode of cartographic expression (Bertin, 1977).

This example demonstrates the nature of the weakness of Bertinian theory. It considerably reduces the cartographer's expressive room for manoeuvre, not allowing certain resources *a priori* that might otherwise

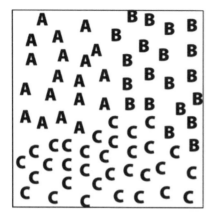 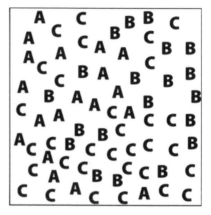

Fig. 1 Shapes, maps, and spaces.

have worked. Instead, it frees other, more 'classic' means to express another dimension of a problem, for instance, that could not have been expressed otherwise.

Bertinian semiotics thus has but one virtue: damage control, in other words to ensure that apprentice cartographers do not make mistakes and do not produce maps that say the opposite of what they intend. However, this comes at the exorbitant cost of limiting cartographic creativity and drastically reducing the possible range of expressions used to represent spaces. Yet, there is no guarantee that this safeguard leads to optimal representation.

Shapes can be both efficient (left image) or inefficient (right image) for mapping territories. Here, efficiency depends on the geographical space to be mapped.

Three cartographic freedoms

After these interesting contributions (and, in any case, precursors to Jacques Bertin), even if cartography has long been an efficiently practised technology, cartography logically became more logically complicated, giving rise to a number of strange debates. So-called 'statistical' cartography has taken on a prominent place in the teaching of cartography, distancing it further and further from the 'culture of image'.

I will now discuss three of these unnecessary complications (or badly-founded debates) and three alternative, critical ways of seeing that return some freedom to cartography.

Choropleth mapping and proportional symbols are possible for all variables. The first opportunity for leeway we identified for a cartographer is to clearly distinguish between the spatial form of the phenomena he wishes to represent and the cartographic form in which he chooses to represent them. This principle of distinction results in the need to build a link between reality and its representation. This is consistent with the idea that mapping does not simplify reality, but rather builds an image that represents an idea we have of reality.

Our intention here is not so much to criticise maps that are too 'respectful' of the punctual, areal, or linear nature of the data they represent as cartographic processes that focus more on the statistical nature of data than on whether or not this nature is geographical. We often hear that so-called 'rate' variables should be represented using choropleth maps (in colour or grey scales), and that 'absolute' data variables require maps with proportional symbols. At the same time, choropleth maps with 'absolute' variables (that is, colouring territories based on the number of such-or-such a thing in such-or-such territory, for example) would also be forbidden. This rule is wrong. It ignores the nature – geographical or otherwise – of rates and is a simplistic idea of cartographic interpretation. Absolute values can always be depicted in colour ranges.

The first reason for this is synthetic: What matters most in a map is the overall structure that emerges. It is the form seen by the observer's eye. And these forms, as we have said, are a result of the cartographer's ability to render the visualisation of graphic objects. Only the overall impression and end result count. However, in a fairly regular 'territorial' frame (which, moreover, is preferable, statistically speaking), the overall structure appears just as clearly on a choropleth map as, for example, on a map with proportional circles. Often it is even better, because of the Euclidean topology of choropleth maps and the shading effects of colour, which can help to define spaces. Finally, cluster effects (see infra) are a way for maps with proportional symbols to recover a bit of graphical leeway in this regard.

The second reason is analytical: if the territorial frame is regular, an absolute variable will automatically be represented as a density (the corresponding density map would be identical), and thereby a variable of geographic rate. If the frame is not regular, then it is still possible to (discretely) indicate the territorial limits to allow for a proper local reading of the map. Either way, if these limits are absent, the reader usually knows that the absolute quantity represented by a colour does not extend over the entire surface of that colour on the map. Intuitively, there is a tendency to consider that, at a given point on the map, the 'local' representative value tends toward that indicated by the colour. In practice, choropleth maps for absolute values usually work very well.

However, regarding rate variables, the reasoning must be pushed to the limits. A rate variable is only geographical (we should even say 'cartographic') if the rate is calculated according to surface unit. This makes it possible to eliminate statistical territorial limits on the map. Otherwise, any other type of rate is actually an absolute magnitude, excepting the objects for which absolute magnitude is uniformly distributed (equal density), which is rare. In other words, an indicator and its choropleth cartography then raises the usual problems.

More generally, any variable can be considered an indicator. One must then decide whether it is possible to give it an actual meaning of density, that is, to allow it to indicate a strictly valid measurement anywhere on the map by erasing the cartographic limits of territories.

Finally, let us note that the idea that quantity variables for territories should be represented by proportional symbols means choosing a position (centring) for these symbols. However, the loss of geographic information caused by this 'pointalisation' process is probably worse than the local inaccuracy caused by choropleth representation of absolute variables, or, as is often the case, interpolation of 'smoothed' or gradients maps.

The proportionality of symbols is arbitrary. A second cartographic belief that needs to be done away with imposes on cartographers a single rule of proportionality between the size mapped and the size of the proportional symbols. The classic rule is to make the surface area of symbols proportional to the value they represent (Bertin, 1977). This rule should, on the contrary, again be seen as pure construction. It is an arbitrary choice that depends on the nature of each cartographic project. In addition to the lack of solid justification for the rule of surface proportionality, several other objections can made regarding it.

The first is elementary : Size is in no way comparable to surface area. Height and width - which are much more easily compared than surface areas - are possibilities, however. The ability to compare is, of course, closely linked to the form of objects. In this way, the surface of a ring is undoubtedly fairly tricky to estimate. And what to make of certain principles that tell us to make the volume of proportional balls proportional to the mapped surface ?! Comparing drawn volumes is quite misleading.

However, there is a second and more interesting objection. Choosing the square root of the mapped value as a function of proportionality serves no other purpose (from a cartographic point-of-view) than to seek a compromise between the (graphic) commensurability of symbols and the reality of the 'weight' they represent. In this specific case, because of the non-linearity of the root function, commensurability is given an advantage to the detriment of comparability. But the opposite choice can also be made.

Take, for instance, maps that represent the size of cities in a country with proportional circles. This is usually the population size and is represented by circles with proportional areas. In this case, small cities have the advantage of better visibility as compared to large ones (square root function). Let us then imagine that we want to represent city sizes by their urbanity, defined as the number u of potential relationships among inhabitants. So, for n inhabitants: $u(n) = n(n-1)/2$. We see that urbanity changes exponentially relative to the population. Indeed, the larger the city's population is, the more weight each additional inhabitant adds in terms of urbanity, since the greater the number of inhabitants, the greater the number of potential relationships. When n is very large, the function $u(n)$ is close to the function $n^2/2$ and thus behaves (increases) like the n^2 function. Why, then, should this magnitude be represented by using a proportionality of symbols according to a square root, that is, according to the function $n^{1/2}$? And what about in the case of balls with proportional volumes, by the function $n^{1/3}$ (cubic root)?

If, on the contrary, we decide that there is a cartographic choice, the following generalisation can be proposed: The size of proportional symbols is calculated by a function such as x^a, where x is the mapped value and a is a power adapted to the nature of the phenomenon and/or to the chosen compromise of representation between commensurability and comparability. If a tends towards 2, we would tend toward a correct representation of urbanity (or associated phenomena). If, however, a is closer to ½, then anti-urbanity is emphasised. To illustrate, let us say that, if a equals 2, a map of cities is a map of building heights, and if a's value is ½, then it represents residential lots.

Every map is a 'cartogram'. Cartograms are maps whose backgrounds seem distorted, much more strangely than the strangest projection.

Cartograms have flourished in recent years, having become quite easy to produce. Yet, they are often still confused with anamorphoses (maps where the distortion itself constitutes all of the information). They are often criticised for their imprecision and the lack of rigour of the distortion methods used (contrary to projection methods), and so on. Cartograms have become mysterious, even esoteric objects for certain cartographers and are often best understood outside of their community.

Cartograms are in fact a universal idea of cartography: More room is given to spaces that matter more with regard to the topic at hand. Technically, they have nothing to do with projections and are independent of them. Classic maps with an equivalent projection – which maintains the surface areas – are therefore cartograms whose distortion variable is the surface area. A classic map with conformal projection that respects angles locally (local shapes) could be redrawn to respect the surface areas using a cartogram.

More generally, every base map can be distorted using an anamorphic function according to variable x^n, where x is the density variable (population for example), and n is a positive or negative power. If n equals 1, a classic cartogram base is obtained. If x is the population, this base is well-enough adapted to take into account phenomena linked to co-presence and urban concentrations – in other words, to reveal cities' inner-workings in detail. If n is negative, an anti-cartogram base is obtained, that is, an inverse cartogram. Calculated, for example, based on the mathematical inverse of population, it is interesting for mapping traffic-related phenomena, because it produces a filamentous base which underscores population areas intruding into the great human 'deserts'. If n equals zero, the base is that of a simple projection map. In one sense, this base is the best for handling telecommunication issues, at least those that introduce ubiquity phenomena that are free of the geography of populations and their movements.

However, we must recall that the general approach of (anti)cartograms is that the distortion of the map's base is only a technique and does not in itself carry any information (unlike 'anamorphoses'). The 'quality' of its distortion is secondary, as it serves only one purpose: To change either the internal sizes (cartogram) or internal forms (anti-cartogram) of a map to produce graphic objects that are relevant to the geographical issue represented, objects whose clarity and sharpness will be enhanced through the use of colour and visual effects (see below).

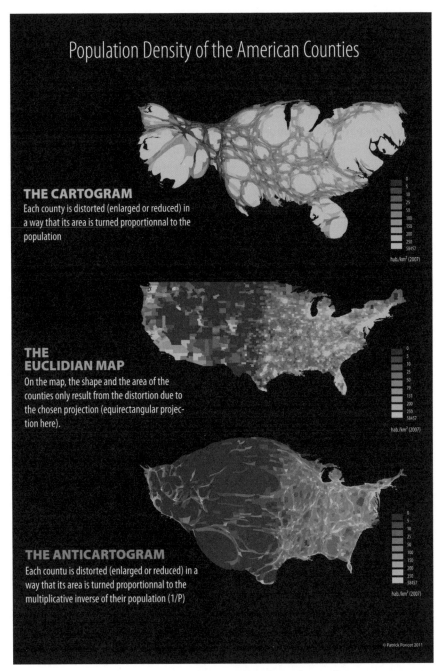

Fig. 2 (Anti)cartograms of population density: copresence, telecommunication, and circulation maps.

Semiological proposition: the map in only four expressive dimensions

Criticising the rigidity of a certain type of cartography is easy. To be fully accepted, it seems useful to propose an alternative. The mediology of the map I proposed here, to replace Bertinian semiology, is therefore based on just four expressive dimensions (versus 'visual variables'): form, size, colour, and visual effects.

Form. Let us recall that the goal of cartography is to facilitate the identification of visual objects of every size – representing places of the problem represented – by how the reader looks at the map. It is therefore natural to try to produce these places through forms that contrast each other, be they the objects' outline shape or the forms that make up the interior, giving it a certain texture. The notion of shape must be considered in the mathematical sense as all of the angle values that define a geometric figure. In a very broad, overarching sense, the concept of *angle* also applies to a frame whose parallel stripes orient the objects it adorns. Beyond this, a simple straight line represents a direction with respect to conventional orientations (page, map edges). This is also true of very beautiful maps of pressure or wind fields, whose segmented figures are reminiscent of the aligning of iron filings around a magnet.

A comparison of figures with acute angles or of territorial units with protruding forms therefore emerges in other visual objects with round, soft shapes. These semiological properties apply not only to cartographic artefacts that may underlie the graphic expression (symbols), but also to features of the basemap itself, such as coastlines, borders, outlines of statistical entities, road webs, and other networks. Hence, the often-pressing need to get rid of basemaps, to reduce them to a strict minimum, or to soften them so as to create the greatest leeway in terms of contrasting forms, undoubtedly the tool of cartographic design par excellence.

Let's also remember that toponymy is also a tool in the cartographer's morphological palette, and that sets of forms govern the optimisation of anti-cartograms.

Size. In the Euclidean world of the map, the notion of size refers directly to the importance of the phenomena represented. A cartographer can therefore, without much difficulty, apply a simple rule: The place where the mapped phenomenon is important should jump off the page. If the mode of expression used is based on a set of forms, then the latter must be of consequent dimension (e.g. large disks or stripes). However, on a more subtle level, this also applies to large spatial entities, which is the basic principle for the anamorphic backgrounds of cartograms: One can magnify places where the intensity of the phenomenon is multiplied by the mass (population, for example) to which it applies.

Let us consider, however, two nuances to better understand the impact of size.

First, the definition of the size of graphic objects is not as simple and unambiguous as its form. The shape of a disk can be based on its diameter, its circumference, or its surface area (see above). A ring, for instance, will have the added dimension of its thickness. For any form, the difference in size will go through a conventional dimension (often vertical). If the form is oriented, it will be according to this orientation.

If we add to this the fact that the proportionality between the size of the visual object and the phenomenon's importance can follow various functions (see above), then we measure the cartographic freedom thus obtained and the importance of verification by image.

Finally, size must be seen as relative to an intermediate size that we would consider important in terms of its visual effect. A form whose size is too close to the proportions of the map itself merges with the basemap and goes unnoticed. This is common with maps that, in attempting to subtly differentiate between small cities, make the proportional circles corresponding to the cities disproportionate (and even tend to be removed from the map).

Colour. Technological considerations of printers that compose the Bertinian semiology by using colour nuances or grey scales must also be abandoned. A return to general colour theory (for example, based on the HSB model: hue, saturation, and brightness) is sufficient to control the use of means of cartographic expression that play on the visibility of graphic objects.

In fact, depending on their graphic environment, small objects can be very visible. Size is not really a modulator of visibility. Colour, however, can both make a place appear or disappear and order spaces by varying contrasts, complementarity, nuances, shades, and scales. Here, the rules of composition are precisely the same as those that define colour relationships, including meaning, such as the contrast between warm and cool colours.

The only real difficulty in the cartographic manipulation of colours is that the range of available colours is generally limited, as similar hues are generally used to express proximity and similarities between places, while their juxtaposition is used to reflect gradients. There often remain only a dozen separately identifiable colours that can produce clear dissociation (red, dark green, light green, dark blue, turquoise, pink, purple, yellow, orange, black, grey, white, gold, silver, and copper). Not to worry, however: The so-called 'four-colour' mathematical theorem, whose extremely difficult proof is, as yet, only experimental (through computers), stipulates that any map made through the tiling of contiguous territories without divisions only requires four distinct colours to distinguish each territory such that no neighbour has the same colour.

To conclude, while white is allowed, it has no intrinsic meaning; it takes on meaning relative to the other colours on the map (the absence of information, the weakness of a phenomenon, a void or full space, especially in a sea of black).

Visual effects. The final expressive dimension of cartographic design is a fairly extensive set of techniques that result from the domestication of visual effects resulting from elementary graphic choices on the map (internal effects) and the relationship to its graphic environment (external effects). The essential idea is to consider all of these effects (shading, for example) not as mere decorations or stylistic features, but as standardised, ordered semiological tools that carry meaning and cannot be summed up simply in terms of size, form, or colour.

While we do not have the room to name them all, here is a possible – though probably incomplete – list of cartographic visual effects: perforation and floating in layering cartography; optical illusions in legends as well as between the perceived colour and the size of entities, for example; effects of volume (false 3D, perspective, aggregates, clustering, and superimposing); transparency, superposition, and shading; lighting; the 'animation' of arrows and symbols; alignments, grids, and modularisations; tears, dismemberments, shreds, and de-solidifications of the basemap; cartograms and anti-cartograms; graphic styles (pencilling, etc.); positive/negative (maps with a black background); background effects; typographic effects; and the use of toponymy for graphic objects.

Easier than people think

In summary:

A map is a representation of space that respects certain, simple, non-restrictive constraints: it holds a specific spatial discourse, lacks planes (foreground, background, etc.) and contains visual objects to which an entire 'apparatus' gives meaning.

Differences between maps mostly depend on their use and their expected impact in terms of communication, even towards itself. If desired, a map can be an instrumental encoding, a linguistic object, or a media-driven language. This corresponds to three distinct 'occupations' in cartography, and amateurs, for their purposes, often do as well as professionals.

Making maps is easier than people think. Faced with an issue of cartographic representation, solutions are often numerous, while 'recipes' are few but their combinations are many. Few combinations are truly 'risky' for transmitting a map's message (even if scientific). Finally, only the result matters and can be used to judge a map's quality: Does the image produced say what you want it to say?

Cartography just isn't what it used to be.

References

Lévy, J. & Lussault, M. (eds.), 2013. *Dictionnaire de la Géographie et de l'espace des sociétés*, 2nd edition, Paris: Belin.

Bertin, J., 1977. *La graphique et le traitement graphique de l'information*, Paris: Flammarion.

Chapter 13

Lost in Transduction: From Digital Footprints to Urbanity

Boris Beaude

On the trail of Italo Calvino's *Invisible Cities*, we recognize the multi-faceted nature of a given urban space, establish a link between individual practices and the city as a whole, explore the non-hierarchical relationship between ideal and material realities and, finally, shed light on the decisive nature of the city's self-visibility. From this perspective, *invisible cities* are probably less fictional than most urban representations, which are generally limited to buildings and transport infrastructures. At best, these representations depict main roads, traffic, and commuting. Calvino, in his own way, emphasized the most important part of urbanity: its complexity.

In 1972, when the work was first published, such complexity was hard to comprehend, other than through literature. Fastidious and expensive studies were needed to perceive individual desires, representations, and perceptions of specific parts of a city. Nowadays, however, we could say that things have changed significantly. The proliferation of digital footprints gives us a unique opportunity to make discreet practices more visible. Through their aggregation and recurrence, these original data provide evidence of the city in the making. Like memories from the digital devices we use, these tracks reflect an increasing part of our *spatialities*. Such a purpose is sensitive and includes many challenges, particularly for the social sciences, which effectively are not disposed to using such 'unusual' data. Yet, digital footprints have been used extensively in recent years. Many artists, designers, computer scientists, and, more recently, physicists have sensed the capacity of this type of data to renew our representations of space.

However, digital footprints do have advantages that are of significant interest to the social sciences. For one, they have the great advantage of being produced independent of the researcher's observation. They are also an exceptional raw data source that reflects a wide range of practices (taking a picture, making a call, moving around, asking for information, rating a place, etc.). However, to actually reflect urbanity, to make *invisible cities* visible, digital footprints must be made explicit. Yet, it is crucial not to betray the individuals who, knowingly or unknowingly, produce these data. In response to this challenge, we should remember: 'We must reflect in order to measure and not measure in order to reflect' (Bachelard, 1934, p. 241).

The potential of digital footprints could thus be summarised as follows: digital footprints *can* reflect the complexity of urban spaces, particularly when individual practices are considered (inhabiting, mobility, identification, and interaction) (Paquot, Lussault, & Younès 2007), and provided we pay special attention to the specific contexts from which they arise. Moreover, because of the diverse contexts, these data would benefit from a subtle association, if our goals are to grasp the complexity of urban practices and show innovative representations of the city.

Thus, particular attention should be given to the production of such images. From digital footprints to representations of urbanity, we will shed light on difficulties relative to each step in the process. As such, digital footprints can renew our representations of urbanity and greatly contribute to the social sciences of the city. We must be aware of both the potential and the limits of such data, give ourselves the means to make these *invisible cities* easier to read, and not succumb to reductionist aesthetics. This data's potential is still largely underexploited, thus producing many meaningless, useless, and inefficient images.

Exploiting digital footprints

Digital footprints are the basis for a large body of works in which the state of the 'art' and the state of the 'research' must be distinguished. These kinds of sources are widely used by computer scientists, designers, and artists who, as mentioned, produce most of the projects and images that use digital footprints. Far from conventional research, the number of these images is actually increasing thanks to the multiplication of data and the development of new means to access and exploit them.

Digital footprints

A first set of works focuses not on space but rather uses digital footprints from telecommunication practices. One of the most impressive projects of this type is Google Flu Trends.[1] In 2010, when demonstrating its data processing capacity, Google announced on a dedicated website that it could anticipate the flu epidemics at least as accurately as, if not better than, the U.S. Center for Disease Control (Ginsberg et al., 2008). Up until now, this example has been one of the most representative of digital footprints' ability to reflect reality. However, it required a considerable amount of data (all the Google search queries relating to the flu over several years) as well as privileged access to this data.

Facebook is another example, although less dramatic. A partnership between Facebook and psychology researchers led to the creation of a Gross National Happiness Index, which was created to reflect the happiness level in a particular country (the United States, in the first step of the project) (Kramer, 2010). The project was based on a semantic analysis of many posts published on Facebook. Although the product of impressive research, the index is actually limited in scope owing to the lack of referents and the numerous biases relating to this particular type of tracking. Nevertheless, the study's authors were able to identify the major periods of happiness as

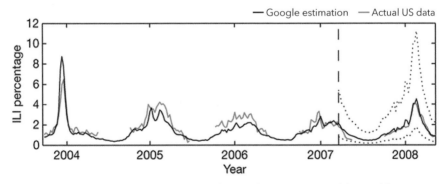

Fig. 1 Google Flu Trends. Source: US Public Health Centers.

[1]   Refer to 'sitography'.

being linked to collective celebrations. The results of the study show the capacity of these data to reflect the world that produces them.

Finally, another set of works focuses on hyperlink networks. Following the example of PageRank, which was created using this approach, many indexes are based on hyperlinks. Hyperlinks are not only useful for ranking webpages; they also help identify clusters among the increasing number of websites. Linkfluence is undoubtedly one of the pioneers in this area. Inherited from academic research, Linkfluence is currently one of the most representative producers of hyperlink mapping, as a private company that maps semantic, relational and temporal activities for specific topics (i.e. advertising or political campaigning) on the Web. In 2005, Linkfluence showed that opponents of the French European Constitution referendum were significantly more active than its supporters, thus showing a clear divergence between the electorate and the media. For the moment, this approach cannot really be considered scientific. It does, however, stress digital footprints' capacity to improve the readability of complex issues.

The spatiality of digital traces

While many digital footprints are specific to the urban space, most are just demonstrations of technological prowess, with no real scientific expectations. The World Touristness Map, created by Bluemoon Interactive in 2009 using pictures from Panoramio, and Visualizing Facebook Friends, the famous map designed by Paul Bulter while interning at Facebook (exploiting 10 million friend connections), are just two examples. While these projects are quite impressive, they cannot properly be interpreted. The New City Landscape Maps by Fabian Neuhaus, a kind of 'tweetography' that offers density maps of tweets published in certain cities including London, New York, Munich, and Paris, is a perfect example of this deficiency.

Other projects are more explicitly related to artistic explorations. Ester Polak's *Real Time Amsterdam* (Figure 2a) (2002), which recorded the movements of 75 volunteers in Amsterdam over 40 days using a GPS) and *Elastic Mapping* (2009), presented in Berlin, are two such examples. Christian Nold's surprising maps are also noteworthy. Since 2004, Nold has been developing the concept of *biomapping*, which consists of geotracking variations in emotion in urban contexts. These projects

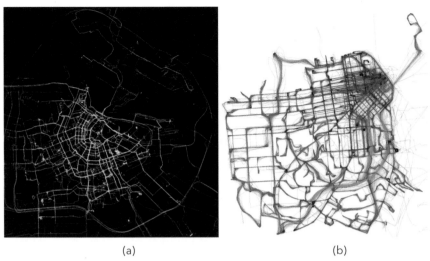

Fig. 2 (a) Real Time Amsterdam – (b) A Day of Muni.
Sources: (a) Esther Polak, 2002, (b) Eric Fischer, 2010.

underline the strong link between digital footprints and digital mapping, embodied perfectly by self-proclaimed 'map geeks' such as Eric Fischer, one of the most prolific in the field. Fischer blurs the frontiers between mapmakers, artists, and programmers. For instance, *Local and Tourists* (2010), *A Day of Muni* (2010), *See Something or Say Something* (2011) and *Paths Through Cities* (2012) combine multiple skills from both cartography and computer science, with a touch of aesthetics. *Archipelago* (2010), by Anil Bawa-Cavia, and *UrbanMobs* (2008), by faberNovel and Orange Labs, which exploit data from innovative sources like Foursquare and cell phone tracking, are other examples of this trend. Besides their deliberate aesthetic aims, these works are more exercises in style than heuristic methods that improve scientific knowledge of cities and urbanity. Scientific approaches require a more systematic characterisation of data, more rigorous methods, and more explicit images.

Following Google Flu Trends, special attention should also be paid to projects managed by companies that exploit the direct or indirect spatial dimensions of their activity. This is the case for *HotMap* (Microsoft Research), which provided visualisation of the most sought-after places on Virtual Earth Search and Live Search Map from January to July 2006. *Tag Maps*, managed by Yahoo! Research (2006), is another example. It exploits data from Flickr, or *SpotRank* from Skyhook, which shows the most frequented places, using a database of known locations of over 700 million

Wi-Fi access points and cell towers. By exploiting various kinds of data, namely search queries, metadata from images, and cell phone tracks, the three companies offer innovative and stimulating representations of space. However, grasping the veritable potential of these projects, which have largely been abandoned and served only for experimentation purposes, is difficult.

Research in the field

In recent years, the potential of digital footprints to apprehend urban spaces has been addressed by academic researchers as well. Several groundbreaking works have even been published in prestigious journals such as *Nature* and *Science*, though they did not go beyond the observation that most individual movement is largely predictable. Using large sample groups (100,000 people over a period of six months [González, Hidalgo, & Barabási, 2008], 50,000 people over a three-month period [Song et al., 2010]), these studies treat individuals like atoms, producing interesting analyses, but with important limitations. They merely confirm established facts, given that working, studying, sleeping, and living are mostly static and regular practices that constitute more than 80% of our everyday life.

Another set of studies focuses more on detailed analysis of individual practices. These studies do not attempt to forecast movement but rather aim to find out where people actually spend their time during an entire day. The impetus was established in 2006, with several projects initiated by separate groups led by Nathan Eagle, Eamonn O'Neill, and Carlo Ratti (Eagle & Pentland 2006; O'Neill et al., 2006; Ratti et al., 2006). These studies concentrated on MIT students, pedestrians of Bath, and inhabitants of Milan. They have initiated a real revival of urban space representations.

These days, digital footprints can be exploited more easily. It seems that most of the data comes from six kind of sources:

1. *cell phones*, by far the most common: Ahas et al., 2010; Bayir, Demirbas, & N. Eagle, 2009; Francesco Calabrese et al., 2010; Nathan Eagle & Pentland, 2009; Nathan Eagle & Sandy Pentland, 2006; Girardin et al., 2009; Girardin, Calabrese, Fiore, Ratti, & Blat, 2008; Girardin, Fiore, Ratti, & Blat, 2008; Horanont & Shibasaki, 2008; Olteanu, Couronné, & Fen-Chong, 2011; Carlo Ratti, Pulselli, Williams, & Frenchman, 2006; J. Reades et al., 2007; Jonathan Reades, Francesco Calabrese, & Carlo Ratti, 2009; Shoval & Isaacson, 2007; Vaccari et al., 2009.

2. *Metadata* (names of places, geographic coordinates, and time codes) from *images* published on websites like Flickr and Geograph: Crandall et al., 2009; Girardin, Francesco Calabrese, Fiore, Carlo Ratti, & Blat, 2008; Girardin, Fiore, Carlo Ratti, & Blat, 2008; Girardin, Vaccari, Gerber, Biderman, & Carlo Ratti, 2009; Hollenstein & Ross Purves, 2011; R Purves & Edwardes, 2011; Rattenbury, Good, & Naaman, 2007; Vaccari, Francesco Calabrese, B. Liu, & Carlo Ratti, 2009; R. Purves & Edwardes, 2011.

3. *GPS* (embedded devices, taxis, buses): Girardin, Francesco Calabrese, Fiore, Carlo Ratti, & Blat, 2008; Neuhaus, 2010; Carlo Ratti, Pulselli, Williams, & Frenchman, 2006; Shoval & Isaacson, 2007; Vaccari, Francesco Calabrese, B. Liu, & Carlo Ratti, 2009, Eric Fisher, 2010.

4 *Bluetooth sensors*: Bayir, Demirbas, & N. Eagle, 2009; Nathan Eagle & Pentland, 2009; Nathan Eagle & Sandy Pentland, 2006.

5 *specific service providers, i.e. velib'* (bike-sharing): Borgnat et al., 2009; Froehlich, Neumann, & Oliver, 2008; Fabien Giradin, 2008.

6. *metadata from posts on social networks, i.e. Twitter*: Phithakkitnukoon & Olivier, 2011; Kalev Leetaru et al., 2013.

Sometimes these data records are supplemented with other information:
- *database* about specific places, i.e. shops and bars, to contextualize the data: Cortright, 2009; Jonathan Reades, Francesco Calabrese, & Carlo Ratti, 2009.
- *small surveys*: Ahas, Aasa, Silm, & Tiru, 2010; Bayir, Demirbas, & N. Eagle, 2009; Nathan Eagle & Sandy Pentland, 2006.

On the whole, these studies represent innovative works with significant prospects. They also contribute to improving knowledge of individual practices in urban spaces, and offer unconventional representations that reveal the complexity of the city through novel aggregations of individual practices (mobility, photography, social networks, etc.).

Each of these studies is limited, however, by numerous biases due to the weak methods and data involved (cf. 2.3.2). Furthermore, as a result of the strong technical skills these methods involve, most of the studies are conducted outside the social sciences. The fact that the data come mainly from social practices is a serious issue, since the significance of the data cannot be seriously confirmed. Lastly, many of these studies have been developed in the context of specific events and have not been tested further, thus reflecting particular and spectacular moments in the life of a city

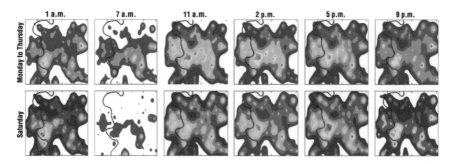

Fig. 3 Cellular Census, Rome (J. Reades, F. Calabrese, Sevtsuk, & C. Ratti, 2007).

and showing exceptional rather than the everyday (*Amsterdam RealTime, Real Time Rome*, and *UrbanMobs*). The recent Live Singapore project, however, developed by the Senseable City Lab, is deeply linked to common urban issues, although its current output remains more spectacular than effective and disconnected from actual individual expectations.

Thus far, no study has offered a transversal approach to digital footprints capable of exploiting their plurality. Moreover, no study has offered strong contextualisation for this innovative kind of data, even though this is the only way to produce usable representations of the city for researchers, urban planners, as well as inhabitants. Several studies do use two types of data to improve the significance of their results: cell phones and Flickr (Girardin, Francesco Calabrese, Fiore, Carlo Ratti, & Blat, 2008; Girardin, Fiore, Carlo Ratti, & Blat, 2008), Flickr and Geograph (Purves & Edwardes, 2011) and several methods of geolocalisation like GPS, Wi-Fi and cell towers (Shoval & Isaacson, 2007). Furthermore, with the exception of a study managed by Foursquare data (Phithakkitnukoon & Olivier, 2011), most studies concentrate on urban intensity more than on urban diversity. The complexity of urban spaces has not yet been extensively studied. However, exploring this complexity remains an important scientific issue with substantial potential.

From digital footprints to urbanity

Excepting the social sciences, digital footprints are receiving increasing attention. In spite of this, it is important to address the potential of urban digital footprints from a social perspective and to assess the significance and capacity of such data to improve knowledge of urban spaces by considering their complexity.

Despite the abundance of studies on digital footprints, few take significant advantage of their potential; too often are they limited to a single source (Flickr, Foursquare, cell phones, etc.). Moreover, these initiatives are generally limited to data-visualisation performances whose challenges are mainly technical, aesthetic, and promotional. This results in many projects being unexploited and unexploitable, further highlighting the potential of digital footprints. The time has come to merge these innovations in a broader perspective with a deeper social outlook, and to develop innovative methods that will help make cities, and urbanity in particular, easier to interpret and grasp.

Digital footprints offer an unprecedented opportunity, as they reflect practices that are quite difficult to grasp (photo shoots, movement, user reviews via web platforms like Yelp, etc.). Such information requires expensive studies, and these studies are generally far from exhaustive. Furthermore, these information sources effectively supplement conventional data (density, commuting, land registry, etc.), whose limitations often render them inappropriate for analysing contemporary uses of urban spaces.

From this point of view, digital footprints offer a remarkable opportunity to renew and complete conventional ways of understanding and analysing the complexity of urbanity. From a large scale to just a few blocks, they help reveal unequal dynamics and the attractiveness that characterises certain neighbourhoods of certain cities. Moreover, because these data reflect specific practices, they show the city from a new perspective much more closely linked to daily activities and the city in the making. One can even assume that, under certain circumstances, digital footprints could significantly improve the readability of large cities and better convey their urbanity than classic indicators such as density or commuting.

It is essential to exploit the potential of digital footprints to better understand urban spaces and their complexity, their intensity, and their dynamics. This means developing a better knowledge of both urban spaces themselves and the means for understanding them. The following issues are of particular importance:
- Identifying digital footprints relative to urban spaces.
- Establishing the limits of each kind of digital footprint (access, computing, interpretation, etc.).
- Creating meaningful indicators for each kind of digital footprint.
- Creating synthetic indicators for urban practices based on these unconventional data.

- Comparing these indicators to regular ones to discern how they complement one another.
- Investigating urban representations from these indicators.
- Depicting the complexity of urban spaces, with a focus on unequal density and diversity, locally (space) and momentary (time), not limited to
  mere partitions of space but revealing subtle gradients of urbanity.

After such investigations, the social sciences will be fully able to take part
in this dynamic, though initiated by information and computer science,
design, and art. Notions such as *digital footprints* and *cellular census* will
be in accordance with the particular requirements of social issues. Questioning the potential of digital footprints in the social sciences is indeed a
prerequisite for considering how such data can help us understand the city
and the complexity of urban spaces.

   Connections between digital technology and cities were identified long
before the use of digital footprints. Several pioneers have clearly shown
the importance of the spatial dimension of digital technologies (Bakis,
2001; Bakis, 1994; 2004; Beaude, 2008; Dodge & Kitchin, 2001; Éveno
& Bakis, 2000; Éveno, 2004a; 2004b; Kitchin, 1998; Mitchell, 1996) and
stressed that digital cities are not merely digital transpositions of urban
space but rather a complex combination of cities and digital technology.
From this perspective, a digital city is rather an extensively connected city,
where digital data and digital services are available to inhabitants (Aurigi,
2006; Dykes et al., 2010). A digital city is more about hybridisation than
virtualisation. At present, it is clear that telecommunication and digital
technology are not alternatives to urban spaces; cities are actually the perfect place for these technologies (Bakis, 2001; Hardey, 2011; Mitchell,
2000). Furthermore, these technologies are not only efficient for reducing
distances but are also extremely useful for managing proximity (Castells,
2001; Éveno, 2004b; Gordon & Silva, 2011).

   The development of ubiquitous computing – that is, the combination
of the seeming disappearance and functional omnipresence of digital technologies (Galloway, 2004; Greenfield, 2006) obliges all stakeholders to
think about the plurality of cities in full consideration of digital technology
(Graham, 2004). From this standpoint, digital footprints are at the heart of
contemporary issues in urban studies, perfectly situated between digital
technologies and cities. However, going from digital footprints to urbanity
is no small step. The road ahead is full of challenges. To avoid losing our
way, it is best to start with the expected target to know where we are going.

Urbanity

In the beginning was the city, although, since the end of the 19th century (and particularly during the second half of the 20th century), increasing urbanisation at the global scale has greatly affected its significance and readability. Nowadays, the notion of city is too limited to convey the contemporary phenomenon of densification, which favours networks, since the significance of the contiguous built-up areas has been steadily decreasing. This is how the 'culture of limit' has gradually disappeared, along with the notions of 'city', 'country', and 'urban' (Choay, 1994). Only the essence of the notion of 'city' has been preserved, that is its specific capacity to improve productivity (Bairoch, 1985), its unrivalled capacity to maximize social interaction (Claval, 1981) and to create physical contact while preserving social distance (Wirth, 1938). In fact, 'the air of the city makes you free' precisely because 'the area of the city makes you free' (Lévy, 1996).

However, this complexity can be grasped through two attributes that perfectly define urbanity : density and diversity (Lévy, 1994). High urbanity can be described as high density and high diversity – two means of improving social interaction. Density is the quantity of *things* present in a given area. The notion of diversity typifies the variety of *things* in a given area, relative to a reference area. Diversity can be intra- or inter-dimensional, that is, respectively, many differences in a specific dimension (services, buildings, individuals) or between many dimensions. In other words, the notion of urbanity describes the urban quality of a given space, the result of the density and diversity of social realities. Hence, we could consider infinite potentials, which could be qualified by various spatial ideal-types (geotypes) that correspond to specific endowments of these attributes.

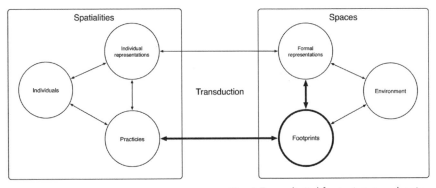

Fig. 4 From digital footprints to urbanity.

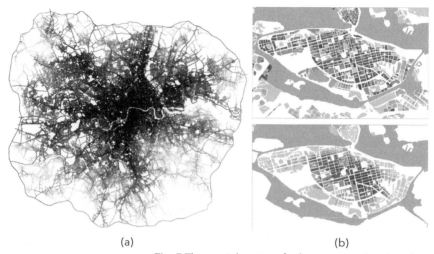

(a)   (b)

Fig. 5 The spatial syntax of urban segregation, London.
M25 (a) and Stockholm (b) (Vaughan, 2007).

For instance, the open-list of geotypes includes central, sub-urban, peri-urban, infra-urban, meta-urban, para-urban and peri-central (Levy, 1994).

Moreover, distinguishing between potential and effective urbanity is essential, in other words, between *a priori* and *a posteriori* urbanity (Lévy, 1994; 1996; 1999). This fundamental distinction emphasizes the fact that it is important not to confuse a city's interaction potential with the actualization of this potential through daily practices. *A priori* urbanity can be grasped thanks to spatial aggregated indicators. For instance, the density and diversity of buildings, inhabitants, shops, and transportation modes are many ways of qualifying *a priori* urbanity. In the architectural field, this issue has been tackled through *space syntax*. This visual method aims to reveal a space's potential through road connectivity (Figure 5a) and density (more recently, Figure 5b).

A priori urbanity is by far the most used, although *a posteriori* urbanity is being increasingly considered, particularly in the context of mobility, urban planning, and even hoarding boards, which require more than just *a priori* expectations. Nevertheless, in cases where data relative to urban practices are not only unattainable or too expensive, they are usually confidential as well. Census and mobility surveys do not actually compensate for this limit, as they generally focus on housing and commuting, which represent the most predictable parts of urban practices. In fact, *a posteriori* urbanity is less exploited than *a priori* urbanity because it is far more difficult to estimate.

This unfortunate difficulty must be overcome, since *a posteriori* urbanity is particularly useful for understanding urban spaces, especially the adequacy between its potentiality and its actuality. The problem stems from the complexity and cost of the apparatus used to assess such urbanity. This presumes access to a considerable amount of data that is constantly being renewed. It also requires considering not only space but time, so as to respect the temporal dimension of spatial practices, as spaces empty and fill according to the time of the day, week, and year (Scalab, 2004).

This issue is not new but has been greatly reconsidered since geolocation–based digital footprints have emerged. During the past decade, new players who were not directly involved in producing urbanity indicators have become by far the largest producers of spatial information, thanks to the massive use of cell phones and GPS- equipped devices (Nova, 2009). Currently, the commercial value of these data is considerable but still confidential. Furthermore, firms such as TomTom, Google, Orange, and Swisscom are not fully aware of this potential, beyond the specific context in which these data have been produced (traffic forecasts, cell phone tower regulation, security, etc.). In this respect, digital footprints based on geolocation are a remarkable opportunity for society to significantly improve the available means for reading, understanding, and managing what has become common space for most of humanity.

Digital footprints do not speak for themselves

The fusion of digital technology with telecommunication in recent years has dramatically improved data computing capacity and thereby innovative services that were formerly unimaginable with analogical technologies. Today, processing capacity is so great that digital technologies are now part of most of our telecommunication devices (radios, televisions, telephones, etc.). The Internet is the most advanced outcome of this merger. Now integrated even in our cell phones, this 'ubiquitous' technology is virtually everywhere. The result is a profound renewal of our environment, which poses a serious challenge to the social sciences.

The spreading of digital technologies to most of our social mediation devices results in a proclivity to leave footprints that are far more visible and greater in number than those usually left by our own bodies. Identifying and exploiting these footprints is clearly less costly, given that they are 'centralised' and easy to manipulate. Digital footprints, and the spatial data produced by digital devices in particular, are not only important in terms of their relative quality but also their quantity, as their number is constantly increasing with the spread of digital technology into daily activities.

This trend, which has been clearly identified in recent years, challenges the quantitative methods used in the social sciences and revives the old debate on the pertinence of such an approach. The current social issue surrounding digital footprints is so-called *big data*, which represents such a vast quantity of data that quality and relevance are supposed to emerge from quantity. *Big data* refers to an unprecedented accumulation of data on individual social practices (Twitter, Wikipedia, Facebook, etc.) (Lazer et al., 2009), historical perspectives (urban statistics) (Bettencourt & West, 2010), newspapers (Leetaru, 2011) and books (Michel et al., 2011).

While opinion remains divided, the potential of *big data* is generally accepted. Although the risk of reductionism and imperialism of the physical sciences, computer science, and mathematics exists, the emergence of *big data* is seen as an opportunity for the social sciences to re-examine its methods (Torrens, 2010) and develop closer relationships with other disciplines (Paradiso, 2011), following the ethno-mining approach (Aipperspach and al., 2006). It is also an opportunity to reconcile quantitative and critical geography, the latter of which only occasionally acknowledges the potential this data has to confirm their assertions (Kwan & Schwanen, 2011). Nevertheless, some social scientists familiar with the subject forewarn the many aporia relative to *big data*. They stress that the social sciences are not characterised by the quantity of data available but its subjective nature, which can be summed up as: facts and data do *not* speak for themselves.

In a recent text, danah boyd and Kate Crawford cite 'six provocations' that perfectly capture the limits of big data (Boyd & Crawford, 2011) and, consequently, of digital footprints.

1. Automating research changes the definition of knowledge, as the instruments used change the whole of social theory (Latour, 2009).

2. Claims to objectivity and accuracy are misleading because quantity cannot transform subjectivity into objectivity.

3. Bigger data does not always mean better data, reminding us of the long-standing tradition in the social sciences of collecting and analysing data, while paying particular attention to sampling mechanisms and question biases. In this respect, 'Without taking into account the sample of a dataset, the size of the dataset is meaningless'.

4. Not all data are equal. For instance, frequency is not equal to intensity, and active footprints are not equal to passive footprints.
5. 'Accessible' does not mean 'ethical'. Most data have not been produced to be massively matched, analysed, and divulged. This makes all the difference between 'being in public' and 'being public'.
6. Finally, limited access to big data creates new digital divides, since the access to these data is often impossible. Most of the time they are indeed confidential, which prevents us from reproducing any study based on such data. Nevertheless, we should bear in mind that, as Derrida said, 'Effective democratization can always be measured by this essential criterion: the participation in and access to the archive, its constitution, and its interpretation' (Derrida, 1996).

A few other 'provocations' can be added to this list. First, correlation is not causality, which is why it is crucial to know the specific production context of any type of data – the minimum requirement for producing any meaning at all. Furthermore, the social sciences cannot aspire to discover social laws comparable to physical laws, since individuals cannot be compared to objects. Reflexivity – that is, self-awareness – makes a major distinction between object and subject. In particular, subjects can change as a result of experience, and act differently in similar conditions. A mere social law can change society; hence any social law appears as nonsense (Popper, 1957). This is probably why Google Flu Trends eventually failed. In the 2012/2013 season, it predicted twice as many doctors' visits as the US Centers for Disease Control and Prevention (CDC) eventually recorded. In facts, the Google Flu Trends consistently overestimated flu-related visits over the last years. It shows that using big data to predict the future isn't as easy as it looks, while GFT is often held up as an exemplary use of big data (Lazer et al., 2014).

Therefore, digital footprints do not speak for themselves, and they require our full attention. The possible analogies that can be made between digital footprints and the practices that produce them must be seriously questioned (Beaude, 2009; 2010). In particular, it is important to stress that they are not 'raw data'. This notion is an oxymoron (Bowker, 2008) that supposes data produced without a socio-technical environment. Thus, it is essential to identify the context, quality, and representativeness of all digital footprints and to distinguish between active footprints (knowingly produced), passive footprints (unwittingly produced), personal footprints (produced for oneself) and social footprints (produced to be shared).

Henceforth, many biases can be identified, one of the most important being the highly unreliable social and spatial sampling of these footprints. Data from cell phones are among the most reliable and most abundant, but are also among the most inaccessible. Conversely, metadata from Flickr are among the least representative but are the most accessible. Major sampling differences can nevertheless be seen for the same type of data (between Flickr and Geograph, for instance [Purves & Edwardes, 2011, Figure 6]). Studies requiring specific devices face another important bias: people must be directly involved in the study (Bayir, Demirbas, & N. Eagle, 2009; Nathan Eagle & Pentland, 2009; Nathan Eagle & Sandy Pentland, 2006). Moreover, these studies have shown that it is difficult to build continuous data given the limited energy autonomy of such devices, of which cell phones are no exception. Furthermore, despite the apparent accuracy of digital footprints, their geolocation is not so reliable. For example, the average accuracy of data produced by cell phones is approximately 320 meters (Francesco Calabrese, Pereira, Di Lorenzo, Liu, & Ratti, 2010) and varies from 3.5 m2 to 8000 m2 in the metropolitan area of Paris (Olteanu, Couronné, & Fen-Chong, 2011). Digital footprints present so many challenges that some researchers have proposed a typology of their specific limits: representativeness, accuracy, certainty, and granularity (Olteanu et al., 2011).

These basic biases remind us how important it is to ask the right questions to the right data – and to know their specific limits. However, Google Flu Trend is an enlightening example in that it shows how the aggregation of data can provide meaningful indicators, if the data are used to answer specific questions with appropriate methods.

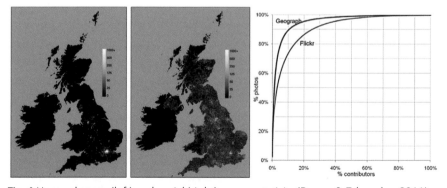

Fig. 6 Unequal space (left) and social (right) representativity (Purves & Edwardes, 2011).

Another example is the strong relationship between a place rating (i.e. a restaurant) and the distance of this place from home. Called 'voting with your feet' by its authors (Froehlich et al., 2006), it provides an interesting nuance to the more extensive notion of 'cellular census' (Reades et al., 2007).

Digital footprints relative to urbanity are not exempt from these biases, but specific methods can help to prevent the majority of them. This requires identifying the various biases for each type of data (pictures, cell phones, social platforms, etc.) and to assess the difficulty there is in obtaining and using them, considering that some of them are particularly strategic or confidential.

Transduction

Digital footprints are all the more important given that they are not a mere reflection of urbanity: they are liable to change it. This phenomenon requires a differentiation between space and spatiality (Figure 4), that is, between space of action and spatial action (Lussault, 2007; Lussault & Stock, 2010). Individuals coproduce space, which is concurrently a support for action. Thus, practices leave footprints in space, which are used to create formal representations (maps, for instance) that become supports for action through individual representations of space. Once digital footprints have been analysed and formalised, they are used in a wide range of devices that help us understand a given city. The emergence of urban representations built from digital footprints is thus a major issue for the potential of urbanity, as they greatly contribute to the actualization of the city.

A distinction must therefore be made between how digital footprints are represented formally (i.e. how they are made visible) and the spatial *transduction* phenomenon (Dodge & Kitchin, 2005), following the works of Simondon and Mackenzie (Mackenzie, 2002). Spatial transduction differentiates the process of representation from the ontogenic process of space. This process follows a positive feedback loop that deeply links practices and digital footprints, since one cannot be the sole consequence of the other. 'Transduction' is the process by which space becomes the environment that leads to its own genesis.

Consequently, the representations of urban spaces that emerge from digital footprints cannot be reduced to a mere evidence of urban practices; they are eminent constructions that emphasize just how devices and arrangements are built together (Merzeau, 2009). Here lies an opportunity to explore urbanity with a renewed and increased acuity, which is crucial if our goal is to identify the advantages and disadvantages of resorting to technical mediations (Latour & Hermant, 1998). Representations do not only simplify reality; rather, they proceed from a set of operations (filtering, standardisation, accentuation, differentiation) that respect conventions within a particular field. Moreover, the process of reduction adds new specific property (Lynch, 1990). Finally, as the last theory of perception suggests, the latter cannot be reduced to simply a passive process. Perception, on the contrary, is a full experience rather than a reception of experiences (Gibson, 1986). In this respect, how we perceive a city while reading a map is also an urban experience. This is why such perception plays a key role in all our representations and in many experiences – territorial or not.

Hence, the study of the relationship between digital footprints and urbanity requires accurate identification of the context in which these footprints are produced (Figures 4, 1) *and* an understanding of how we can manage the process that takes us from footprints to formal representations of urban spaces (Figures 4, 2). In particular, we must focus on the technical devices involved, as well as the individuals who produce and use them in urban spaces. Particular attention should also be paid to the algorithms used and their ethical and political dimensions, as footprints have become a subtle component of the city through transduction.

The importance of algorithms has actually been stressed in recent years, following Lawrence Lessig's work. In *Code and Other Laws of Cyberspace* (1999), Lessig stresses the importance of code, highlighting the main forces that regulate people's behaviours as well as the production of data: markets, laws, norms, architecture, and code. Rob Kitchin and Martin Dodge transposed this concept to space, developing the notion of Code/Space (Dodge & Kitchin, 2005; 2011) to describe the increasing dependence between spaces and codes. However, they did not apply this notion to representations, but essentially to usual functional urban devices (traffic regulation, airports, etc.).

The spread of digital devices to all urban spaces (Galloway, 2004; Greenfield, 2006) has resulted in the proliferation of digital footprints, calling us to seriously question this new kind of data and not wait for a major failure to realize how important they are (Thrift, 2004; Thrift & French, 2002). In recent years, many scientists have attempted to underline the power code has to shape the world. For instance, Stephan Graham proposed the notion of *software-sorted geographies* while suggesting increased attention to a *spatial politics of code* (2005).

A rigorous analysis of all digital footprints is thus required to improve their ability to contribute to strong indicators of urbanity. With this in mind, we must be as cautious with digital footprints as we are with conventional data sources, and consider their respective qualities. Many experimental studies in different urban spaces must be carried out to understand the strengths and limits of this kind of data. Furthermore, each digital footprint must be systematically qualified – from its sources to rigorous representations of urbanity – as a precondition for any study. Each type of source considered should be subject to a specific survey of individuals who have been actively or passively involved in their production.

Following the example of social networking sites studies (Boyd & Ellison, 2007; Hargittai, 2007), we must characterise the users of these devices to better define what we can expect from digital footprints. This is particularly important, as many ICT usage studies have shown the importance of context. However, when we consider *volunteered geographic information* issues (Elwood, 2008; Flanagin & Metzger, 2008; Goodchild, 2007) or *naïve geography* (Egenhofer & Mark 1995), the context is always decisive for understanding the true potential of these data.

The four steps proposed by Ola Söderström for analysing images (context, production, use, and materialisation) (2000) should also be applied to all productions that involve digital footprints. Moreover, the performative propensity of representations (Lussault, 1998; 2007) would be greater – and hence more insidious. Digital footprints are not immune to the 'reality effect'. Thus, *transduction* via digital footprints must be considered with great care. Otherwise, the proliferation of digital footprints and the resulting representations will greatly alter urban representations, thus changing the city in an unexpected way.

Note: This text is strongly related to a research conducted in collaboration with Nicolas Nova (Head, Switzerland).

References

Ahas, R. et al., 2010. 'Daily rhythms of suburban commuters' movements in the Tallinn metropolitan area: Case study with mobile positioning data.' *Transportation Research Part C: Emerging Technologies* 18[1]: 45–54.

Aipperspach, R. et al., 2006. *Ethno-Mining: Integrating Numbers and Words from the Ground Up*. Berkeley: EECS Department, University of California, Berkeley.

Aurigi, A, 2006. 'New Technologies, Same Dilemmas: Policy and Design Issues for the Augmented City', *Journal of Urban Technology* 13[3]: 5–28.

Bachelard, G., 1934 [1967]. *La formation de l'esprit scientifique*, Paris: Librairie philosophique J. Vrin.

Bakis, H., 2001. 'Understanding the geocyberspace: a major task for geographers and planners in the next decade', *Netcom* 15[1-2]: 9–16.

Bakis, H., 2004. 'La géographie des Technologies de l'Information et de la Communication. Perspectives', *Netcom* 18[1-2]: 3–9.

Bakis, H., 1994. 'Territoire et télécommunications. Évolution de la problématique et perspectives : de l'effet structurant aux potentialités d'interactions au service du développement urbain et régional', *Netcom* 8[2].

Bayir, M., Demirbas, M., & Eagle, N., 2009. 'Discovering Spatio-Temporal Mobility Profiles of Cellphone Users', in WoWMoM, 2009.

WoWMoM 2009. IEEE International Symposium, World of Wireless, Mobile and Multimedia Networks & Workshops, 2009. IEEE International Symposium on a IS - SN - VO -, IEEE, p. 1–9.

Beaude, B., 2009. 'Crime Mapping, ou le réductionnisme bien intentionné', *Espaces-Temps.net*.

Beaude, B., 2010. 'Espace de la carte, espace de la ville. Des analogies à la coexistence', in Zreiked Khaldoun (ed.), *Nouvelles cartographies, nouvelles villes. Hyper-Urbain.2*, Paris: Europia.

Beaude, B., 2008. Éléments pour une géographie du lieu réticulaire. Doctoral dissertation, Université Paris 1-Panthéon Sorbonne.

Bettencourt, L. & West, G.. 2010. 'A Unified Theory of Urban Living', *Nature* 467[7318]: 912–913.

Borgnat, P. et al., 2009. 'Spatial analysis of dynamic movements of Vélo'v, Lyon's shared bicycle program', Warwick: European Conference on Complex Systems.

Bowker, G., 2008. *Memory Practices in the Sciences*, Cambridge: MIT Press.

Boyd, D. & Ellison, N., 2007. 'Social Network Sites: Definition, History, and Scholarship', *Journal of Computer-Mediated Communication* 13[1]: 210–230.

Boyd, D. & Crawford, K., 2011. 'Six Provocations for Big Data', *SSRN eLibrary*.

Calabrese, F. et al., 2010. 'The Geography of Taste: Analyzing Cell-Phone Mobility and Social Events', in Patrik Floréen, Antonio Krüger, et Mirjana Spasojeviceds (eds), *The Geography of Taste: Analyzing Cell-Phone Mobility et Social Events*, Berlin, Heidelberg: Springer, pp. 22–37.

Castells, M., 2001. *The Internet Galaxy: Reflections on the Internet, Business, and Society*, Oxford: Oxford University Press.

Cortright, J., 2009. 'Walking the Walk: How Walkability Raises Home Values in U.S. Cities', in CEOs for Cities, <http://blog.walkscore.com/wp-content/uploads/2009/08/WalkingTheWalk_CEOsforCities.pdf>

Crandall, D. et al., 2009. 'Mapping the World's Photos', WWW '09: Proceedings of the 18th International World Wide Web Conference: 761–770.

Dodge, M. & Kitchin, R., 2001. *Mapping Cyberspace*, Oxford: Routledge.

Dodge, M. & Kitchin, R., 2005. 'Code and the Transduction of Space', *Annals of the Association of American Geographers* 95[1]: 162–180.

Dykes, J. et al., 2010. 'GeoVisualization and the Digital City', *Computers, Environment and Urban Systems* 34[6]: 443–451.

Eagle, N. & Pentland, A., 2009. 'Eigenbehaviors: Identifying Structure in Routine', *Behavioral Ecology and Sociobiology* 63[7]: 1057–1066.

Eagle, N. & Pentland, A., 2006. 'Reality Mining: Sensing Complex Social Systems', *Personal & Ubiquitous Computing* 10[4]: 255–268.

Egenhofer, M. & Mark, D., 1995. 'Spatial Information Theory: A Theoretical Basis for GIS', in Frank, Andrew & Kuhneds, Werner (eds.), *Lecture Notes in Computer Science*, Berlin, Heidelberg: Springer, pp. 1–15.

Elwood, S., 2008. 'Volunteered Geographic Information: Future Research Directions Motivated by Critical, Participatory, and Feminist GIS', *GeoJournal* 72[3-4]: 173–183.

Fischer, E., 2010. 'Personal geography' maps. http://www.flickr.com/photos/walkingsf/sets/72157628738161697/

Eveno, E. & Bakis, H., 2000. 'Les géographes et la société de l'information. Des effets pervers d'un champ réputé a-géographique', *Géocarrefour*: 7–9.

Eveno, E., 2004a. 'La géographie de la société de l'information: entre abimes et sommets', *Netcom* 18[1-2]: 11–87.

Eveno, E., 2004b. 'Le paradigme territorial de la société de l'information', *Netcom* 18[1-2]: 89.

Flanagin, A. & Metzger, M., 2008. 'The Credibility of Volunteered Geographic Information', *GeoJournal* 72[3-4]: 137–148.

Froehlich, J. et al., 2006. 'Voting with Your Feet: An Investigative Study of the Relationship Between Place Visit Behavior et Preference', in *Lecture Notes in Computer Science*, pp. 333–350.

Froehlich, J., Neumann, J., & Oliver, N., 2008. 'Measuring the Pulse of the City Through Shared Bicycle Programs', in *Proceedings of UrbanSense08,* Raleigh: International Workshop on Urban, Community, & Social Applications of Networked Sensing Systems, pp. 16–20.

Galloway, A., 2004. 'Intimations of Everyday Life: Ubiquitous Computing and the City', *Cultural Studies* 18[2-3]: 384–408.

Gibson, J., 1986 [1979]. *The Ecological Approach to Visual Perception,* Mahwah, NJ: Lawrence Erlbaum Associates.

Ginsberg, J. et al., 2008. 'Detecting Influenza Epidemics Using Search Engine Query Data', *Nature* 457[7232]: 1012–1014.

Girardin, F. et al., 2009. 'Quantifying Urban Attractiveness from the Distribution and Density of Digital Footprints', *International Journal of Spatial Data Infrastructures Research* 4: 175–200.

Girardin, F. et al., 2008. 'Leveraging Explicitly Disclosed Location Information to Understand Tourist Dynamics: A Case Study', *Journal of Location Based Services* 2[1]: 41–56.

Girardin, F. et al., 2008. 'Digital Footprinting: Uncovering Tourists with User-Generated Content', *IEEE Pervasive Computing* 7[4]: 36–43.

González, M., Hidalgo, C., & Barabási, A., 2008. 'Understanding Individual Human Mobility Patterns', *Nature* 453[7196]: 779–782.

Goodchild, M., 2007. 'Citizens as Sensors: The World of Volunteered Geography', *GeoJournal* 69[4]: 211–221.

Gordon, E. & de Souza e Silva, A., 2011. *Net Locality*, New York: John Wiley & Sons.

Graham, S., 2005. 'Software-sorted geographies', *Progress in Human Geography* 29[5]: 562–580.

Graham, S. (ed.), 2004. *The Cybercities Reader*, Oxford: Routledge.

Greenfield, A., 2006. *Everyware: The Dawning Age of Ubiquitous Computing*, San Francisco: New Riders.

Hardey, M., 2011. 'The City in the Age of Web 2.0: A New Synergistic Relationship Between Place and People', *Information, Communication & Society* 10[6]: 867–884.

Hargittai, E., 2007. 'Whose Space? Differences Among Users and Non-Users of Social Network Sites', *Journal of Computer-Mediated Communication* 13[1]: 276–297.

Hollenstein, L. & Purves, R., 2011. 'Exploring Place Through User-Generated Content: Using Flickr Tags to Describe City Cores', *Journal of Spatial Information Science* 0[1]: 21–48.

Horanont, T. & Shibasaki, R., 2008. 'An Implementation of Mobile Sensing for Large-Scale Urban Monitoring', in *Proceedings of UrbanSense08,* Raleigh: International Workshop on Urban, Community, and Social Applications of Networked Sensing Systems, pp. 51–55.

Kitchin, R., 1998. *Cyberspace: The World in the Wires*, New York: John Wiley & Sons.

Kitchin, R. & Dodge, M.. 2011. *Code/Space: Software and Everyday Life*. The MIT Press.

Kramer, A., 2010. 'An Unobtrusive Behavioral Model of "Gross National Happiness"', in ACM- Chi '10, *Proceedings of the 28th International Conference on Human Factors in Computing Systems*, Atlanta: ACM, pp. 287–290.

Kwan, M. & Schwanen, T., 2011. 'Quantitative Revolution 2: The Critical [Re]Turn', *The Professional Geographer* 61[3]: 283–291.

Latour, B. & Hermant, E., 1998. *Paris ville invisible*, Paris: La Découverte.

Latour, B., 2009. 'Tarde's Idea of Quantification', in Candea, M (ed), *The Social After Gabriel Tarde: Debates and Assessments*, Oxford: Routledge, pp. 145-162.

Lazer, D. et al., 2009. 'Computational Social Science.' *Science 323*[5915]: 721–723.

Lazer, D. et al., 2014. 'The Parable of Google Flu: Traps in Big Data Analysis', *Science* 343(6176), 1203–1205.

Leetaru, K., 2011. 'Culturomics 2.0: Forecasting Large-Scale Human Behavior Using Global News Media Tone in Time and Space', *First Monday* 16[9].

Leetaru, K. et al., 2013. 'Mapping the Global Twitter Heartbeat: The Geography of Twitter,' *First Monday* 18[5].

Lessig, L., 1999. *Code and Other Laws of Cyberspace*, New York: Basic Books.

Lévy, J., 1994. *L'espace légitime*, Paris: Presses de Sciences Po.

Lévy, J., 1996. 'La ville, concept géographique, objet politique', *Le débat* [92].

Lévy, J., 1999. *Le tournant géographique*, Paris: Belin.

Lussault, M., 1998. 'Images [de la ville] et politique territoriale', *Revue de G*éographie de Lyon 73[1]: 45–53.

Lussault, M., 2007. *L'homme spatial*, Paris: Seuil.

Lussault, M. & Stock, M., 2010. 'Doing with Space: Towards a Pragmatics of Space', *Social Geography* 5[1], pp.11–19.

Merzeau, L., 2009. 'Du signe à la trace: l'information sur mesure', *Hermès* 53: 23–29.

Michel, J.B. et al., 2011. 'Quantitative Analysis of Culture Using Millions of Digitized Books', *Science* 331[6014]: 176–182.

Mitchell, W.J., 1996. *City of Bits: Space, Place, and the Infobahn*, Cambridge: MIT Press.

Mitchell, W.J., 2000. *E-topia*, Cambridge: MIT Press.

Neuhaus, F., 2010. 'UrbanDiary: A Tracking Project Capturing the Beat and Rhythm of the City: Using GPS Devices to Visualise Individual and Collective Routines within Central London', *The Journal of Space Syntax* 1[2]: 336

Nova, N., 2009. *Les médias géolocalisés: comprendre les nouveaux espaces numériques*, Limoges: FYP Editions.

Olteanu, A.M., Couronné, T., & Fen-Chong, J., 2011. 'Modélisation des trajectoires spatio-temporelles issues des traces numériques de téléphones mobiles', in *SAGEO '11*, Paris: International Conference on Spatial Analysis et GEOmatics.

O'Neill, E. et al., 2006. 'Instrumenting the City: Developing Methods for Observing and Understanding the Digital Cityscape', in Dourish, Paul & Fridayeds, Adrian (eds.), Ubicom 2006. *Lecture Notes in Computer Science*, Berlin, Heidelberg: Springer, pp. 315–332.

Paquot, T., Lussault, M. & Younès, C., 2007. *Habiter, le propre de l'humain*. Paris: La Découverte.

Paradiso, M., 2011. 'Information Geography: A Bridge Between Engineering and the Social Sciences', *Journal of Urban Technology* 13[3]: 77–92.

Phithakkitnukoon, S. & Olivier, P., 2011. 'Sensing Urban Social Geography Using Online Social Networking Data', Barcelona: AAAI Workshop on Social Mobile Web.

Popper, K., 2002 [1957]. *The Poverty of Historicism*, Oxford: Routledge.

Purves, R.S. et al., 2011. 'Describing Place Through User Generated Content', *First Monday* 16[9].

Rattenbury, T., Good, N., & Naaman, M., 2007. 'Towards Automatic Extraction of Event and Place Semantics from Flickr Tags', *Proceedings of the 30th Annual International ACM SIGIR Conference on Research and Development in Information Retrieval*: 103–110.

Ratti, C. et al., 2006. 'Mobile Landscapes: Using Location Data from Cell Phones for Urban Analysis.' *Environment and Planning B: Planning and Design* 33[5]: 727–748.

Reades, J. et al., 2007. 'Cellular Census: Explorations in Urban Data Collection', *IEEE Pervasive Computing* 6[3]: 30–38.

Reades, J., Calabrese, F., & Ratti, C., 2009. 'Eigenplaces: Analysing Cities Using the Space-Time Structure of the Mobile Phone Network', *Environment and Planning B: Planning and Design* 36: 824–836.

Shoval, N. & Isaacson, M., 2007. 'Tracking Tourists in the Digital Age', *Annals of Tourism Research* 34[1]: 141–159.

Song, C. et al., 2010. 'Limits of Predictability in Human Mobility', *Science* 327[5968]: 1018–1021.

Söderström, O., 2000. *Des images pour agir: le visuel en urbanisme*, Paris: Payot.

Thrift, N., 2004. 'Remembering the Technological Unconscious by Foregrounding Knowledges of Position', *Environment and Planning D Society and Space* 22 [1]: 175-190.

Thrift, N. & French, S., 2002. 'The Automatic Production of Space', *Transactions of the Institute of British Geographers* 27[3]: 309–335.

Torrens, P.M., 2010. 'Geography and Computational Social Science', *GeoJournal* 75[2]: 133–148.

Vaccari, A. et al., 2009. 'Towards the SocioScope: An Information System for the Study of Social Dynamics Through Digital Traces', in ACM GIS '09, *Proceedings of the 17th ACM SIGSPATIAL International Conference on Advances in Geographic Information Systems*, New York: GIS '09, pp. 52–61.

Vaughan, L., 2007. 'The Spatial Syntax of Urban Segregation', *Progress in Planning* 67[3]: 205–294.

Zook, M.A., 2001. 'Old Hierarchies or New Networks of Centrality?: The Global Geography of the Internet Content Market', *American Behavioral Scientist* 44[10]: 1679–1696.

Websites

Amsterdam RealTime – http://realtime.waag.org/

Archipelago – http://www.urbagram.net/archipelago/

Biomapping – http://biomapping.net/

Elastic Mapping – http://nimk.nl/nl/elastic-mapping-live-performance-esther-polak

Facebook – Gross National Happiness – http://apps.facebook.com/usa_gnh/

Google Flu Trends – http://www.google.org/flutrends/

Hotmap - Microsoft Research – http://hotmap.msresearch.us/

Linkfluence – http://fr.linkfluence.net/insights-2-0/atlas/

Live Singapore – http://senseable.mit.edu/livesingapore/exhibition.html

New City Landascape Maps – http://urbantick.blogspot.com/2010/01/new-city-land-scapes-interactive.html

PersonalGeography–http://www.flickr.com/photos/walkingsf/sets/72157628738161697/with/6644014421/

Real Time Rome – http://senseable.mit.edu/realtimerome/

Revealing Paris Through Velib' Data - http://www.girardin.org/fabien/tracing/velib/

SpotRank - Skyhook – http://www.skyhookwireless.com/spotrank/

Tag Maps - Yahoo! Research Berkeley – http://tagmaps.research.yahoo.com/

UrbanMobs – http://www.urbanmobs.fr

Vizualizing Facebook Friends – http://paulbutler.org/archives/visualizing-facebook-friends/

World Tournistness Map – http://www.bluemoon.ee/~ahti/touristiness-map/

Chapter 14

Augmented Reality and the Place of Dreams

André Ourednik

The classic, physical idea of space is built on the paradigm of exclusivity: two objects cannot occupy the same place at the same time. This logic merits challenging through the exploration of augmented-reality technologies. The foundations of cartographic representation are being upset as Borges' *aporia* of 1:1-scale map becomes a practical possibility.

In Herzog's *Fitzcarraldo* (1982), Klaus Kinski, his eyes deep in another world, stands on the shore of a river and says: 'Everyday life is only an illusion, behind which lies the reality of dreams'. According to him, this is what the Jivaro Indians believe. In his own dream, *Fitzcarraldo* sees his boat climbing over the hill to reach another river, in order to sail downstream, loaded with latex to be transformed into money at the river's end. The money, in turn, is traded for Fitzcarraldo's dream: an Italian opera master singing in the midst of the Amazon jungle. He envisions a place of aesthetic ecstasy in a world of fierce competition for resources and land.

There is a gap between *Fitzcarraldo* and the Jivaros, as they do not share the same dream. However, what unites them is their will to inhabit the world – not according to what there *appears* to be there, but according to what *ought* to be. In geomatics, knowledge about what there is in space is organized into layers of spatial information. *Fitzcarraldo* and the Jivaros strive for existence in spatial layers they could call their own. Their struggle is hard, at the beginning of a century characterized by *monospatial* logics in which only one dream can come into being in a given place. The boat cannot sail on *and* be sacrificed to the river. The Amazonian forest cannot be an object of industrial conquest *and* the newfound Eden. Aristotelian logic does not offer the poetic lenience of Heraclitus' 'and', by which 'we step *and do not* step into the same rivers'[1] twice. In this paper, I argue that we might do so again. A new logic of spatial experience is emerging with the development of a technology called 'augmented reality'. The latter offers a renewed lenience to spatial exclusiveness. How much lenience, however, is also to be discussed.

The emergence of augmented reality

'Augmented reality' entered into our lives as both a concept and a possible experience of our world. As a concept, it is directly related to 'virtual reality', a term that, in fact, has been in use since the 19th century, for instance to describe the effect of fables and parables in literature,[2] the experience of memory,[3] or the role of imagination as an incentive to leisure travel.[4] In this classical definition, 'virtual' is not contrasted with 'real', but rather *actual* (*see* Waldenfels, 2008: 231). In its current meaning, which refers specifically to a computer-based experience, the expression was first used in 1989 by Jaron Lanier,[5] co-founder of the first company to sell 'virtual reality' goggles and gloves, and more recently co-developer of the Kinect device for the Xbox 360. Even in the more recent use of the expression, 'virtual realities' are thought of as worlds of experience that *could* be real, but that have not been made quite real yet. For cost, safety, temporary technical limitations, and other reasons, their demiurges only 'simulate' them in a virtual *representation*.

---

[1] *Hoc est, quod ait Heraclitus: In idem flumen bis descendimus et non descendimus.* (Seneca, *Letters*, 58)

[2] Fables and parables, in *The Illustrated Family Journal*, J. Clayton (ed.), London: 1846, p. 148.

[3] Upham, T. C. (1857). *Letters aesthetic, social, and moral, written from Europe, Egypt, and Palestine*. H. Longstreth, p. 76.

[4] Simpson, A. L. (1861). *Pioneers: or, Biographical sketches of leaders in various paths*. T. Nelson and Sons, p. 42.

[5] Technological developer, Jaron Lanier is also a harsh critic of the social impact of collaborative web technology. See, e.g. Lanier, J. (2011). *You Are Not a Gadget: A Manifesto*. Vintage.

The first papers to mention the idea of *augmenting* reality appeared slightly later, in the early 1990s (McKey et al., 1993; Feiner et al., 1993). Unlike mere virtual reality, augmented reality is thought to present a virtual world that enriches, rather than replaces, the real world, instead of blocking [it] out (Feiner et al., 1993). Shortly after the term was coined, 'augmented reality' superseded 'virtual reality' as an object of public interest.[6] Whether the real world could indeed be blocked out, replaced, or even slightly augmented is another question. The 'coiners', however, did not ask this question, a point to which I shall return before the end of the text. Of main interest, however, is what augmented reality has become, and to what extent it could change our understanding of space, politics, and social relations.

Augmented reality as a sociotechnical rhizome

Regarding AR purely as a software innovation would obscure not only its historic and cultural relevance but also the very way in which it functions. It is more appropriate to see AR as a *sociotechnical structure*[7] made of at least three categories of components: a mobile device, a specific space, and a human actor.

Mobile devices as augmenting filters

The *mobile device* is the most tangible component of AR, a kind of augmenting filter between a subject's senses of perception and the perceived world. In this respect, the Walkman of the 1980s is also a type of AR, though the current use of the AR concept is limited to the augmented *visual* experience.[8] AR consists in the 'laying of dynamic and context-specific information over the visual field of a user' (Manovich, 2006). The technical possibility of doing so is afforded by a combination of micro-cameras

---

[6] In August 2009 already, the number of Internet searches for the newer 'virtual reality' totals only half of those for 'augmented reality'. Since 2013, interest for both terms is equal. Source: Google Trends.

[7] The notions of *actor network* (as used in the works of Michel Callon, Bruno Latour, John Law, and others) and the *rhizome* (as used in the works of Gilles Deleuze and Félix Guattari) could also be used to describe it.

[8] This restriction of the concept of AR to the augmented vision can be interpreted in terms of a domination of the visual experience in the modern conceptualization of the body and the lived world.

and portable flat screens in most smartphones. The image recorded by the camera is 'augmented' by overlaying computer-generated images of 3D objects. The next sociotechnical step in AR is the marketing of head-mounted *wearable computers* to the public (*cf.* Barfield/Caudell 2001).[9] The near future may introduce image generation to contact lenses or directly into the user's nervous system through integrated micro-devices that transmit stimuli to the optic nerve. Whatever the mobile device used, AR induces the perception of new objects in an already-existing spatial reality. The reality being augmented, however, is always a *specific* space.

The local space and the World Wide Map

Two broad categories of space can be augmented by AR: local or global.[10] An example of local space augmentation can be found in the work of Swiss artist Camille Scherrer (2008) (Figure 1), a book in which images climb out of the pages when looked at through an augmenting filter. In this case, the augmenting figure's location is strictly determined by the spatial reference provided by the book itself. Other examples of local AR define the spatial reference based on *fiduciary marks*, such as QR tags or other wall-applied stickers, or *natural feature tracking* (*see* Uricchio, 2011, 31ff.).

Global ARs function in the same manner, but their spatial reference is a *World Wide Map*.

I wish to call 'World Wide Map' the common referential system of geographical coordinates by which global society locates all things on the surface of Earth. In its foundations, the system is not new – the first use of such coordinates dates back at least as far as Hipparchus of Nicaea (2nd century B.C.; Thrower, 2008: 23). But, as in the case of the World Wide Web, the concept alone is not enough. In order to function, this locating instrument also requires a widespread cultural consensus around the ideas of longitude and latitude, which was only reached in the 19th century (*ibid.* 38). Even today, its locating capability is not a given; it is only assured by a complex socio-technical structure that the concept of 'map' alone does

---

[9] Google has been selling its glasses in the USA since May 2014, with moderate success. Producers of similar products include Epson (Moveiro Smart Glasses), Optivent (ORA-1 Digital Eyeware), or Vuzix (M100 Smart Glasses).

[10] We should accordingly speak of local AR and global AR. To distinguish the two, the developers of the AR application Layar use the terms *vision*-based or *geolocation*-based AR (LAYAR 2012).

Fig. 1 Camille Scherrer, 2008, *Le monde des montagnes*. The spatial reference of the augmenting objects in this example is the page of the book.

not quite describe. 'World Wide Map' seems a more appropriate term for this impressive locating rhizome.

Without the World Wide Map, AR could not exist beyond the local scope, since computers would not be able to calculate where to position the augmenting objects. The World Wide Map thus upholds the monospatial logic. But, as we shall see, it is also a condition of its overcoming. To get a better idea of its nature, we can consider it as consisting of two components:

- A *conceptual framework*, made of a spherical system of longitudes and latitudes whose coordinates are linked to points on the surface of the earth via a complex projection.[11]
- A *material system* of satellites and ground-based emitters, whose combined signals, considered within the context of the framework, assign a unique *position* to any device capable of receiving and interpreting them, *i.e.* of processing this plurality of signals into a spatial coordinate. The USA-based Global Positioning System (GPS) is the

---

[11] The quality of the projection between the geode (the actual physical form of the planet Earth), its ellipsoid model, and its spherical coordinate system is the expertise domain of a specific branch of the earth sciences called *geodetics*. This projection is constantly recalculated to account for continental drift and other phenomena.

most popular.[12] Other systems, such as the collection of spatial data from local Wi-Fi networks, likewise contribute. The device also provides information on its orientation with respect to Earth's surface and to the cardinal directions (*see* Uricchio, 2011), generating a particular view of the World Wide Map.

The World Wide Map provides a unique space in which every object is assigned a place. But it is also a geometrical abstraction. As such, it locates not only physical objects but rather anything with a pair of coordinates attached to it. In fact, anything we can possibly imagine. Unlike impenetrable physical space, the World Wide Map can accommodate an unlimited number of objects into a single point. GIS professionals, used to working with 'layers' of spatial data, experience this feature on a daily basis without according much attention to its singularity. As a World Wide Map, the world can be draped in countless such layers, and thus multiplied into as many spaces of cognitive experience: the geological space, the demographic space, the economic space, the climatic space, the space of political boundaries of today and of the distant past, etc.[13]

For a long time, these layers could be observed only from a zenithal perspective, outside of the human subject. The map that says 'you are here' says so looking down at your location, while you stand there and look all around and above you. In this respect, classic maps should bear the inscription 'you are *there*', as *here* is only where *you* perceive yourself as being standing. Through augmented reality, however, the *here* of the map and the *here* of the observer can be merged into a single point of view. In other words, the abstract experience of space *as a map* can be integrated with the visual, kinetic, acoustic and olfactory experience of space made by the *human body*. The map is brought to the subject's own, ground-level perspective, and the image of reality *becomes* part of reality, with no perspective

---

[12] The Russian ГЛОНАСС (Глобальная Навигационная Спутниковая Система) and the European Galileo are the most prominent competitors of GPS. The first is not implemented in most large public devices, but many do use ГЛОНАСС as a geopositioning alternative. Galileo will only be available to the general public in 2020. It is worth noting here that its very existence was subject to political tension between the EU and US until 2004 (China and India, however, provided strong support for Galileo). Even on the global level of the World Wide Map, a plurality of spaces is possible. Yet, even at this level, this plurality remains in conflict with the monospatial logics serving the interest of specific nation states.

[13] For impressive examples of ancient map projections over contemporary GIS, see the *David Rumsey Map Collection*, http://www.davidrumsey.com/view/google-maps (visited on 2014-11-24).

shift in projection or scale. AR makes real the fictional map of the Empire at a 1:1 scale that has haunted the cartographic imagination since the 19th century (Carroll, 1893: 169;[14] Borges, 1946; see Baudrillard, 1981; Eco, 1992). With one difference: in AR, there is not one but many possible images of the Empire, including images of what the Empire had been or *could* be. In the augmented Empire, there are multiple empires, each one with its own set of visible 3D objects superposed on the image captured by the camera of a mobile device. Looking through the eye of the beheld, the observer can dwell in his own Empire, or, in more technical jargon, in the 'layer' of spatial information of his choice or making. These new degrees of freedom bring us to the last component of AR: the individual human actor.

Human actors

The one thing that can be said about reality is that it is a condition whereby something appears to someone. This implies that the individual observer is a necessary component of any reality, including an augmented one. By perceiving a reality, the human actor participates in its making. With the introduction of AR, however, the actor acquires two extra degrees of freedom. First, he can choose which of the many *possible* realities becomes *actual,*[15] that is, perceived *here and now* in his own augmented space. Second, he is empowered to add his own augmenting objects, thus promoting his 'dreams' to realities, possibly shared by others. Later, we shall discuss some examples of the technical frameworks in which he can do so.

---

[14] – 'That's another thing we've learned from your Nation,' said Mein Herr, 'map-making. But we've carried it much further than you. What do you consider the largest map that would be really useful?' – 'About six inches to the mile.' – 'Only six inches!' exclaimed Mein Herr. 'We very soon got to six yards to the mile. Then we tried a hundred yards to the mile. And then came the grandest idea of all! We actually made a map of the country, on the scale of a mile to the mile!' – 'Have you used it much?' I enquired. – 'It has never been spread out, yet,' said Mein Herr : 'the farmers objected: they said it would cover the whole country, and shut out the sunlight! So we now use the country itself, as its own map, and I assure you it does nearly as well' (Carroll 1893, 169).

[15] N.B.: The 'actual' and the 'virtual' are two distinct categories of the real or, in P. Lévy, states of being distinct from the real. Proust, quoted by Deleuze, sets up the distinction, defining memory as virtual: Real but not actual, ideal but not abstract. See Gilles Deleuze, *Différence et répétition*, Paris: PUF, 1969 (*Difference and Repetition*. New York: Columbia University Press, 1994) ; Pierre Lévy, *Qu'est-ce que le virtuel*, Paris: La Découverte, 1995 (*Becoming Virtual: Reality in the Digital Age*, Plenum Trade, 1998).

The socially shared aspect of AR is most essential here, as we are dealing not with the actualisation of an individual hallucination but with a shared spatial experience. In AR, each human actor becomes a creator of possible realities that can be actualised by *others*. The World Wide Map and mobile devices discussed above are the conditions for this sharing.

Now, one might argue that such sharing is already possible in the reality called 'physical space', for instance through works of art. Indeed, it is possible, but only to the extent that the 'physical space' permits. This space is impenetrable and, as far as our planet is concerned, finite. This means that it cannot hold more spatially-extended objects than its own scope allows, and even less so in the limited number of places that are easily accessible to human spectators. Only AR allows for a plurality of objects of sensory and first-person experience to be situated in the same place.

Overcoming spatial exclusiveness

> 'Si supponga ora che ciascun suddito afferri un lembo della mappa e lo ripieghi progressivamente rinculando: si raggiungerebbe una fase critica in cui la totalità dei sudditi si troverebbe addensata al centro del territorio, sopra la mappa, sostenendone i lembi ripiegati sopra la testa. Situazione detta di catastrofe a scroto, in cui l'intera popolazione dell'impero rimane rinchiusa in un sacculo trasparente, in situazione di stallo teorico e di grave disagio fisico e psichico. I sudditi dovranno dunque, a mano a mano che avviene il ripiegamento, saltare al di fuori della mappa, sul territorio, continuando a ripiegarla dall'esterno, sino a che le ultime fasi del ripiegamento avvengano quando più nessun suddito giace nel sacculo interno.' (Eco, 1992)[16]

---

[16] "Now suppose that each subject grasps a bit of the edge of the map and begins folding it, while retreating further and further. A critical point would be reached at which the subjects would all be crammed together at the center of the territory, standing on top of the center of the map and supporting its folded edges above their heads: a situation aptly termed scrotum catastrophe, as the entire population of the empire is enclosed in a little transparent sac, in a situation of theoretical stalemate and of considerable physical and psychological discomfort. The subjects must therefore, as the folding gradually proceeds, leap instead outside the map and onto the territory itself, where they will continue folding from outside, until the final stages of the folding, when no subject remains inside the sac." Eco, U. (2013). On the impossibility of Drawing a Map of the Empire on a Scale of 1 to 1, How To Travel With A Salmon: and Other Essays. Vintage Books.

Let us take a step back and consider the actual progress that has resulted from this transformation. One of our dominant ideas about space is the *principle of impenetrability*, according to which two bodies cannot coexist in the same place at the same time. In the Hellenic intellectual sphere of influence, this principle already appears in Aristotle's *Physics* (Book IV), from which it radiates throughout history, constantly reformulated and supported by new and imaginative arguments. French philosopher Jean de Jandun, for instance, teaching Aristotle at the beginning of the 14th century, argues that if *two* things could share the same space, then an infinite number of things could as well. For him, this implies that the whole universe could be held within a single millet seed, which he rejects as an absurdity (Grant, 1978 : 552).

In Aristotle's *Physics*, the principle of impenetrability already appears in its most radical form. First, he builds a strong link between existence and spatiality. Space is that 'without which nothing else can exist' (*Physics* IV, 1); something lacking a place *is not*. Second, the author of *Physics* does not admit the existence of void, which implies that anything that exists must *make room for itself* somewhere, where something else already is. Third, space is everywhere, inside and outside of things, so that there can be only one space. Thus anything that claims to exist must occupy a single place – the Aristotelian *topos* – in the one and only space that is the universe.

If we sum up these views, the principle of impenetrability translates into what can be called a principle of *spatial exclusiveness*. We can take as an example the finite amount of space comprised between the Earth's surface and its upper atmosphere. A consequence of the Aristotelian point of view, then, is that anything that claims to *be* must find its unshared portion of this space or renounce its existence. The argument may resemble a philosophical speculation, with no consequence for social life. But seeing it as such would be a gross underestimation of the impact of physical worldviews on politics. For example, when Hobbes – incidentally a fierce critic of the political teachings of Aristotle – wrote *Leviathan* in the 17th century, he started his treatise by presenting his atomistic worldview. In his universe made of moving atoms that only remain in motion, humans too persist in a similar fashion and, in so doing, become each other's 'wolves' – in Hobbes' famous quote. The whole construction of *Leviathan* is rooted in the need to overcome this 'state of nature'. His text remains one of the founding cornerstones of the concept of the modern State.

In a similar way, the image of space as a container filled by physical bodies all occupying their exclusive positions is not only relevant for
physics. *Anything* we imagine as a possible experience for a human being
must be situated somewhere in this spatial container. How self-evident
this idea was for ancient scholars becomes well apparent in the depictions
of the mythical realm of the Christian Paradise. This realm is imagined
neither as a-spatial, nor as other-worldly, but as concretely situated on the
surface of the globe, namely in far-eastern Asia, as depicted, for instance,
in St. Beatus' *Terrarum Orbis* map from the 8th century. It is still as much
situated in Dante's 14th-century representation, merely displaced to the
outermost 'celestial sphere' that encompasses the Earth, according to a
cosmology that Dante directly borrows from Aristotle.

Aporias that are rooted in this conception of space do not, of course,
go unnoticed by scholars. A most obvious aporia lies in explaining the
motion of a body through a space *already filled* with other bodies. This
problem finds its solution in the idea of the three-dimensional void, evoked
by Nemesius in the 3rd century B.C., but only adopted definitively in the
17th century (Grant, 1978: 561). While the problem of the movement of
bodies is solved in this manner, the concept of void also brings along other
unsolved problems, such as explaining the propagation of electromagnetic
waves through a medium-less space.

An equally aporetic question is that of the place of the human *mind*. If
every portion of space is occupied by either a body or a void, where can the
mind be? Descartes attempted to answer that question by placing the mind
apart in the spaceless realm of the *res cogitans*, but without ever providing a satisfactory explanation of how such a mind acts on spatial matter.
Still facing the same problem in the mid-18th century, Julien Offray de La
Mettrie dismisses Cartesian dualism, and in doing so, equates mind with
matter. Thus is La Mettrie's human-machine born.[17] Its conceptual emergence is also rooted in the premise that only that which occupies its *own
portion of space* can *exist*. The obsession of locating thought (and dismiss-
ing psychological theories that do not focus on doing so) persists today in
bioneurology. This locating imperative does not concern only the mind,
but anything that is subject to thought and analysis. There is, as Heidegger
(1950) wrote, a metaphysics of rigor, an injunction to project all objects
of thought on a ground-plan (*Grundriss*) of natural processes. I argue that

---

[17]   *See* La Metterie, J. O. de. (1748). *Homme machine*. Paris: Frédéric Henry.

the concept of an impenetrable space is a fundamental component of this ground-plan. Even today, the idea that anything that claims to *be* must be *somewhere* in *space* where *nothing else is* persists. This view is not circumvented even in contemporary theories of *emergence* or *supervenience* which, while recognising some degree of ontological or at least semantic existence of material macrophenomena, basically agree on a monistic view of space and its exclusive location imperative.

The struggle for reality to overcome the limits of space

Now, if we apply the principle of impenetrability to the space in which humans dwell, anyone who claims to exist in a portion of space seems to be expected to exclude all those that claim to share it. This applies to persons, groups, civilizations, or any product of human creation. Understanding reality as something fundamentally spatial, and space as something impenetrable and finite, sets the basis for an existential *competition for reality*. A society living in one single and impenetrable space is like the psychiatric patient 'caught up in actuality', incapable of projecting oneself into virtual realities, such as one's own future, or to account for the life experience of others (*see* Waldenfels, 2008, 232). Such 'virtualization of reality' is only possible when we consider not only the possibilities within our world or possible rearrangements of this world, but also *possible worlds and possible spaces*, in which we cross over *like into another world* (ibid, 233).[18] Even Lefebvre, who wishes to see the planetary space as a collective artwork of humanity, thinks of this space in the singular (1974: 484–485), deeming artwork itself just another object of conflict. Indeed, being incapable of understanding the coexistence of two distinct realities in the same place leaves only three manners of dealing with other realities: their negation by existential assimilation, their reduction to nothingness, or their spatial expulsion. In the social world, spatial exclusiveness translates into *spatial exclusion*. My point is that this exclusion can only be overcome if the limits of space are lifted – an act in which AR could play a significant role.

Depending on the space we are dealing with, of course, the abrogation of limits requires different solutions. The existential competition of

[18] Our translation.

biological organisms, for example, can only be set aside if the environmental resources needed for their existence *as* biological realities were unlimited. This can be achieved either by increasing the land's productivity, finding other ways of keeping biological bodies alive, or by redefining what biological reality is. All three solutions are open to scientific and fictional speculation of all types. Less speculative, however, is what global AR already offers: the possibility of stacking multiple objects of spatial sensory experience into the same place. With AR, 3D objects such as works of art, monuments, symbolic structures, and architectural elements in general can share the same space.

This is important because space is one of the universally approved repositories of *symbolic capital* (*see e.g.* Bourdieu, 1989: 21). The accessibility of places, their relative positions, the ideas associated with their toponyms, and individuals' actual frequentation of them all make space into a scale of values. In a reality comprised of only one space, this scale is monistic; in other words, only one scale of values is possible, and actors of all sizes – from individuals to institutions – compete to define it. A plurality of world values is only possible if we recognise a plurality of spaces (see Aase, 1994). I argue that AR offers the possibility of a situated sensory experience of this plurality at many scales of humans' relationships to space. Some architects, for instance, point out that AR allows for the reintroduction of an iconographic dimension to objects, without making them into vectors of ideological conformism. Manovich (2006) writes: 'If the messages communicated by traditional architecture were static and reflected the dominant ideology, today's electronic dynamic interactive displays make it possible for these messages to change continuously, making the information surface a potential space of contestation and dialog, which functions as the material manifestation of the often invisible public sphere'. In AR, architecture and mapping converge. Architecture is no longer limited to monistic physical space but develops in a plural space composed of spatially superposed maps and thematic map layers. By opening up this plurality, AR opens up a world beyond the struggle for reality in symbolic space. Let us now consider some concrete examples of implementation.

Implementation and examples of uses: aesthetics as a political process

Several software applications for iPhone or Android devices have popularized mobile global AR as recently as 2009. Some only allow for the visualisation of augmented realities, while others allow users to create them collaboratively. From this point of view, we can distinguish between AR and *collaborative AR* (CAR), [19] much as we would distinguish between maps and collaborative maps. The most important CAR 'browsers'[20] today are Layar, Wikitude, and Junaio. In May 2014, the three companies reached first agreements towards a cross-platform interoperability of their applications.[21] Although the attention of Layar's developers now seems to have shifted to view-based local AR (see below), all three applications still offer a multilayer framework that allows not only for the visualization of geolocated AR layers, but also their creation by third parties. Some of these third parties do not develop final layers, but layer creation systems that allow even users with weak computer skills to augment reality with their own objects, from simple 2D tags to fully-extended 3D objects. In March 2011, there were over 470 layers in Layar. This number had reached over 14,500 by October 2012.[22]

Most existing layers are still limited to the localisation of already occupied physical places: you are often guided to shops, fast-food eateries, bus stops, and popular touristic attractions. Some projects, however, do take creative advantage of this empowerment.

One such project is *ARTags* (Letoqueux *et al.,* 2012), an interface for geolocated drawing available for all three of the browsers mentioned above. The application literally builds wall upon wall: it drapes space with more space, providing a new drawable surface. *ARTags* has a 'first come, first served' logic, an implicit homestead principle whereby the drawings, once created, remain, making the space they occupy unavailable to others. Nevertheless, it has the benefit of offering a second space whose existence

---

[19] The term 'collaborative augmented reality' was coined as early as 2002 in the context of human-machine interface research (Billinghurs/Kato 2002).

[20] The term 'AR browsers' results from a semantic shift from the notion World Wide Web 'browsers'. We could call them World Wide Map 'browsers'.

[21] Dirk Grotten. (2014-05-28). Layar, Metaio and Wikitude Now Include AR Interoperability. https://www.layar.com/news/blog/2014/05/28/layar-metaio-wikitude-now-include-ar-interoperability/ Viewed 2014-11-25.

[22] Source: http://www.layar.com/layers/ viewed in March 2011 and in October 2012. In November 2014, the list of layers is only searchable through the mobile browser.

makes conflict between official planners of the urban space and its self-proclaimed 'taggers' less inevitable. Already here, AR becomes an open challenge to a territorial logic of exclusion, as discussed above. In the long term, more elaborate forms of such AR traces left by urban users could become inspiration to the physical planners of the city.

A more elaborate example of AR as an alternative social space is Sander Veenhof's and Mark Skwarek's permanent exhibition between the walls of the New York Museum of Modern Art (Veenhof & Skwarek, 2012). As the artists put it, 'the show is happening in augmented reality, and will therefore not be visible to regular visitors of the MoMA'. In fact, it exists 'only' as an AR-layer, yet occupies floors 1 to 6, virtual floors 7 and 8, and the garden. The exhibit 'opened' on October 9, 2010. The project's deeper meaning becomes clear when one considers the importance of the MoMA as a spatial instrument of social recognition of art and artists. What can or cannot become part of its collection is the decision of an institutional power that confers its value to art. This power itself, of course, is not bound to a single person or museum but results from a highly pluralistic process involving media, collectors, art investors, scholars, artists, and other actors. However, once its judgment has been passed, it is written in the spatial fabric of history, and becomes hard to contest. In Veenhof and Skwarek's work, this artistic legitimacy, so solidly anchored in a controlled portion of space – i.e. in the territory of legitimate art – is subsumed. The plurality of logics capable of conferring value to art is re-assessed. Following this example, any alternative group of artists and/or art viewers can meet in a parallel space in which the positions of centrality and periphery are redistributed.

But AR as a means of technical circumvention of established power relationships can easily surpass the realm of art. A political slogan is a slogan, even if it is spray-painted on a hyper-wall. And it is as difficult to erase AR graffiti as it is to prevent the spread of political 'tweets'. The role of new media must not be exaggerated in the current state of technology,[23] but as media become more pervasive and more intertwined with the physical experience of space, we are looking towards a future in which more delicate and far-reaching examples of political action in AR emerge. Take, for example, a place in the antique city of Jerusalem,

---

[23] In the recent 'Arab Spring', for instance, new media's role was, at first, highly mediatised, but later questioned following deeper research. See, e.g., Aday, S., Farrell, H., Lynch, M., Sides, J., & Freelon, D. (2012). Blogs and bullets II. New Media and conflict after the Arab Spring. *Peaceworks (United States Institute of Peace)*, (80).

whose very toponym is laden with a persistent and symbolic conflict. The Hebrews call it *Har haBáyith*, the Arabs *Haram al-Sharif* and the English-speaking world knows it as the Mount of the Rock. Currently, it is the location of the Noble Sanctuary (*Haram al-Sharif*) and of the *Al-Aqsa* mosque. It is also the historically-attested location of the Temple of Solomon, which some spatial actors would like to rebuild. In an exclusively monospatial logic, the reconstruction of the past architectural element cannot circumvent the destruction of existing ones. From this perspective, present and past territories cannot be synthesised without martial undertones. But if we throw AR in the equation, could not a hyper-Temple of Solomon offer a solution to this impasse? This suggestion is easily dismissed on many grounds, but let us not judge too quickly. An AR reconstruction of a building destroyed in 70 CE by the Romans can definitely exist in the same place as the contemporary structures that currently occupy it. Of course, considering the limited capabilities of today's AR technology, this solution seems as irrelevant as building a miniature model of the 'real' thing. However, as the ontological gap between material and digital lived space[24] grows thinner (see 2.2), there might be a point at which certain issues regarding the symbolic appropriation of space could become quite unreal.

Could not, then, the West Bank Barrier also be made transparent? Regarding such questions, contemporary technology is both despairing and exalting; despairing because its solutions are desperately easy to implement in the near future yet would only be effective if they spread to all spaces, including the space of water or food supply, and exalting because it allows – at least momentarily – for the suspension of our spatial aporias. It is also dangerous, since spaces tend to act on other spaces. Dreams are programs that are more efficient when formulated with precision, and more compelling when they are concretely experienced. The Jivaros manage to transport Fitzcarraldo's boat over the hill, but they also send it down the rapids as such is the will of their god.

But let us leave behind the question of uncertain futures and consider how AR relates to our pasts. From this point of view, it can be seen as an extreme form of an urban palimpsest (Corboz, 1983). An example of this is the Berliner Mauer layer (Gardeya, 2010), an AR reconstruction of the historic scar on Germany's capital. For an AR-device owning stroller, it is a highly suggestive approximation of what the Wall must have felt like

---

[24] Throughout this text, I use the term 'lived space' in the sense of Bollnow, O.F. (1961). *Lived-Space. Philosophy Today*, 5(1), 31–39.

Fig. 2 La Frontera de los muertos border memorial. Border fence near the Lukeville
crossing in the Organ Pipe Cactus National Monument.

during the 30 years of its existence. AR, in this case, becomes an instrument of collective memory. Other layers give concrete form, even to historical facts that are less present in the collective conscience.

One such example is the *Border Memorial: Frontera de los Muertos* (Freeman 2011; Freeman & Skwarek, 2012), dedicated to the thousands of migrants who have died along the U.S./Mexico border, largely as a consequence of the U.S.'s 'prevention-through-deterrence' policy, enforced since early 1994, and which involves thousands of border patrol agents, multiple physical barriers, and the use of advanced electronic surveillance equipment (Cornelius, 2004).[25] While, in earlier decades, border-crossers' deaths were mainly 'limited' to road accidents and homicide, the subsequent periods show an alarming +1000 % increase in deaths due to hypothermia, dehydration, sunstroke, and drowning, mainly as a result of the more dangerous routes taken to avoid this new surveillance system (*ibid*). Due to

[25] See Cornelius, W. A. (2004). Death at the Border: Efficacy and Unintended Consequences of
US Immigration Control Policy. *Population and Development Review*, *27*(4), 661–685.

the remote locations, many of the bodies are never found. Those that are simply become death toll statistics. The *Frontera de los Muertos* memorial is an attempt at giving them a more pregnant reality. Removed remains are *re-placed* in the landscape, in 3D, in the form of Mexican *calaca* – a figure of a human skeleton commonly used for decoration during the Mexican Day of the Dead.[26] In this case, AR not only brings uncomfortable truths on the surface of physical space, but yields a deeper consciousness and understanding of statistical data by transforming it into a sensory experience that is not only visual, but also requires movement and physical presence in the specific environment in which the 'data' became a fact.

Bodies and algorithms: points of view beyond the traditional map

The obligation to move one's own body in a specific environment is what unifies the examples of AR use we have just seen. It is also what distinguishes the 2D and 3D visualisations used in standard geographic information systems from AR browsers like Layar, Wikitude, or Junaio. Classic maps, much like navigation systems such as Google Earth and Bing Maps, put us in an immobile posture. In AR, you move through the physical world; it is only this movement that produces the reality you observe. As William Uricchio expresses it, 'the point of view is embodied, constant, and synonymous with the viewing subject' (2011 : 32). AR does not provide an omniscient reality. It does not treat phenomena with objective distance. This, in my view, is precisely what gives an AR element like the Mexican *calaca* in Freeman & Skwarek's Border Memorial more empathic salience. Only our existence *as bodies*, subjects of pleasure and pain, gives us an *understanding* of the existence of other human beings – and by 'understanding', I mean an inner representation of the *other* as an ethical subject; one who I am not but who I could be (Ourednik, 2010, §1.4.4).

Yet – and herein lies its second specificity – AR gives your body *new* spaces, freeing it from its mono-spatial condition. At the same time as it forces you, as a body, to move to see or alter the maps – thereby participating in the construction of a new spatial reality – it frees you

---

[26] More recently, a scaled AR replica of the region has been 'installed' on the MoMA terrace in collaboration between J.C. Freeman and M. Skwarek. See: <http://www.markskwarek.com/Border%20Memorial_Frontera%20de%20los%20Muertos1_4.html>

from confinement in a single space striated with territories and borders
of established powers. Despite its embodiment, AR is as plural as the
map layers that compose a geographic information system. AR spaces
are maps because they are constructed with an explicit symbolic spatial
language and are based on an analogical relationship to other spaces. But
they are more than maps because of their 1:1 scale, in which the plurality of possible maps proper to cartography meets the sensory salience of
architecture. Like collaborative maps, they require the participation of
many individuals to be written but, like cities, they require as many individuals to be read. They turn the World Wide Map into a world in which
many worlds are possible. Or do they really *turn*?

One unifying power perhaps still looms in the depths of AR. It is the
hidden *algorithmic processing* layer (*see* Uricchio, 2011) that constantly
calculates the relative positions of objects and that binds the plurality of
our augmented bodies into a unique structure. Because of its hidden character, the algorithmic layer has the power to determine the meaning of
the word 'body': room for smells and sounds, for instance, has not yet
been made in AR worlds. The visual dimension of the embodied experience dominates. Although the algorithmic layer allows for multiple viewpoints, we should also be aware of the particular understanding of spatial
experience it conveys. The algorithm itself is a point of view, a fact that is
sometimes overlooked. As the ontological gap between AR and our everyday spatial experience shrinks, the algorithms that make AR possible will
require as much attention as the misleading map projections so criticised
by the cartographers of the 20th century.

What 'reality' exactly is being augmented?
An ontological stopover on the way
to an augmented space

Before I conclude, let us return to a consideration relative to AR that I raised
at the beginning of this text. The question is: to what degree can AR be considered *real*, and how it relates to other realities. Are augmented realities
simply 'added' to some other, basic, unalterable reality? Answering this
question is as difficult as distinguishing between 'natural' and 'artificial'
(*see* Waldenfels, 2008: 190–206). On the one hand, 'augmented reality' is
undoubtedly a necessary term: its widespread collective use allows us to
collectively reflect on the future of a socio-technical construction process

that has already begun. But on the other hand, it is also a problematic, and, frankly speaking, rather unfortunate term. Indeed the very idea of 'adding' to reality implies an ontological view in which reality appears as a *set of things*. Such is, of course, the etymological meaning of 'reality' (*res*, the thing; *realitas*, someone's property). But since the 17th century at least, the English word 'reality' has borne another meaning, which is best expressed in the German *Realität* vs. *Wirklichkeit*. While *Realität* is rooted in the thing itself, *Wirklichkeit* is rooted in the idea of effect (*Wirkung*). Reality as *Wirklichkeit* is not a *set* of things but rather a *process* – or, specifically, a fundamentally indeterminate process that can only be understood as a coming-into-being of things contingent on an observational stance. Reality *happens* as reality-related subjects 'subjectify' themselves, and concomitantly objectify their existence, which appears as a constantly varying set of objects. To some degree, these objects can be shared among subjects, through the mediation of language or other means, to which belong also geographic models. But even this shared reality is a process, and not a finite set that anything could augment.

The very concept of AR confines reality in *Realität*. In so doing, it regresses towards the worldview of ontological realism – to which positivist science also subscribes – according to which all subjects *ultimately* share one unique and finite set of things – in other words, an 'absolute reality' (*see* Waldenfels, 2008: 212). In this worldview, anything beyond this *absolutum* is considered a dream or illusion, despite AR's efforts to link those 'illusions' to the reality it augments. The coiners of the term have thereby failed to point out that the only 'reality' actually being augmented is not a *reality*, but rather the physical model of an impenetrable space (§ 3). The great irony – and the great contribution – of 'augmented reality' is that it builds on this model while providing an escape from its reduction. It restores the *plurality* of spaces we need to arrive at an understanding of reality. Perhaps we should call it 'de-reduced reality', or simply 'augmented physical space'.

Neither reality, nor space is given

Despite its unfortunate name, the sociotechnical phenomenon known as 'augmented reality' has allowed for a major paradigmatic shift with regard to our being-in-space. From an AR standpoint, what earlier critics called alienated 'spectacle' (Debord, 1967) or 'simulacrum' (Baudrillard, 1981) suddenly has a radically different ontological and sociological status (*see* Lapenta, 2011). *Mediated information* can no longer be considered a realm in which humans are alienated from their relationship to others and the plurality of their sensory experience of the world. Not only is information itself increasingly produced in a decentralized manner through direct participation, it is also becoming increasingly holistic from a sensory standpoint. Compared to other collaborative frameworks, such as collaborative publishing or collaborative mapping, collaborative augmented realities allow us to share a common kinetic experience. They also allow us to alter environments, filling them with new sensory facts. Despite being limited to sight and movement, the involvement of other senses can be expected in the near future, further closing the ontological gap between 'material' and 'digital' lived space. At least in the examples we have seen, ARs are not confined simulacrums that merely absorb human action, but rather new modes of world-making that, as such, offer a potential for world-change (*see* Bourdieu, 1989: 23).

What AR is already changing is our understanding of space. The possibilities they afford remind us that neither reality nor space is given, but that space – like time – is only a modal concept by which individuals relate to their lived world and to each other. They remind us of the inherent plurality of this relatedness by breaking down the barriers of spatial monism and its logics of spatial exclusiveness and exclusion, partially opening an escape from the logics of power 'sedimented' in physical space. They make the symbolic appropriation of multiple spaces a sensory reality and, in doing so, multiply inhabited spaces, making room for the reality of dreams between the layers of everyday life.

References

Aase, T.H., 1994. 'Symbolic Space: Representations of Space in Geography and Anthropology', *Geografiska Annaler Series B Human Geography*, 76(1), 51–58.

Aristotle, 1930. *Physica, The Works of Aristotle v. 2*, trans. R. P. Hardie & R. K. Gaye, Oxford: Clarendon Press.

Baudrillard J., 1981. *Simulacres et simulation*, Paris: Galilée.

Barfield, W., & Caudell, T., 2001. *Fundamentals of Wearable Computers and Augmented Reality*, Oxford, New York: Taylor & Francis.

Billinghurst, M., & Kato, H., 2002. *Collaborative Augmented Reality*. Working paper, <http://masters.donntu.org/2012/iii/akchurin/library/article9.htm>

Bourdieu, P., 1989. 'Social Space and Symbolic Power', *Sociological Theory*, 7(1), 14–25.

Borges, J. L., 1946. 'Del rigor en la ciencia' *Los Anales de Buenos Aires*, March 1946, p. 53.

Carroll, L., 1893. *Sylvie and Bruno Concluded*, London, New York: MacMillan and Co.

Corboz, A.,1983. 'Le territoire comme palimpseste', *Diogène*, (121), 14–35.

Debord, G., 1967. *La Société du spectacle*, Paris: Buchet-Chastel.

Deleuze, G., & Guattari, F., 1980. *Mille Plateaux*, Paris: Minuit.

Eco, U., 1992. Dell'impossibilità di costruire la carta dell'impero 1 a 1. *Il secondo diario minimo*, Milan: Bompiani.

Feiner, S., Macintyre, B., & Seligmann, D, 1993. 'Knowledge-based augmented reality' *Communications of the ACM*.

Freeman, J.C., 2012. 'The Border Memorial: Frontera de los Muertos', <http://www.layar.com/layers/bordermemorial> (visited on 2014-11-25).

Freeman, J.C., & Skwarek, M, 2012. 'Border Memorial: Frontera de los Muertos', <http://bordermemorial.wordpress.com> (visited on 2014-11-25).

Heidegger, M., 1950 [1938]. 'Die Zeit des Weltbildes', *Gesamtausgabe. Bd 5. Holzwege*, Frankfurt: Klostermann, pp. 75–114.

Gardeya, M.R, 2010. 'Berlin Wall 3D', *Hoppala: Mobile Augmented Reality* [blog], April 14th 2010, <http://www.hoppala-agency.com/article/berlin-wall-3d> (visited on 2014-11-25).

Herzog, W., 1982. *Fitzcarraldo* [film], Peru, West Germany.

JUNAIO, <http://www.junaio.com> (visited on 2014-11-25)

Lapenta, F., 2011. 'Geomedia: on Location-Based Media, the Changing Status of Collective Image Production and the Emergence of Social Navigation Systems, *Visual Studies*, 26(1), 14–24.

Lash, S., & Urry, J., 1994. *Economies of Signs and Space*, London: Sage.

LAYAR, 'Augmented reality: Layar Reality Browser', <://www.layar.com>(visited on 2014-11-25)

Lefebvre, H., 1974. *La production de l'espace*, Paris: Anthropos.

Letoqueux, R. et al., 'ARTags', <http://www.artags.org> (visited on 2014-11-25).

MacKay, W., et al. 1993. 'Augmenting Reality: Adding Computational Dimensions to Paper', *Communications of the ACM*, 36(7): 96–7.

Manovich, L., 2006. 'The Poetics of Augmented Space', *Visual Communication* 5(219).

Ourednik, A., 2010. *L'habitant et la cohabitation dans les modèles de l'espace habité*, PhD Thesis, Lausanne: EPFL.

Scherrer, C., 2008. *Le monde des montagnes*, Diplome project, Lausanne: ECAL.

Uricchio, W., 2011. 'The Algorithmic Turn: Photosynth, Augmented Reality and the Changing Implications of the Image, *Visual Studies*, (261), 25–35.

Thrower, N J W, 2008. *Maps and Civilization: Cartography in Culture and Society*, 3rd ed., Chicago: The University of Chicago Press.

Veenhof, S. & Skwarek, M., 2012. 'MoMA AR exhibition', <http://www.layar.com/layers/moma> (visited on 2014-11-25).

Waldenfels, B., 2008. *Grenzen der Normalisierung, Studien zur Phänomenologie des Fremden 2, Erweiterte Ausgabe*, Frankfurt: Suhrkamp.

WIKITUDE, <http://www.wikitude.org> (visited on 2012-10-07)

After Cartography

Tim Ingold

I

At a recent workshop I attended, participants were divided into two groups, A and B. I found myself in Group A. We stood in the hallway of a rather lovely building – home to Aarhus University's Research Centre on Learning and Technology – where the event was taking place. Each of us was given a copy of a map on a single A4 sheet. Our task was to determine how to instruct the members of Group B on using this map to find their way around the building. This sounded simple enough until we took a look at the map and discovered, to our dismay, that it was for a completely different building from where we were! In fact, the plan was for a school building, probably dating from the early twentieth century, with its premises quaintly divided between girls' classrooms and facilities on one side and boys' on the other. Both had a main entrance and hallway, but beyond that the two buildings – the school on the map and the villa we were in – had nothing whatsoever in common. What trick, we wondered, had been played on us? How were we to proceed?

After some deliberation, we resolved to turn the tables on our colleagues in Group B. Handing them the copies of the map, our instruction was for them to find their way around the map by means of the building. They were, in other words, to imagine themselves as inhabitants of the map, and to use the building to guide themselves around it. Much fun was had in the attempt, but it also left everyone feeling sorely perplexed. It was like taking a trip behind the looking glass, where nothing was as it seemed. Behind the glass, everything we thought was real was just a representation; everything we thought was a representation turned out to be real. The map became the territory and the territory the map. And the question this raised in our minds was precisely the central question of this book: are the territory and the map really that different? Do they fall on opposite sides of an unassailable ontological division between the reality of the world and its representation, or do they exemplify comparable realities – each of which can serve as a guide, template, or surrogate for the other?

An example from the other side of the world, and from a very different cultural context, might help to put the dilemma in perspective. Among Aboriginal people of Australia's Northern Territory, young men have traditionally been educated into the lore of the land and its formation through the contemplation of paintings done on sheets of bark. These paintings have been described by analysts as 'maps' of the land, although to the uninitiated eye, there would appear to be no more of a match between the land and any particular painting than there was for us, in our workshop, between the villa we were in and the school plan we were given. The painting offers no obvious clues for finding one's way. Yet Aboriginal elders, in their instruction of novices, play the same trick that we in Group A played on Group B. Rather than using the painting to help find their way in the land, novices are told to inhabit the painting and to use the land as their guide. The painting, evidently, is not to be understood as a representation at all. It is rather the visible revelation, or manifestation, of an inner truth – a truth even more real than the reality we see – which was established by ancestral beings in that eternal era of world formation known as the Dreaming.

Aboriginal praxis posits a kind of ontological continuum, from the outermost manifestations of the Dreaming to its innermost truth, and in the course of their instruction, novices are led on an inward path, rather like peeling an onion, such that each successive peel provides a guide for making sense of the next one. The outermost layer, however, lies in the immediate apprehension of land itself. Along with the experience of moving around in the land and observing its fauna and flora, this apprehension provides the clues for understanding the most figurative of the paintings. It is the figures in the paintings, and their relative dispositions, that provide the clues for understanding paintings that seem more abstract and geometric, but which – in Aboriginal cosmology – come ever closer to the inner truth of the Dreaming. These latter paintings, from which all figurative elements have been stripped away, are the most condensed, the most powerful, and the most radiant. And precisely because they stand more as condensations or radiations than as representations of truth, I had initially been critical of their comparison – in anthropological accounts – to maps.[1]

Subsequently, however, while reading up on the history of maps in the monastic tradition of medieval Europe, I was surprised to find unexpected parallels. Like young men in Aboriginal Australia, monastic novices were instructed by their mentors to inhabit paintings that resembled maps and that were even known by this term, as *mappae*. There were maps of the world which offered little or no clue to its actual geography, and maps of cathedrals and other sacred structures – many of which were never built. These maps were understood, just like Aboriginal paintings, not as representations of reality but as the manifestations of divinely inspired cosmogeneration, the prolonged contemplation of which could open a pathway for the novice to the knowledge of God. Again, the physical earth and its sacred buildings, and the observations and experiences they afforded, comprised the outermost figurations of divine order, on which novices could draw for guidance in their contemplative inhabitation of the maps. This contemplation, in turn, could introduce them to depths of understanding that would not otherwise be accessible.[2]

Perhaps, then, it is acceptable to describe Aboriginal paintings as maps after all, but only on condition that we drop the cartographic premise that the map is, by definition, the representation of an objectively given reality, tied to it by relations of verisimilitude. As is well-known, the idea that the earth affords a solid base or substrate, a *tabula rasa*, upon which human beings have enacted and inscribed the drama of history, is an essentially modern one, immortalised in the words of Immanuel Kant: 'the world is the substratum and the stage on which the play of our skills proceeds'.[3] Thenceforth the map no longer seemed to undergird the world or to channel insight into its fundament, but rather to overwrite it, much as the mind

---

[1]   The key source on Aboriginal paintings to which I refer is Morphy (1991). For my critique, see Ingold (2011: 202–205).

[2]   Ingold (2011: 198–202).

[3]   Kant (1970: 257).

– in the episteme of modernity – came to overwrite the material universe. For the modern subject, to aspire to truth is not to enter into the world or to plumb its depths but to take our distance from it, to view it from afar or, as we say, 'objectively'. Being human, we moderns insist, means knowing the world in a way no other creature does, by setting ourselves up on its far side, whence it appears alien, opaque, impenetrable, insensitive to our needs, and resistant to our investigations. We call it 'nature'.

This move, however, leaves us saddled with a profound existential dilemma. Surely, as human beings, individuals of the genus *Homo*, we are made of the same stuff, treading the same ground and breathing the same air as all living creatures. And yet our very specificity, denoted by the appellation *sapiens*, lies in the renunciation of our earthly existence, in breaking through the bounds of nature that hold all other species captive. In essence, the nature of being human is to exceed our human nature, to be more than the creatures we nevertheless hold ourselves to be. Yet how can we be simultaneously both *Homo* and *sapiens*, within nature and beyond it? It is akin to being asked to leave our house while yet remaining within, as if we could look back and see ourselves through the window, still going about our business at home. The very same duplicity, however, afflicts our concept of the Earth as both the matrix of habitation and as the planet. Viewed from the far side, the earthly home is inverted to become a solid globe. Looking back, we see ourselves like ants, condemned to crawl upon its outer surface. Inhabitants of the Earth, we are but exhabitants of the globe.[4]

II

On the planetary surface, as the philosopher Martin Heidegger exclaimed on first seeing pictures of the earth photographed from space, there is nowhere for a body to *be*: 'There is no place for *Dasein* on the planet', he exclaimed.[5] Nor, for the same reason, is there a place for contemplation on the modern map. For the very inversion that turns the earth into a globe also turns the map into a projection of the global surface. In this inversion lies the origin of cartography. In the words of Augustin Berque, a pioneer of environmental philosophy and landscape geography, it heralded the death

---

[4] Ingold (2011: 113–114).
[5] Heidegger, in Wolin (1993: 103). See also Lazier (2011).

of the cosmos and the birth of the universe, or the replacement of the world *around* us with a world *without* us – objective, exterior, and indifferent to our concerns.[6] Or to put it another way, it turned the ratio between nothing and everything, zero and the infinite, inside out. In so doing, it created the horizontal as a plane of indifference, a tabula rasa. To elaborate: in the cosmos, zero is a point of infinite concentration, an emplaced centre into which everything is drawn and which, in turn, radiates the potency of this concentrate into its surroundings. We could think of it as a kind of black hole, from which the world opens up on the inside, in its plenitude. But in the universe, zero is a point of infinite distantiation, where things vanish into a horizon that can be neither reached nor crossed. It is not right here where we *are*; it is infinitely far away.

As an experiment, try multiplying zero times infinity. If every zero represents a particular concentration of the infinite, then what you get from their multiplication is the fullness of the phenomenal world, taken from every possible centre. This is the logic of the hologram, of which every point or pixel is not one fragment of a totality but the positional enfoldment of a world in becoming, a condensation of those relations and processes of which it is the momentary outcome. But this holographic logic is not the one that most respondents, schooled in Western mathematics, are inclined to apply. They will insist that if you multiply zero by anything, the result is still zero. This is because they are thinking of a universe as what the physicist David Bohm would call an *explicate*, rather than an *implicate*, order. In the *implicate order*, as Bohm puts it, 'everything is enfolded into everything'.[7] But in the *explicate order*, everything exists in-itself, outside everything else, as a bounded and finite entity in the infinitude of space. In this sense, as Patrice Maniglier explains in Chapter 2, every entity, thus contained, is its own continent, and to say that any multiple of zero remains zero, even to infinity, is simply another way of expressing the idea that in the explicate order, space itself, minus all the continents that occupy it, is a boundless void. We can count and multiply the continents, but infinite space without continents to fill it is pure nothingness.

There is, however, an alternative way to approach the experiment, in terms not of the substantive or material contents of the universe but rather of its scalar projection. Take an entity of known dimensions. Divide these dimensions by two, then three, and so on – allowing that number continually

---

[6] Berque (2013: 51).
[7] Bohm (1980: 149).

to increase. The bigger the divisor, the smaller the entity, and as the former approaches infinity, the latter approaches zero. It follows that if the procedure is reversed, we can – by a multiplication of zero and infinity – bring the object back to its original, finite size. This, of course, is exactly what happens in linear perspective. Out at sea on a clear day, a distant ship may be observed to sink beneath the horizon: first the hull goes down, and then the masts, until the vessel disappears altogether from sight. We know why this happens: it is because of the curvature of the earth. But if the earth were completely flat, then the ship would not sink beneath the horizon but rather shrink into a point that would eventually become so tiny as to be indiscernible. This is the so-called vanishing point. Linear perspective projects the world as if the earth were flat. Its horizon, therefore, is not a function of the curvature of its surface but is defined as the line connecting all possible vanishing points from the fixed-point perspective of a viewer placed on a flat earth.

On the horizon of projection, zero is infinitely far. On the vertical picture plane, the horizon figures as a straight line. In multiplying zero by infinity, however, we can retrieve all points on the horizon line and restore them to the foreground, where they reappear as the entities or continents they once were. In so doing, we create the plane of horizontality, orthogonal to the picture plane, upon which all things can be measured, enumerated, and plotted. That is, they can be mapped in the strictly cartographic sense. And yet, as we have seen, by inverting the ratio between zero and infinity, and by turning the cosmos into a universe, we have not only entered the self-imposed exile of pure subjectivity; we have also turned the horizontal into a tabula rasa, a plane of indifference. Now there are two kinds or aspects of indifference, says philosopher Gilles Deleuze, 'black' and 'white'.[8] The white is the indifference of an isotropic surface, upon which rest bodies that have no determinate connection to it. The black is the indifference of the bodies towards this surface. Like severed limbs on a battlefield, bodies are indifferent to where they lie on the surface; the surface is indifferent to the bodies scattered upon it. Now the cartographic map, in Deleuze's terms, is black on white. The earth that we inhabit, however, is not. So what must we do to the earth to render it mappable?

[8]   Deleuze (1994: 28).

III

Recall that in a move which defined the modern era, Kant compared the earth to a stage upon which is placed everything that might form the object of our perception, like properties and scenery on the boards of the theatre. In the hands of Karl Marx, Kant's stage became a place of work. The earth, Marx declared, 'provides the worker with the platform for all his operations, and supplies a field of employment for his activity'.[9] For Marx, what gave the earth its use-value as an instrument of labour also allowed it to qualify – in the eyes of the founder of ecological psychology, James Gibson, writing over a century later – as having an *affordance*. It is 'stand-on-able', he said.[10] Not only are people supported by the surface of the earth; so also, according to Gibson, is everything else. For Gibson, it was self-evident that when we speak of the ground, we are referring to the surface of the earth. And this ground, he contends, is 'the literal *basis* of the terrestrial environment'.[11] As such, it is cluttered with all the objects that rest upon it, much like furniture on the floorboards of an otherwise empty room. There are hills and valleys, trees and boulders, houses and caves. However, just as the floor, in Deleuze's terms, is indifferent to the furniture placed on it, in Gibson's scheme, the ground is indifferent to the manifold features that make up an environment.

In effect, the surface of the earth has here been rendered as a tabula rasa from which all variations or differences have been erased, only to be remodelled as free-standing objects placed *upon* it. This erasure and remodelling, as we have seen, is what renders the surface cartographically mappable. In this regard, it is instructive to compare what Western thinkers such as Kant, Marx, and Gibson have to say about the surface of the earth with the views of Tadashi Suzuki, one of the foremost figures in contemporary Japanese theatre.[12] Evidently, Japanese and Western traditions cleave to quite different understandings of the ground. In the Japanese understanding, the ground is not a platform of support but a source of growth and nourishment. The floorboards of the traditional Japanese house, Suzuki tells us, virtually grow into the inhabitants who walk them, just as did the trees from whose wood the boards were made once grow

---

[9]   Marx (1930: 173).
[10] Gibson (1979: 127).
[11] Gibson (1979: 10, emphasis in original).
[12] Suzuki (1986: 21).

from the earth. Here the ground is no more indifferent to the trees than are floorboards to people; rather, trees and people grow from the earth and from boards, respectively, in an ongoing process of differentiation. However, as traditional, wood-floored houses are giving way in Japanese cities to internally carpeted Western-style apartment blocks, the once strong and positive orientation to the ground is being eroded. Nothing can grow from the concrete floor of an apartment block. And for Suzuki, this is a matter of regret.

The distinction that we are getting at here – so vividly highlighted in Suzuki's contrast between traditional and modern flooring in Japan – is effectively between the ground of differentiation and the ground of indifference or, if you will, between the respective grounds of *becoming* and *being*. The ground of being, as we are inclined to say, is hard, providing a solid but inert foundation for the objects that rest upon it, and the activities that are conducted across its surface. It is worth noting that exactly the same metaphor is imported into our thinking about the human mind, when neuropsychologists, for example, speak of the mind's 'hardware' as offering a neural *substrate* capable of supporting various kinds of cognitive operations, including those involved in speech and manual tool-use. In the very division between the hardware and the software it supports, the separation of knowing from being, of *sapiens* from *Homo*, is replicated and reinforced. No wonder there is so much talk of 'mapping' brain functions! Just imagine, then, what would happen if we were to think of the grounds of human knowledge as something more like the floorboards of a traditional Japanese house, or, with Deleuze and his collaborator, Félix Guattari, like a field of long grass,[13] or like the earth itself.

In treading the earth, writes philosopher Alphonso Lingis, 'we do not feel ourselves on a platform... but feel a reservoir of support extending infinitely in depth'.[14] With the ground of becoming, it is this depth of support, affording rootedness and growth, rather than the hardness and rigidity of a surface which affords neither, that counts. Like growing roots, the inhabitants of this ground – let us not call them human beings but rather human becomings[15] – do not move *across* a hard, preformed surface, as do actors on a stage or game pieces on a gaming board. They rather find or push their way *through* the ground and, in so doing, contribute to its

---

[13]   Deleuze and Guattari (2004: 17).
[14]   Lingis (1998: 14).
[15]   Ingold (2013b: 8–9).

ever-emergent texture. This is the kind of movement that I have elsewhere called *wayfaring*[16] – a movement that seeks not to connect pre-determined points or territories but rather, at every moment, to keep on going. That is to say, it is a movement or a relation – amounting to the same thing – which goes not between but along. Where the movement of ready-made being is across and between, the movement of becoming is through and along. This is also the difference that Deleuze and Guattari are making in their insistence upon a distinction between the *map* and the *tracing*, except that they confuse everyone by using these familiar terms to mean the precise reverse of that to which we are accustomed.[17] It is to this that I now turn.

IV

Tracing, for Deleuze and Guattari, entails the transposition or axial projection of an already given array upon a surface, or perhaps a layered series of surfaces, at different orders of resolution. This is what we would call mapping. Contrariwise, what they call mapping is what we would call tracing – namely, drawing a line, treading a track or following a path; or more generally, inscribing a movement into a medium that is viscous enough to retain the passage in its wake, at least for a while. Thus does the medieval reader trace the letters of the scribe, the novice calligrapher the gesture of the master, the hunter the movement of his prey, the wayfarer the footsteps of predecessors. In every case, the trace does not represent the original but rather enters into it with yet another line, inserted into the weave. It is, as Deleuze and Guattari say of what *they* call the map, 'an experimentation in contact with the real', an improvisatory movement that is at every moment responsive to the tendencies of things.[18] That is to say it *corresponds* with them. By correspondence, I do not mean a matching or equivalence of mutually substitutable forms, but the way in which becomings, in their movements and their growth, answer to one another, as does the orchid to the wasp – to cite one of Deleuze and Guattari's favourite examples.[19]

---

[16]   Ingold (2007: 75–76).
[17]   Deleuze and Guattari (2004: 13–15). This distinction is discussed by several of the contributors to this volume including Patrice Maniglier (Chapter 2), Marie Ange Brayer (Chapter 3), and Jacques Lévy (Chapter 8).
[18]   Deleuze and Guattari (2004: 13).
[19]   On correspondence, see Ingold (2013a: 105–108; 2015: 154–158).

Despite getting the terms backwards, Deleuze and Guattari highlight a contrast of paramount significance. For the map and the tracing are not interchangeable. It is one thing, as they say (but with the terms reversed), to put tracings on the map; quite another to plug the map back into the tracings. The first is a movement of territorialisation; the second is a movement of de-territorialisation. Consider, for example, the peculiarly human activity of walking. The artist Richard Long is famous for walking lines into the landscape. Reflecting on the significance of Long's work, architectural theorist Francesco Careri argues that his walking is an action that 'draws a figure on the terrain and therefore can be reported in cartographic representation'.[20] But this procedure, Careri notes, can also be applied the other way around, when Long draws a figure on a paper map and goes on to walk it in the landscape. In the first case he maps out the tracings that he has first made with his feet; in the second, he traces on foot what has first been put on the map. But what happens in this second case? For Careri, it is the exact opposite of the first. In it, the figure drawn in the landscape is a projection of the one drawn on paper. In effect, the surfaces of the paper and of the landscape are of a kind, making of the latter 'an immense aesthetic territory, an enormous canvas on which to draw by walking'. Each walk, Careri explains, adds 'one more layer'.[21]

In much the same vein, prehistorians often liken the landscape to a palimpsest, an ancient parchment, that 'has been written on and erased over and over again', in the words of archaeologist Osbert Crawford, one of the originators of the metaphor. Roads, field boundaries, woods, farms, and all the other products of human labour, according to Crawford, are the letters and words inscribed on the land.[22] But the key term here is *erasure*. It is as though with each successive intervention, the slate was wiped clean or covered over to create a fresh surface – a tabula rasa – prior to the act of inscription. Prehistory can then be read as the succession of inscribed surfaces, much as history can be read in the successive pages of a book. To my mind, however, this image of layering is profoundly misleading. For the ground is not like a canvas or parchment. It is not rolled out for people to draw, write, or walk on. It is rather matted, more like felt, from all the roots and runners, paths and tracks, of the countless life-forms which make up its texture. Or as Deleuze and Guattari would say, it is constituted not

---

[20] Careri (2002: 150).
[21] Careri (2002: 150).
[22] Crawford (1953: 51).

stratigraphically but rhizomatically. To walk a path is not to add another sheet to the pile but to weave another strand into the texture.

It follows that when Long walks a line that he has first drawn on a map, it is not the mirror reflection of what he does when he draws a line on a map that he has first walked on the ground. Tracing from a map and mapping from a trace are not the same. One starts from a territorialised world of layers, pages or sheets, and ends with the open weave – or what I have called the 'meshwork'[23] – of the ground. The other starts from the deterritorialisation of the meshwork and ends with the layering, or hierarchical superpositioning, of the map. A line on a cartographic map is indifferent to the surface on which it is drawn, as is the surface to the map. The line does not grow or issue from the surface, nor does the surface receive the line into itself. Traced on the ground, however, the path marks a line of differentiation. Or as Deleuze would put it, in walking a path, the line continually differentiates itself from the ground without the ground differentiating itself from the line.[24] If the ground were a palimpsest, to return to Crawford's metaphor, then we would have to think of it as one whose surfaces, far from having been prepared prior to each act of inscription through the erasure of previous markings, were continually built up from the markings themselves. Every surface would then be a tissue of lines.

V

Perhaps we could find a parallel for such a palimpsest in the Australian Aboriginal paintings to which I have already referred. These paintings are formed of lines that imbue the bark surfaces with spiritual power. For initiates, peeling back the paintings reveals an inner truth. But that truth *is* the ground, it is not *below* ground. A bias in the English language, which equates the surface with superficiality, inclines us always to look beneath the surface for inner meaning, rather than to dwell in the surface itself. But surfaces, too, can be 'deep', in that the more you abide with them, the more you see. It is precisely in this respect that the ground differs from the map. It is also why we are not deceived even by the most perfect, eye-trumping cartographic representation, albeit on the scale of one to one. As Gibson realised, there is an acid test that always enables us to tell a representation

---

[23] Ingold (2007: 80–82; 2011: 63–94).
[24] Deleuze (1994: 29).

for what it is. It lies in 'whether you can discover new features and details by the act of scrutiny'.[25] The real world is inexhaustible; there is no limit to what can be found. Whatever the point reached in one's explorations, it is still possible to go further. However, the map contains only such information as has been added to it. No amount of scrutiny will reveal what is not there.

This does not mean that the world is more complex than the map, or that the map, in selecting a few details for representation, is a simplification of the world. On the contrary, I want to suggest that of all the judgements we might want to make about a world, complexity or simplicity is not one of them. It can only be a judgement about the way this world is described or represented. Suppose, for example, that I want to draw a tree with as much accuracy as I can. Should I draw every leaf? Impossible! Instead, I compromise by using a lot of short pencil marks to produce an overall 'leaf effect'. This, you might say, amounts to a simplification. But does the falling of leaves in autumn simplify the tree? Or do the snows of winter, as they cover the cracks and furrows of the ground in a smooth blanket, simplify the landscape? Such questions cannot be answered with a yes or no; rather the questions themselves seem inappropriate. For the world presents itself to us not as a multitude of particulars but as a field of endless variegation. The last thing we would say of the tree, standing gaunt against the winter sky, or of the snow-covered ground, is that it has lost some of its particularity.

For another example, imagine the surface of a pond on a still day. The water, disturbed only by the boatmen that skim its surface, is smooth as glass. In it, you see a world upside down: the blue sky, the scattered clouds, the foliage of trees growing close to the water's edge. You also see the colourations of the bottom, the variations of silt content and possible underwater vegetation, all of which modulate the surface patina. And of course you see the boatmen, and the intersecting ripples they create, visible from the ways they catch the light. The whole world, it seems, is in the surface of the pond. Yet that surface is neither complex nor simple. As we have already seen of the ground of walking, it cannot be factored into separate, superimposable layers. The closest approximation, on paper, would be to a painting in water colours in which – although the artist may have alternated between the different hues of his palette – every wash of

---

[25] Gibson (1979: 257).

colour so impregnates the surface that it runs into every other.[26] Even the most detailed painting, however, would fail Gibson's test for reality. For unlike the pond, one can look at it but not into it. It presents only the illusion of transparency and depth.

In short, the problem of particularity, and with it of complexity, arises only at the point of capture, when we seek to make a tally of the world, to reckon with it, to measure and describe. Then, and only then, do singularities become particulars, converting variegation to variety, difference to diversity, history to identity. With this, we can return to a question I posed earlier. What must we do to the earth to get it onto the map? The answer is that we must measure it. To measure the earth, of course, is the literal meaning of geometry. Evidently, cartography and geometry are joined at the hip. The first geometers were the surveyors of Ancient Egypt who, after every annual flood of the Nile, would measure out and reapportion the land by stretching ropes between stakes driven into the ground. Indeed they were known, by profession, as 'rope-stretchers'.[27] The cathedral builders of medieval Europe did the same when they laid out the foundations for their works, again by means of cords and stakes.[28] Even today, methodical gardeners use pegs and string to mark their beds and ensure that their vegetables are planted in neat, straight lines. Ancient Egyptian surveyors, medieval European builders, and modern gardeners are all geometers, but what would it take for them to become cartographers as well?

VI

Let me return momentarily to the path of the walker. How does it compare with the geometer's stretched rope? Both the path and the rope traverse the ground. While the path is determined by a movement, wayfaring, the lie of the rope is determined by its stoppages – that is by the stakes that fix its ends. Although the path continually differentiates itself from the ground, without ever parting from it, the rope is perfectly indifferent to the ground above which it is suspended. In both these respects, the rope anticipates the cartographic line. Two further transformations were required, however. One was to bring the line 'back down' to the surface on which it now

---

[26] On the indivisibility of the surface of water and the parallel with water-colour painting, see Gunn (2002: 104–105).

[27] Ingold (2007: 159).

[28] Pacey (2007), see also Ingold (2013a: 55–56).

appears as a drawn mark, connecting points rather than stakes; the other was to convert the variable ground into a horizontal and isotropic plane. Ever since cartographers thus got the world onto the map, the ambition of planners, architects, and engineers has been to impose the order of the map onto the world. They have done this through a combination of erasure, hard-surfacing, and construction. Between them, the bulldozer, the concrete-mixer, and the crane are the most potent and ubiquitous embodiments of cartographically driven world-making. The first levels the ground so as to make it as blank and homogeneous as an empty sheet, the second lays a solid foundation or substratum on which everything can rest (yet from which nothing can grow), the third adds components on top.

There is, however, another side to this. Today's cartographers are no longer the expert draughtsman they once were. Many have instead become modellers, entrusted with the management of immense and growing datasets. By and large, maps serve merely as programmatic visualisations that enable us to see the data at a glance. Every datum, however, is a stoppage, a determination, the equivalent of a stake in the ground. What gets onto the map, to quote Deleuze and Guattari, 'are only the impasses, blockages, incipient taproots, or points of structuration'.[29] For them, this is what makes the map (which they call the *tracing*) so dangerous. The accumulation of data is tantamount to the suffocation of life. For in imposing the order of the map onto the world, we have smothered the earth with our constructions. There is surely a connection between our insatiable appetite for data-mining and the profligacy with which we refill the earth with waste. We take out information without meaning and give back commodities without use. Geographic information systems and landfill, alongside the super-digitisation of the map and the overloading of the territory, are two sides of the same coin. There is excess on both sides. Suffocated by data and having smothered the earth, we are no longer able to correspond with it.

Where now? What prospects can there be for the map, now that it has been so thoroughly absorbed into corporate regimes of data management and control? Can cartography turn upon itself and undo the inversions of modernity? Could the maps of the future liberate us from the tyranny of data? Might they enable us to listen to the earth and to receive with good grace what it has to give? Can they help us give back what we owe, rather than dumping that for which we have no further use? Can they restore the

---

[29] Deleuze and Guattari (2004: 15).

infinite to where we are? Could they even restore the cosmos? Is there any cause for hope?

As the essays collected here show, there is no shortage of alternatives, some of which seem to return to medieval or even indigenous understandings of the map as a focus for cosmic contemplation, while simultaneously scrolling forward to digital futures that – far from blocking our passage – restore movement, life, and growth to our apprehension of the world. To adopt a term suggested by Emanuela Casti (Chapter 6), this might call for a new kind of metrics, *chorographic* rather than cartographic: a metrics that is paced out in the actual movements of inhabitants as they make their ways through the world, and that replaces the topography of Cartesian space with the topology of the meshwork. In chorography, to adopt a phrase from Marie-Ange Brayer (Chapter 3), measurement – as in the walker's pacing the earth – is its own measure; or in the words of philosopher Gaston Bachelard, cited by Boris Beaude (Chapter 13), 'we must reflect in order to measure and not measure in order to reflect'. Perhaps, with Brayer, we can imagine maps that are as rhizomatic as the worlds they both describe and simultaneously bring forth, where any division between reality and its representation would be swallowed up in a movement of becoming. In such a movement, the map both goes beyond what is and yet falls short of what will be: it is neither a representation of the present nor a plan for the future but a pulling away from both. Perhaps map and territory will ultimately become interchangeable. Perhaps the map will even become what Deleuze and Guattari say it is. Then, having turned upon itself, having become everything that it presently is not, will it still be cartographic?

References

Berque, A. 2013. *Thinking Through Landscape*, trans. A-M. Feenberg-Dibon. Abingdon: Routledge.

Bohm, D. 1980. *Wholeness and the Implicate Order.* London: Routledge & Kegan Paul.

Careri, F. 2002. *Walkscapes: Walking as an Aesthetic Practice.* Barcelona: Editorial Gustavo Gili.

Crawford, O. G. S. 1953. *Archaeology in the Field.* London: Praeger.

Deleuze, G. 1994. *Difference and Repetition*, trans. P. Paton. New York: Columbia University Press.

Deleuze, G. and F. Guattari 2004. *A Thousand Plateaus: Capitalism and Schizophrenia*, trans. B. Massumi. London: Continuum.

Gibson, J. J. 1979. *The Ecological Approach to Visual Perception.* Boston, MA: Houghton Mifflin.

Gunn, W. 2002. *The Social and Environmental Impact of Incorporating Computer Aided Design Technologies into an Architectural Design Process*, Unpublished doctoral dissertation, University of Manchester.

Ingold, T. 2007. *Lines: A Brief History.* London: Routledge.

Ingold, T. 2011. *Being Alive: Essays on Movement, Knowledge and Description.* Abingdon: Routledge.

Ingold, T. 2013a. *Making: Anthropology, Archaeology, Art and Architecture.* Abingdon: Routledge.

Ingold, T. 2013b. Prospect. In *Biosocial Becomings: Integrating Social and Biological Anthropology*, eds. T. Ingold and G. Palsson. Cambridge, UK: Cambridge University Press, pp. 1–21.

Ingold, T. 2015. *The Life of Lines.* Abingdon: Routledge.

Kant, I. 1970. A translation of the Introduction to Kant's *Physische Geographie.* In *Kant's Concept of Geography and its Relation to Recent Geographical Thought*, ed. J. A. May. Toronto: University of Toronto Press, pp. 255–264.

Lazier, B. 2011. Earthrise; or, The Globalization of the World Picture. *The American Historical Review* 116(3): 602–630.

Lingis, A. 1998. *The Imperative.* Bloomington: Indiana University Press.

Marx, K. 1930. *Capital*, vol. 1, trans. E. and C. Paul. London: Dent.

Morphy, H. 1991. *Ancestral Connections: Art and an Aboriginal System of Knowledge.* Chicago, IL: University of Chicago Press.

Pacey, A. 2007. *Medieval Architectural Drawing: English Craftsmen's Methods and their Later Persistence (c.1200–1700).* Stroud: Tempus.

Suzuki, T. 1986. *The Way of Acting: The Theatre Writings of Tadashi Suzuki*, trans. J. T. Rimer. New York: Theatre Communications Group.

Wolin, R. (ed.) 1993. *The Heidegger Controversy.* Cambridge, MA: MIT Press.